DI058778

Backfire

Backfire

A Reporter's Look at
Affirmative Action

BOB ZELNICK

Regnery Publishing, Inc.
Washington, D.C.

Library of Congress Cataloging-in-Publication Data

Zelnick, Bob, 1940–
    Backfire : a reporter's look at affirmative action / by Bob Zelnick.
        p. cm.
    Includes bibliographical references and index.
    ISBN 0–89526–455–2
    1. Affirmative action programs—United States. I. Title.
HF5549.5.A34Z45 1996
331.13'3'0973—dc20   96-13733
                                                        CIP

Published in the United States by
Regnery Publishing, Inc.
An Eagle Publishing Company
422 First Street, SE, Suite 300
Washington, DC 20003

Distributed to the trade by
National Book Network
4720-A Boston Way
Lanham, MD 20706

Printed on acid-free paper.
Manufactured in the United States of America

Designed by Dori Miller

10 9 8 7 6 5 4 3 2

Books are available in quantity for promotional or premium use. Write to
Director of Special Sales, Regnery Publishing, Inc., 422 First Street, SE, Suite
300, Washington, DC 20003, for information on discounts and terms or call
(202) 546-5005.

To the memory of my parents,
David and Lillian Zelnick,
and to my wife,
Pamela,
with and for a lifetime of love.

CONTENTS

ACKNOWLEDGMENTS

This book takes a strong stand on a controversial subject and would not have been possible without the help and support of many who agreed with my point of view, many who disagreed with it, and others who felt the issue worthy of fair and honest treatment regardless of the author's conclusions.

Al Regnery, the publisher, asked me to follow the subject wherever it led, a mandate every reporter yearns for, and one for which this reporter is deeply grateful.

Ron Goldfarb, my agent, helped shape the initial proposal and, in that critical stage, played the much needed role of editor.

Richard Vigilante, my editor at Regnery, combined personal warmth and support with rigorous demands that the book meet the burdens of proof it had established for itself and that it do so with intellectual clarity and, where possible, style.

Patricia Bozell, my copy editor, improved the product with every slash and caret of her pencil. With commendable sangfroid, David Dortman kept the whole process moving along.

At the outset of the project I enlisted the aide of two second-year law students at my alma mater, the University of Virginia Law School. During the next eighteen months Devin Scahumburg and Gregg Schultz performed their assigned tasks with great competence, commendable punctuality, and tremendous good humor. This project would not have been successful without their help, and now, as they graduate, both carry my everlasting gratitude and confidence that their own careers will prosper from the same sort of commitment and integrity they showed me.

During the course of this project the Hoover Institution at Stanford University provided me with two short-term fellowships which greatly facilitated my work on the West Coast, and for that, my thanks go to President John Raisian and Senior Vice President Tom Henrikson.

I should like to thank Adeen Postar of the Georgetown University Law School who arranged for me to have courtesy access to Georgetown's law library throughout the project.

Broderick Johnson of the House Committee on Economic and Educational Opportunity tried to cure me of my errant ways and also arranged interviews with Reps. William L. Clay and Melvin R. Watts of the Congressional Black Caucus. To all three I am deeply appreciative, as I am to David Bositis of the Joint Center for Political and Economic Studies, whose expertise in the area of voting rights is matched by only a handful of the nation's more learned academicians.

Jeffery A. Norris, Larry Lorber, Leonard Biermann, and Charles R. Mann were particularly generous with their time in helping me understand both the workings of the Labor Department's Office of Federal Contract Program (OFCCP) Review and corporate attitudes toward affirmative action, although I am certain each of them would dispute certain of my own conclusions. John Fox of the Palo Alto law firm Fenwick and West assembled much of the *Affirmative Action Workbook* made available to me and also provided additional written analysis.

Frank Erwin provided a great deal of both time and material on the issue of job testing.

Patrick J. Rocks, chief assistant corporation counsel for the city of Chicago, provided me with a number of legal documents—all in the public realm I hasten to add—relating to that city's police and fire departments' employment litigation.

Andrew Morris, at the time, editor of the *Cornell Daily Sun*, provided much in the way of background material and worked on my itinerary at Cornell. Lisa Horn helped research the 1969 black student takeover of Willard Straight Hall. Cornell's chief archivist Gould Coleman provided me with exclusive access to interview transcripts he had assembled from the period. Richard Wagner of the Industrial and Labor Relations school at Cornell walked me through that school's admission process in great detail and made additional material available to me. Professor Larry I. Palmer acquainted me with his efforts to end residential segregation at Cornell. And my young friend Chris Montgomery offered, over the course of several meetings, a strong defense of affirmative action at the university level. Also, Peter Warren of the National Association of Scholars called my attention to a good deal of important information on higher education issues.

Louise Dudley of the University of Virginia's public affairs office provided me with hard-to-get information on that school's affirmative action program and also organized a number of helpful interviews on "the grounds."

Mark Staton, a former president of the Jefferson Society at the University of Virginia, organized an extremely valuable meeting for my benefit on the subject of student race relations.

President Albert Shanker of the National Federation of Teachers took time from a busy schedule to reflect on issues pertinent to my chapter on elementary and secondary education. Peter Schmidt of *Education Week* was helpful in pointing me toward that journal's coverage of relevant issues.

Of the many who helped me gather material for the chapter on the California Civil Rights Initiative, I am particularly grateful to Ward Connerly, whose insight into the political dynamics of the situation was invaluable, and to Joe Gelman, who, during a period of personal uncertainty and travail, welcomed me into his home and shared important background information on the history of the referendum effort. Mirian Avalos of the Los Angeles consulting firm Hamilton and Rabinowitz was filled with suggestions—all of them good—as to which people I ought to interview in California.

Several people took the time to read specific draft chapters and offer constructive criticism. In many cases, they had also helped me to acquire the information I then proceeded to misinterpret. Both for their initial and subsequent help, and specifically to exempt them from any responsibility for errors in the final product, I should like to thank the following:

On affirmative action and employment: Farrell Bloch.

On job testing: Professor Frank L. Schmidt and James C. Sharf.

On university issues: Dean Emeritus David B. Lipsky and Professor Ron Ehrenberg of Cornell University. Also, Frank Vinik, formerly with the University of California at Berkeley and a graduate attorney from the University of Virginia Law School.

On voting rights: Professor David Ian Lublin of the University of South Carolina.

On voting rights, mortgage lending, and minority set-asides: William L. McGrath of the House Constitution subcommittee.

On minority set-asides: Mike Kennedy.

On mortgage lending and insurance: Professor Anthony Yezer of the George Washington University and Andy Sindler.

I am also deeply grateful to President Roone Arledge of ABC News for the many personal courtesies extended to me over the years.

My wife, Pamela, and three daughters, Eva, Dara, and Marni, offered the kind of support and encouragement throughout this project that only a loving, close-knit family can provide. With her older sisters away at college, Marni, in addition, provided a great deal of material help, overseeing my many battles with the computer, coaching me gently where possible, sternly where warranted, and preparing several of the charts on her own when my own technical incompetence became more than she could bear. Pam critiqued several chapters and also waded through a daily assortment of newspapers and magazines over the course of eighteen months, providing me with what—certainly at the price—was a splendid clipping and filing service, while somehow managing to keep her real estate work going. Both wife and daughters provided vigorous intellectual challenges to my own conclusions, and I am far from certain even at this point that each would accept my views without some dissent.

But then again, there is nothing new about that.

Backfire

1

A QUESTION OF
DISCRIMINATION

When the University of California at Berkeley routinely admits African American students with lower grades and SAT scores 200 points lower than Chinese Americans who are rejected, there is nothing fancy or esoteric about what the university is doing: it is discriminating against Chinese Americans on the basis of race. When the Department of Defense (DOD) requests bids for a road construction contract at the White Sands missile range and then informs a white bidder that the contract is "sheltered" for the benefit of racial minorities, DOD has discriminated on the basis of race. When, under pressure from the U.S. Department of Justice, the state of North Carolina draws a congressional district with no substantial purpose in mind other than to include sufficient black voters to elect a black congressman, white voters have been discriminated against. And when a white firefighter in Birmingham, Alabama, who finished eleventh among those taking a promotion exam for lieutenant is passed over in favor of a black who finished ninety-fifth, that white fireman has also suffered discrimination on the basis of race.

Americans of all races and political persuasions in overwhelming numbers disapprove of any sort of officially sanctioned race discrimination. As practiced today, affirmative action discriminates on the basis of race, gender, or ethnicity against whites, males, and other unfavored groups. And yet today this official discrimination is one of the most pervasive and powerful of government social policies, denying Americans jobs, career and educational opportunities, even handicapping their ability to bid on government contracts unless they fit into one of the preferred racial or ethnic categories.

Supporters of such discrimination have argued that it is "benign" and, as such, distinguishable from the more virulent forms of race discrimination practiced in the past. Indeed, the argument runs, this past discrimination has so disadvantaged blacks as to make an assortment of modest preferences a practical necessity. Whatever its merits, and available evidence suggests they are dubious, the approach fails on legal grounds. Despite recurring dissents, the Supreme Court has specifically and repeatedly held that neither past official discrimination nor current generalized societal discrimination justifies special treatment by the government for members of the afflicted group who have, as individuals, suffered no harm.

But despite the Court's increasingly clear rejection of discrimination in principle, affirmative action remains pervasive today, just as in 1964, ten years after *Brown v. Board of Education,* Jim Crow still ruled the South. Facing both political and legal rejection, those who would perpetuate the current affirmative action regime have danced gingerly roundabout the core issue to do battle with a series of straw men, to cite ills their remedies do not address, and to broaden the community of beneficiaries in the hope of improving the political odds. So far, they have been remarkably successful.

That was the approach President Clinton took in his address on affirmative action delivered at the National Archives Rotunda on 19 July 1995. The speech announced the conclusions of an Affirmative Action Review undertaken by the White House as the Supreme Court wrestled with the issue of minority preferences in federally subsidized construction contracts. By the time the review was completed, the Court had held in the *Adarand* case that such preferences can be applied only as remedies for specific discrimination and even then only when narrowly tailored to redress past abuse. Although both the Affirmative Action Review and a separate Justice Department analysis of the Court's holding acknowledged that the decision called into question a number of federal programs, the president, undeterred, continued his administration's support for affirmative action, making only such adjustments as were essentially dictated by the Court decisions.

Mr. Clinton acknowledged that many believe "affirmative action always amounts to group preferences over individual merit," and that "it demeans those who benefit from it and discriminates against those who are not helped by it." He continued: "But I believe that if there are no quotas, if we give no opportunities to unqualified people, if we have no reverse discrimination, and if, when the problem ends, the program ends, that criticism is wrong." This has become the standard defense: Concede that affirmative action would be wicked if it contained any of its essential elements, proclaim that henceforth the government will practice only affirmative action that lacks the very discriminatory policies that make it affirmative action, and then continue as before. So might poll taxes have been defended a few decades ago; indeed, that is how everything from poll taxes to many school segregation schemes were defended—by denying they had any discriminatory purpose.

Mr. Clinton's formulation of the issue was itself an oxymoron: if we have no discrimination against whites or other unprotected categories—so-called "reverse discrimination"—then we, in fact, have no affirmative action, since affirmative action, by its very definition, involves preferring one race, sex, or ethnic group over another. A contract that is closed to nonminorities clearly fits this definition. So does one which grants, say, a 10 percent bonus to a contractor who chooses a minority subcontractor. Even colleges and universities that purport to make race nothing more than a "tiebreaker" or "plus factor" are engaging in what the president calls "reverse discrimination"; most, in fact, go a good deal further in preferring blacks and Hispanics over far more qualified whites and Asians. It is, in short, a logical fallacy to assume that one race, sex, or ethnic group can be preferred without another being disadvantaged.

The president then defined the scope of the problem in a manner certain, if not calculated, to broaden the political constituencies beholden to affirmative action and to ensure that neither the problem nor the program would ever end. "The unemployment rate for African Americans remains about twice that of whites. The Hispanic rate is still much higher. Women have narrowed the earnings gap, but still make only 72 percent as much as men do for comparable jobs. The average income for an Hispanic woman with a college degree is still less than the average income of a white man with a high school diploma."

Now there are many reasons why black unemployment rates exceed white rates, why a diminishing residual disparity exists between male and female earnings, and why Hispanic women earn less than white males, but few of them have to do with rampant discrimination in the workplace. Such factors as education, scores on achievement tests, family structure, drug use, involvement with the criminal justice system, the attempt by many able women to accommodate both home and career, and language facility are all far more important in the view of every economist who has studied the matter seriously. And problems not rooted in discrimination cannot be cured by affirmative action. As June O'Neill, director of the Congressional Budget Office, and Harold Orlans have written, "Affirmative action is afflicted by gigantism. A single idea, discrimination, cannot adequately explain the greatly varied conditions and economic statistics of groups composing a majority of the population."

Contrary to the suggestion implicit in the president's statement, it is also widely acknowledged that affirmative action does little to help those most in need. Economist Glenn Loury of Boston University describes affirmative action as "a small tax corporate America pays to the black elite." University admissions and scholarships grounded in race preferences inordinately reward the black middle and upper classes. So do government-mandated set-asides, because the unemployed black or the person receiving something at or close to the minimum wage is rarely in a position to bid on a government contract whatever the preference involved. Professor Steven Carter of the Yale Law School has acknowledged that "[t]he degree of support for affirmative action in the professions bears no relation to the degree of one's concern about black people who are worst off, for the programs do them little good."

Increasingly, black scholars and community activists have come to acknowledge that behavioral problems in the inner city are far more responsible for poverty than external discrimination. Robert L. Woodson, Sr., president of the National Center for Neighborhood Enterprise, has testified: "This poverty is not the result of external circumstances but of irresponsible choices and chances taken by individuals. It includes poverty resulting from drug and alcohol addiction (which is a factor for as much as 60 percent of our homeless population) and out-of-wedlock births. Research reveals that 22 percent of children from one-parent families will be in poverty for seven years or more, compared with 2 percent from two-parent families."

In his brilliant study, *The Truly Disadvantaged*, University of Chicago sociologist William Julius Wilson describes how the era of equal opportunity for black people with an education and professional training or skill has, perversely, brought even greater misery to those left behind. In the "bad old days" of job and residential segregation, most black doctors, lawyers, teachers, clergymen, and skilled workers continued to reside in the inner city, providing structure and leadership to their communities. But as they prospered and moved away, criminals, drug dealers, and other less desirable elements took over. As a result, Wilson writes, "if strong norms and sanctions against aberrant behavior, a sense of community, and positive neighborhood identification are the essential features of social organization in urban areas, inner-city neighborhoods today suffer from a severe lack of social organization." The implication of Wilson's analysis is not, of course, that society should revisit its segregationist past, but rather that a new generation of community leadership is needed, one which spends more time addressing the life choices made by inner-city residents and less time fashioning irrelevant remedies that address the discrimination of a bygone day. As liberal sociologists David O. Sears and Donald R. Kinder have acknowledged, "[o]ver the past 30 years, white opposition to equal opportunity has sharply declined. On voting rights, schools, public accommodations, housing and employment practices, segregationist sentiment has all but disappeared. White America has become, in principle at least, racially egalitarian—a momentous and undeniably significant change."

The president's assurance that nothing in affirmative action suggests that benefits are to be bestowed upon the "unqualified" is a variation of the old debater's trick of constructing and demolishing a straw man to distract attention from the point at issue. Discrimination is practiced when race is weighed as an independent factor in admissions, employment, promotion, or dismissal. The beneficiary of such discrimination may or may not be qualified for the position in question. But all too often, he is *less qualified* than the victim of race discrimination. And the enforcers of affirmative action do not stop there. For much of the past generation one of the pillars of the affirmative action establishment has been the assault on objective standards of merit. In practice, this has taken the form of attacks on employment tests, promotion exams, SATs, teacher and student competency tests, ability grouping, academic tracking, and job skills certification procedures. Currently, blacks and Hispanics tend to score less well on standardized objective tests than do whites and Asians despite vast and costly government programs designed to close the gap. As a result, the mere administration of such tests and procedures is said to have a *disparate impact* on blacks and Hispanics. And this can be legally justified, in the employment context, only by business necessity as defined by the government—including the agencies seeking to perpetuate affirmative action. But an employer who uses a test that fails to meet the government's none-too-clear definition of business necessity is guilty of discrimination even though his intent was merely to select the most competent employee regardless of race.

Once discrimination is established, a vast assortment of remedies—many more punitive than remedial—can be imposed on the offender by the government or the courts, including back pay, hiring or promotion quotas, or other special activities designed to increase the number of minorities in future hiring situations. For that reason, the affirmative action establishment loves the theory of disparate impact and has sought to extend the doctrine to areas as remote from employment as mortgage lending and home insurance. For the same reason, endorsing antidiscrimination laws while opposing affirmative action—as many well-meaning commentators have done—can be a trap, unless discrimination is defined as *disparate treatment* rather than *disparate impact*. Conscious and deliberate acts of discrimination are and ought to be subject to the full weight of the law. But applying objective standards rooted in common sense or historic practice that happen to impact disproportionately on those unable to meet them ought not open the door to massive federal intervention.

Enforcing federal affirmative action policies—including those, like the Voting Rights Act, which are not technically affirmative action but which share many of the same underpinnings—requires a vast and intrusive bureaucracy. Every employer with more than fifteen workers is bound by the Civil Rights Act of 1964 not to discriminate on the basis of race, sex, or national origin, a process supervised by the Equal Employment Opportunity Commission (EEOC). Every federal contractor or subcontractor with fifty employees and doing $50,000 worth of business with the federal government must have its own affirmative action plan, setting forth minority hiring goals and timetables—something very close to a quota system—or must accept the government's version, compliments of the Labor Department's Office of Federal Contract Compliance Program (OFCCP) Review. The racial practices of banks, mortgage companies, and insurance companies come under special scrutiny, a task divided among the Federal Reserve Board, the Office of the Comptroller of the Currency, the Department of Housing and Urban Development, the Department of Justice, and others. The Small Business Administration serves as a clearinghouse certifying the credentials of minority businesses to participate in set-aside programs. Agencies such as the Pentagon, as well as the individual uniformed services, have departments devoted to ensuring that numerical goals for minority contractors are met, not to mention their own recruitment and promotion goals. And, of course, a special election unit at the Department of Justice backed by the Civil Rights Division supervises or closely monitors state and local election procedures either under its original 1965 mandate to prevent the disenfranchisement of blacks or the 1982 amendments which effectively require the creation of "majority–minority" districts, that is, districts including enough minority voters to virtually ensure the election of a minority candidate.

The massive federal enforcement machinery gives lie to the notion, conveniently propagated by affirmative action advocates, that the policy is just a trivial inconvenience to the white majority and other disfavored groups, rather like some legislator's favorite pork program. To the contrary, the issue of race preferences imposed by legislation or administrative fiat is at the core of this nation's value system and, unless checked, is likely to become an even more searing and divisive issue in the decades ahead as the number and political power of minorities increase and each group vies for its own designated slice of the pie.

Many find it offensive for government to have ventured so far in the direction of racial preferences. Andrew Sullivan, the editor of *The New Republic,* complains that "[l]iberalism was once the creed that said you were equal before the law. Parentage, gender, race, religion: none of that mattered. The individual citizen was what counted. Now, in extending the power of government further and further, in regulating the precise percentages of racial and other minorities in a whole range of activities and places, liberalism has become the very force it was born to oppose."

Sullivan, an Englishman, should not be surprised. In a very real sense, today's liberal federal establishment is the true successor to the British imperialists of yesteryear. The sun never sets on its administrative empire. No power may ever be yielded so long as some rationale exists for its exercise. No law should ever pass from the books for having achieved its purpose so long as a single alleged grievance can be cited to support its retention. No insult is too trivial, no cause too remote from effect, no public reaction too allergic ever to suspend the remedy. Long after the battle has been won, the command still functions, thriving on old war stories and the ethic of an earlier day.

Given a devotion to equal outcomes at all costs, it is a very small step from the demolition of objective merit criteria to the proposition that race itself equals merit, a notion inherent in many of the corporate diversity programs still somewhat in vogue, but even more prevalent in the academic community. Few professional school honors carry both the prestige and practical clout of the notation *"Law Review"* on a graduate resume. For generations, students in the top 5 percent to 10 percent of the first year law school classes have been invited to compete for a position on the publication that reviews important developments in the law and publishes scholarly articles. The successful competitor must be a good researcher and a competent writer with a flair for precision and accuracy. Upon graduation, he or she can choose among the best clerkships and the most lucrative prestige firms.

A few years ago, some University of Virginia law students complained that inviting only those to compete who did well their first year unfairly excluded the "late bloomers" who acquired the knack for taking law exams a bit later. So the *Virginia Law Review*—one of the nation's best—allowed students to "grade on" after their first year. But some still complained, this time that while they were not master test takers, they were excellent researchers and writers and should be allowed to compete on that basis. Once again, the editors yielded and a number of students were permitted to "write on" to the publication.

Unfortunately, in the fifteen to twenty years since blacks had been admitted to the formerly segregated institution, not a single one had ever made the *Law Review*. Anxious to change that situation, the editors considered "lowering the floor" for grade eligibility and adding a few points for "diversity," but, except for one black student, whose superb credentials had him on track for a position even under the old standards, no others were likely candidates. So the editors came up with the "Virginia Plan" for minority participation on the *Law Review*. Now each year, twenty-five student scholars "grade on" to the *Law Review*, fifteen "write on," and five—nearly all minorities—"plan on." The plan has proved controversial, and each year some staff members and other white "near misses" urge return to a purely merit-based system. But change is considered unlikely because a recent survey by the *Law Review* found that at least half the publications among the nation's top twenty law schools now select staff members whose preeminent qualification is the color of their skin.

Such activity finds intellectual shelter in the writings of the so-called critical race theorists, whose guiding philosophy is the deconstructionist notion that equal justice, including job selection by merit, in a racist society keeps blacks and other minorities in their place and is thus wholly unsuited to their needs. High on their agenda is the acceptance of blacks on the faculties of the nation's leading universities and law schools even if their academic credentials are sparse, and their published observations on racial issues not up to traditional standards of scholarship. Instead, as Professor Alex Johnson of the University of Virginia Law School has written, "When the scholar of color speaks to any racial issue, such as affirmative action... her viewpoint will be greatly informed as a result of her different experiences in our society as a person of color."

Harvard Law School's Randall Kennedy, by no means a conservative, finds this more an attack upon academic standards than institutional racism. "I do not want race-conscious decision-making to be naturalized into our general pattern of academic evaluation," he writes. "I do not want race-conscious decision-making to lose its status as a deviant mode of judging people or the work they produce."

When a policy like racial preferences becomes infected with ideology, its adherents often seem impervious to mounting evidence that it is a dismal failure if not downright counterproductive, even when judged by its own goals. Since 1972 the National Association of Black Social Workers has opposed transracial adoptions, calling such adoptions "a form of genocide" and claiming, "Black children belong, physically, psychologically, and culturally in black families in order that they receive the total sense of themselves and develop a sound projection for the future." Backed by white liberals, the organization has influenced dozens of states and the federal government into policies that make transracial adoptions terribly difficult. Since 40 percent of all children available for adoption are black, the result has been to condemn tens of thousands of these children to languish in state institutions or foster homes when white couples are ready and eager to become their adoptive parents. And to what end? A twenty-year study of black children adopted by white families conducted by Professor Rita Simon of American University found these children to be better adjusted, far better cared for, and no less conscious and proud of their racial heritage than black children adopted by blacks or remaining in foster care. As Elizabeth Bartholet of the Harvard Law School observed, "The evidence is overwhelming that delay or denial of permanent placement injures children both in the short and the long term. At the same time, there is not a shred of evidence that transracial placement poses any problem for the children involved." At the initiative of Congress, long-standing legal bias against transracial adoptions seems in the process of being erased.

Other examples are legion. The creation of majority–minority voting districts, at the insistence of the black political establishment and its white liberal supporters, has cost about a dozen Democratic seats in the House of Representatives, contributed to the Republican party takeover of the House and a corresponding loss of Black Caucus political power, accelerated the migration of white Southerners to the GOP—greatly increasing its representation in Southern state legislatures—and undermined, at both the state and federal levels, political objectives favored by most blacks.

In elementary and secondary education, black ideologues, again backed by many white liberals, continue to demand black role models and Afrocentric curricula, though no evidence to date suggests that either has produced superior results. To the contrary, experienced teachers—white or black—who themselves perform well on standardized achievement tests, together with school administrators who demand regular attendance, do make some difference, although given the conditions of poverty, out-of-wedlock births, drug usage, and high crime afflicting the inner city, there are limits even to what the best teachers and administrators can accomplish. As for the virtues of Afrocentrism, few can match the assessment of Arthur Schlesinger, Jr.:

> The West needs no lectures on the superior virtue of those "sun people" who sustained slavery until western imperialism abolished it (and, it is reported, sustain it to this day in Mauritania and the Sudan), who still keep women in subjection and cut off their clitorises, who carry out racial persecutions not only against Indians and other Asians but against fellow Africans from the wrong tribes, who show themselves either incapable of operating a democracy or ideologically hostile to the democratic idea, and who in the tyrannies and

massacres, their Idi Amins and Bokassas, have stamped
with utmost brutality on human rights."

Race preferences create dangerous precedents. Lance Morrow,
the brilliant essayist for *Time* magazine, has warned that the "supposedly virtuous high road of race preference has taken the nation
into dubious terrain." Compensatory unfairness may have surface
appeal. But, in the end, it is "a flirtation with the devil, a
deepening reliance on the principle that formed the foundation of
slavery, the Ku Klux Klan, and Jim Crow. This was the position at
the center of apartheid and Hitler's Nuremberg laws." Strong language, to be sure. But racial preferences enshrined into law are the
first cousins to black separatism and black supremacy. They legitimize a sense of victimhood that entitles the bearer to hold
grudges against individuals who did him no harm. Blacks entitled
to enter Columbia University as a form of compensation are also,
it seems, entitled to say of Jews, "Lift up the yarmulke, and what
you will find is the blood of billions of Africans weighing on your
heads." Surely, some currently feel, a race entitled to a preference
because whites hold a disproportionate number of managerial
positions or because whites and Asians command disproportionate
representation at the more selective universities is entitled to control the places of business in its own neighborhood. Surely, such a
race has the right to protest the proliferation of Korean-owned
grocery stores or a Jewish clothier planning to expand into space
occupied by a black record shop. The fire at "Freddy's" in Harlem
may have been set by a demented black racist, but the predicate
was laid by black activist Al Sharpton, whose protest demonstration claimed that it was somehow illegitimate for a Jew to expand
his business in a black neighborhood. And the philosophical home
for racial entitlements resides in the assortment of race preference
programs managed by the federal and state governments.

The fathers of the civil rights movement understood the danger. Challenged in the early 1960s by the black separatist views of Malcolm X, Martin Luther King warned that "black supremacy is as dangerous as white supremacy.... God is not interested merely in the freedom of black men and brown men and yellow men. God is interested in the freedom of the whole human race." And Kenneth B. Clark, the distinguished sociologist whose studies on the psychological effects of segregation helped persuade the Supreme Court in 1954 to overturn segregation in Southern schools, told a *New York Times* interviewer in 1995, "I don't believe in preferential treatment. To me that is a form of racism."

Whether in jobs or in university admissions, racial preferences have an effect opposite what had originally been intended in that they reinforce prevailing stigmas of black inferiority and create a predisposition toward separation. Glenn Loury has written that champions of race preferences have "a great investment in the idea of America as a closed society in which 'people of color' regardless of their individual merit suffer systematic disadvantage in the competition for economic and social benefits." This "exhibitionism of nonachievement," he warns, becomes self-fulfilling.

Justice William O. Douglas recognized a similar danger in university admissions, warning in a 1974 case, "A segregated admissions process creates suggestions of stigma and class no less than a segregated classroom, and in the end it might produce that result despite its contrary intentions." Experience at hundreds of college and university campuses proves how prescient were Douglas's concerns.

Again, this should surprise no one. Such scholars as Donald Horowitz of Duke University, Myron Weiner of MIT, and Thomas Sowell of the Hoover Institution, who have studied race preferences in societies as diverse as Indonesia, Malaysia, Sri Lanka, and Nigeria, have found that uniformly they do not work and often produce results opposite to those intended. Sowell has shown that temporary, targeted preferences invariably expand to other groups or other fields such as employment, university admissions, government contracts, and political representation. The beneficiaries are invariably already comfortably ensconced in the middle or upper classes. Fraudulent claims for benefits multiply. Societal polarization is accentuated producing consequences from political backlash to civil war. In the end, the so-called remedy helps nothing.

In sum:

- Affirmative action is the practice of racial discrimination against whites or other nonfavored ethnic groups.
- It favors the less qualified over the more qualified.
- It is a systematic attack upon objective merit selection criteria.
- While increasing black enrollment at selective universities and expanding somewhat the pool of black entrepreneurs, it has brought few employment, educational, or income benefits to those most in need of help, and has distracted attention from the real causes of misery among inner-city blacks.
- As an ideology as much as a program, it has proven impervious to overwhelming evidence that it is counterproductive.
- It legitimizes negative stigmas and panders to the darker instincts of racial animosity.
- It has been broadened for political purposes to include beneficiaries who lack the historical claim of blacks for relief.
- It has shown a marked lack of success in other societies.
- Increasingly, it is being challenged successfully in the courts and in the political arena.

Why then does it persist? For one thing, a fair chunk of today's affirmative action regime evolved quietly, at times even while those responsible for authorizing or implementing it assured the public they were doing no such thing. Sponsors of the 1964 Civil Rights Act said repeatedly that reverse discrimination as well as numerical hiring goals and timetables were the furthest things from their minds. They also included a provision in the law purporting to protect the rights of employers to set standards as high as they would like and to use standardized tests to measure applicant qualifications. The first minority set-aside program was quietly inserted as an amendment to a noncontroversial bill in the late 1970s.

In practice, an assertive Equal Employment Opportunity Commission and compliant Supreme Court implemented the disparate impact standard that played such havoc with employment testing even as the Court itself claimed to be disallowing reverse discrimination. A far-reaching executive order created yet another agency (OFCCP) to implement and oversee affirmative action in the community of government contractors and subcontractors. The first out-and-out quota came out of an attempt by Richard Nixon's secretary of labor, George Shultz, and his assistant secretary, Arthur Fletcher, to correct the racially exclusionary policies of the Philadelphia building trades. In one way or another, each of these policies or decisions was ratified time and again by Congress. In 1982, Congress also transformed the Voting Rights Act from a statute sweeping aside Jim Crow practices that had prevented blacks from voting across the South into a requirement widely interpreted as requiring the entire country to redraw electoral districts and procedures to elect the maximum number of blacks and Hispanics.

Underlying these efforts is a consciousness of the massive wrongs done to blacks by this society and the notion that, if one must err, it ought to be on the side of too much redress rather than too little. Charles V. Hamilton of Columbia University has articulated brilliantly the unique nature of the black experience in this country. Yes, he agrees, other immigrant groups suffered injustice and indignity, but they had come voluntarily. However bleak their early experience, their situation was usually better than it had been in the "old country." They were grateful toward their adopted country. They were prepared to work hard and achieve in the private sector with no expectation that government was obliged to make their path easier.

On the other hand, "[b]lacks had to cease being property before they could acquire it." They alone suffered not just oppression and discrimination but dehumanization. By necessity, they looked to the central government for relief. The talent and energy of their leaders were devoted not to commercial enterprise, not to enhancing the community's wealth through private effort, but to waging the legal and political battles necessary to secure the most basic human rights.

For blacks and for whites, then, the battle for civil rights became not only a commitment to freedom and justice, but also a measure of themselves as human beings. But when that battle was won and the issue became affirmative action rather than equality before the law, affirmative action became what Shelby Steele has called an "iconographic" public policy. This is a "policy that ostensibly exists to solve a social problem but actually functions as an icon for the self-image people hope to gain by supporting the policy." For whites, supporting the policy was a mark of social virtue, for blacks, racial power. Thus, advocates were loathe to abandon the policy even as its failure became manifest. "The perniciousness of an iconographic policy is that you cannot be against it without seeming to be against what it purports to represent," Steele added. "The white who argues against affirmative action looks like a racist and the black looks like an Uncle Tom."

But a hard look at affirmative action today shatters the icon. There is no moral virtue in supporting a policy that corrupts the values it purports to serve. Nor is there any power in clinging to the rafters of a sinking ship.

2

A FAILED APPROACH

The extent to which affirmative action has expanded minority employment in skilled positions is unclear. The academic literature suggests that before 1974, minority employment growth in contractor firms was predominantly in unskilled positions. Since 1974, there is evidence of modest occupational advance in contractor firms. But some researchers think this may be the result of biased reporting....

—The White House Affirmative Action Review

The dirty little secret is that affirmative action doesn't work.

It is not a secret to those who study such matters for a living. Virtually every objective study, from academic, government, or professional sources, reaches the same conclusion: for all the fuss over affirmative action, the enormous impositions of government power, and the anger generated, the benefits to black workers are marginal at best. Affirmative action—i.e., efforts to require that minorities be hired in numbers approximating their "availability" in the relevant labor force—have virtually no effect on black unemployment or wage rates. In the larger scheme of things, this suggests that the effect on employment may even be negative. After all, this costly, intrusive effort has drained billions of dollars from the corporate sector over the years, money which otherwise might have gone toward such job-creating activities as research, capital formation, marketing, product improvement, and expanded plant capacity.

By contrast, there is general agreement among economists that desegregation and the outlawing of positive, overt discrimination, best represented by the Civil Rights Act of 1964 which dismantled the Jim Crow regime in the South, had an early and positive impact on black wage and employment rates there. A less than unanimous but still substantial plurality of economists would argue that the act, by attacking the erection of such artificial barriers as race, religion, or national origin (and later, gender), has had some good effect in the North as well, though the far earlier proliferation of Northern state laws banning employment discrimination and a somewhat more liberal social order had, to a substantial extent, already changed the landscape.

Crucial to the entire discussion of the issue is the distinction between nondiscrimination and various forms of affirmative action. As the term implies, nondiscrimination simply involves treating prospective and current employees according to objective standards that take no special account, positive or negative, of race or gender. There are a variety of "soft" affirmative action measures that hardly violate the notion of nondiscrimination. These include efforts to "expand the pool" of minority applicants while, in the end, judging all by objective criteria—for example, placing ads for available jobs in the black media or sending company recruiting teams to historically black colleges and universities. Such affirmative action efforts are so uncontroversial as to form no part of the angry discussion over what has become one of the nation's most controversial policies. The sort of affirmative action that is increasingly under challenge in the political arena and the courts goes farther and has two prongs, both designed to provide minorities with an advantage they would not have under simple nondiscrimination. The first involves the destruction of standards that are neutral on their face but that have a "disparate impact" upon minorities. Standardized tests that measure intelligence or academic potential are frequently attacked, not for lack of fairness, but rather because blacks and Hispanics tend to do less well than whites and Asians. Educational attainments, prior experience, even minimum competence to perform the job in question, as opposed to having the potential to be trained to perform it, are also under constant assault.

The second prong involves more blatant efforts to favor minorities. An employer may establish or be ordered to establish quotas, or, far more frequently, "goals and timetables" for achieving a designated percentage of minorities in its workforce. Race can be made a "plus" factor or "tie breaker" in hiring or promotion, or even layoffs. Minority applicants may be "normed," rated only against each other for purposes of obtaining a percentile score and then matched against whites whose far higher raw scores have been given a percentile rank based only on their comparison to other whites. "Diversity" can become the order of the day, with minority status given weight as an added job credential.

Even without a lawyer's knowledge of employment law or the Equal Protection Clause of the Fourteenth Amendment, common sense and an understanding of English would compel the conclusion that tossing out objective standards because relatively fewer blacks and Hispanics tend to meet them or making race an advantage in hiring, promotion, or layoffs are themselves forms of discrimination. To make such discrimination palatable to the law and to public opinion, government and sympathetic courts have attempted over the years to establish a structural foundation capable of supporting it. That foundation involves finding victimhood, that the minorities in question have been disadvantaged by previous or ongoing discrimination to the point at which equal treatment merely compounds the results of that discrimination and the only equitable relief involves preferential treatment for some indefinite period. This notion was articulated by President Lyndon B. Johnson in his memorable 1965 Howard University address:

> You do not take a person who for years has been hobbled by chains and liberate him, bring him to the starting line of a race and then say, "You are free to compete with all the others," and still justly believe you have been completely fair.

Or, as Supreme Court Justice Harry Blackmun argued in the historic *Bakke* case:

> In order to get beyond racism, we must first take account of race. There is no other way. And in order to treat some persons equally, we must treat them differently. We cannot—we dare not—let the Equal Protection Clause perpetuate racial supremacy.

However noble the intent, the result has been to produce a looking-glass world where fairness is reflected as unfairness and discrimination as equality. Among those agencies charged with civil rights enforcement, the world has become a search for victims entitled to some form of special inoculation from ordinary business practices, the application of merit standards, the traditional workings of the marketplace.

Almost every federal agency has some department that deals

with race and gender discrimination, but the Labor Department's Office of Federal Contract Compliance Program (OFCCP) Review, the Equal Employment Opportunity Commission (EEOC), and the Civil Rights Division at the Department of Justice have the broadest jurisdiction.

The Civil Rights Division was set up in the late 1950s to administer that era's rather toothless series of civil rights acts purporting to protect the right to vote. Forty years later its twenty-six lawyers form part of "the largest law firm in the nation," who scrutinize the entire spectrum of civil rights issues, ranging from enforcing the Voting Rights Act, to initiating its own investigations of alleged racial discrimination in mortgage lending and home insurance, to suing corporations for alleged discrimination in hiring or promoting minorities.

Both EEOC and OFCCP have their roots in Title VII of the Civil Rights Act of 1964 and were broadened and strengthened in 1972. While other sections attack racial discrimination in housing, transportation, education, and public accommodations, Title VII bans discrimination against individuals on grounds of race, color, religion, or national origin by employers with at least fifteen employees and by labor unions and employment agencies of any size. By 1972 educational institutions as well as state and local governments were brought under the act and gender discrimination was added to the list of forbidden practices. That year too EEOC was given the right to initiate legal action to remedy discriminatory practices rather than simply mediate or lobby the Civil Rights Division to sue.

While well over half the nation's labor force work for employers covered by Title VII, only 36 percent work for employers with one hundred or more employees. These larger employers are required to file annual "EEO-1" (Equal Employment Opportunity) reports with the agency, listing their employees in each job by race, gender, and ethnicity. An employer whose numbers are "wrong," in the sense of having statistically significantly fewer minorities or women in particular jobs than their local "availability" would suggest, runs the risk of an EEOC complaint or a class action lawsuit by plaintiffs claiming to be victims of a "pattern and practice" of discrimination.

As a result, the EEOC was an important player in many of the early job discrimination battles. Its near pathological opposition to employer-administered aptitude tests which had a "disparate impact" on minorities helped define one of the most important and long-running conflicts in the area of employment law. And it managed rather early to develop a statistical approach to the question of when an employer could be found to be "underutilizing" available minority personnel—the percentage employed must be sufficiently low to have only a 5 percent probability of occurring by chance. This was at least marginally acceptable to business.

In recent years, however, the EEOC has largely run out of cases of much precedential value due primarily to the virtual elimination of rampant institutional employment discrimination. Instead, the agency has become bogged down with tens of thousands of individual complaints, most involving promotions or layoffs. An American Bar Association survey between 1972 and 1987 found that only 19 percent of the employment discrimination lawsuits focused on hiring, while 59 percent alleged discrimination in termination and 22 percent in pay, promotion, or employee benefits. Practitioners in the field and industrial psychologists offer complementary explanations for the disparity between complaints based on hiring versus the other causes. First, a job applicant may have few expectations about being hired, no information at all on the circumstances of his rejection, and little or no contact with others similarly situated. And second, confronted with the pressure to make the numbers look "right," employers will often hire the marginally qualified, in effect postponing the day of reckoning until decisions on promotions or layoffs are demanded. As a result, wrote psychologist Linda Gottfredson of the University of Delaware, "Employers who think they are avoiding litigation by exercising preferential treatment in hiring are likely to have a rude shock when promotion time rolls around. Not only are blacks likely to have performed less well on the average if they were selected under lower standards, but jobs higher in a job ladder typically are more *g* loaded [require higher intelligence], which aggravates the dilemma."

OFCCP is the watchdog subagency within the Labor Department that was responsible for administering President Lyndon B. Johnson's 1965 Executive Order 11246—the most important affirmative action document in the government. It demands that covered employers take "affirmative action" to provide equal opportunity regardless of race, religion, or national origin. Later expanded to include gender, the order now covers nearly 200,000 government contractors and subcontractors hiring about 26 million people, just under 24 percent of the total labor force. Those not in construction—about half the total figure—must file annual affirmative action plans with the agency. Imperious, intrusive, confrontational, ideological, unsophisticated, intellectually dishonest, and hugely expensive, the OFCCP has contributed little to the economic lot of African Americans or other minorities. For all its zeal, it cannot perform the sort of alchemy that would transform those lacking education, skill, and sustained work experience into good employment risks. And, for identical reasons, very much the same could be said about the current EEOC and the Civil Rights Division at Justice.

Again, the reason OFCCP fails is because its entire mission today rests upon the faulty premise, well described in 1990 by economist June O'Neill—now director of the Congressional Budget Office—that due to racial discrimination, "significant numbers of minorities, or women, who can qualify for better paying jobs in the contractor sector, are outside, or inside at lower paying jobs, or unemployed." O'Neill is one of several economists in recent years who has had the intellectual courage to demonstrate that the differences in earnings between black and white males who appear to have similar credentials may still reflect real and important differences. For example, in the Armed Forces Qualification Test, administered to millions of draftees and volunteers over the decades, white males at every level of educational experience—from five to six years of elementary school through completion of four years of college—do substantially better than black males who have completed the same amount of schooling. Indeed, the performance of white high school graduates is only a few points below that of black college graduates. O'Neill attributes the results to "differences in the quality of schools attended and in family background." Her conclusion is diametrically opposed to the fundamental premise on which the OFCCP operates: "[i]t follows that, on average, blacks and whites with the same educational level may not be viewed as equally productive by nondiscriminating firms."

The statistical evidence is overwhelming that affirmative action has barely touched, let alone helped, the vast majority of blacks. According to the most recent statistics compiled by the federal government, black families had a real median income of $21,550 in 1993, not statistically different from their 1969 income of $22,000. The 1993 median income of white families was $39,310, higher than their 1969 level of $35,920. The ratio of black:white median family income was 0.61 percent in 1969 and had declined to 0.55 percent in 1993, reflecting in part the larger drop in black families maintained by married couples. By contrast, between 1969 and 1993, black families headed by married couples gained 31 percent in family income, from a median of $26,860 to $35,230, which is from 72 percent to 81 percent of the white level.

In 1993, 31 percent of black families and 8 percent of white families were poor; in 1969, 28 percent of black families and 8 percent of white families were poor. One-third of all black persons were poor in 1993, similar to their 1969 poverty rates of 32 percent. Among whites during the same period, there was a slight increase in poverty, from 10 percent in 1969 to 12 percent in 1993.

In 1993, of the 13.9 million blacks in the labor force, 12.1 million were employed and 2 million were unemployed. Blacks furnished 10.9 percent of the labor force, 10.2 percent of the employed, and 21 percent of the unemployed. The situation has held remarkably constant throughout the affirmative action era. White male employment ratios for those sixteen and over were 1.2 times those of black male employment ratios in every year from 1972 to 1993, except for 1.1 percent in 1971 and 1972, and 1.3 percent in 1982 and 1983. Just as strikingly, the hourly wage rate gap between blacks and whites, which shrank appreciably between 1940 and 1970, nearly doubled between 1976 and 1990, from a difference of 6.8 percent to 12.4 percent.

In its review which concluded that affirmative action had justified its continuation, the Clinton White House relied most heavily on the work of economists James Heckman of the University of Chicago and Jonathan Leonard of the University of California at Berkeley. But upon closer inspection, the work of both authors actually makes the case that affirmative action has accomplished little or nothing.

Heckman has collaborated with a number of fellow scholars, most notably John J. Donahue III of Northwestern University Law School and Orley Ashenfelter of Princeton University, in studies tracing the jagged rise of black income during the course of the twentieth century. Rather than a "continuous" process, Heckman found it to be "episodic," with decades of stagnation punctuated by sharp increases, triggered by such events as the opening up of high wage manufacturing jobs during the Second World War. One of the periods of high growth began a year after Congress passed the Civil Rights Act of 1964 and lasted through most of the 1965–75 decade, but only in a single region. For the nation as a whole, in 1965, the median earnings of full-time black male workers were .62 percent of those for white male workers. This rose to .72 percent by 1975 before leveling off and falling back to 69 percent by 1987. But when the national figures were broken down and assessed region by region, a strikingly different picture emerged. In the South, black full-time male workers made significant gains during the 1965–75 period, rising from 54 percent to 66 percent of comparable white wages, while in the Northeast, Midwest, and West there were hardly any changes.

This phenomenum was documented in Heckman and Donahue's definitive 1990 study, "Continuous Versus Episodic Change: The Impact of Civil Rights Policy on the Economic Status of Blacks," published in the *Journal of Economic Literature*. In it they write of the period 1965–89: "For the non-South, there is virtually no improvement in the earnings deficit of black men during the 24-year period. In contrast, Southern blacks experienced sharp relative gains over the decade 1965–75, with virtual stagnation thereafter." The authors attribute this gain to the impact and enforcement of the 1964 act, which broke apart the regime of segregation that had existed throughout the South since Reconstruction ended and closed certain categories of jobs to blacks up to and including all but the most menial in the entire textile industry. In South Carolina, for example, prior to the Civil Rights Act, it had been illegal "[i]n the business of cotton textile manufacturing in this state to allow or permit operatives, help, and labor of different races to labor and work together within the same room, or to use the same doors of entrance and exit at the same time, or... to use the same stairway and windows at the same time, or to use at any time the same lavatories, toilets, drinking water buckets, pails, cups, dippers or glasses."

After the 1964 act, the textile industry was quickly opened to black workers, as were other industries across the South. In the words of Heckman and Donahue, "Substantial numbers of Southern employers appear to have been willing to gain access to the cheap supply of black labor, but required the excuse of federal pressure to defy long-standing community norms regarding employment of blacks." In his study with Ashenfelter, Heckman found that in the five-year period, 1965–70, the ratio of black:white male employees working for any given employer increased 20 percent more in the South than in the rest of the country. And the probability that an employer with no black workers in 1966 would have at least one in 1970 was 14 percent greater in the South than nationally.

All of this is entirely consistent with mainstream economic theory as well as historical precedent. Gary Becker, who won the Nobel Prize for Economics in 1992 for his analysis of nonmarket behavior, has propounded a "theory of discrimination" which holds that absent legal sanction, individual employers may develop a "taste for discrimination," which, in economic terms, translates into "a willingness to forfeit income to avoid transactions that involve members of the minority group." Discrimination costs employers who discriminate because they pay a higher price for dealing only with workers, clients, suppliers, or customers of the more favored race or ethnic group. Competitive pressure makes it unlikely that those with an uncompromising "taste for discrimination" can survive.

Becker's theory is, of course, an economic model, like the simple demand curve, which postulates valid economic theory but assumes a level of knowledge and mobility that in fact exists only imperfectly in the contemporary marketplace. It may also understate the coercive power of social pressures in the "real world" which can perpetuate employer discrimination even among those with a scant personal "taste for it"—witness the virtual exclusion of Jews by the "WASP" Wall Street law and investment banking firms well into the 1950s and 1960s. Professor Richard A. Epstein of the University of Chicago Law School may, therefore, be stating the case too emphatically when he writes, "What no one should fear is a set of social practices against any group that are not propped up by state power and domination. Within markets, a single person can deviate from the norm and guarantee enormous profits by catering to that section of a market that is left unexploited by others."

Still, history does show that Jim Crow laws were passed not to reinforce the decisions that were being made in the marketplace but to preempt them. For example, economic historian Jennifer Roback has shown that Jim Crow labor laws enacted in the Southern states during the post-Reconstruction period were designed not to reinforce practices already in existence but to make employers stop hiring black workers at the expense of more highly paid whites. Similarly, a central purpose of the Davis Bacon Act of 1933, which effectively required federal contractors to pay union scale wages on the job, was to prevent contractors from hiring lower paid black workers from the South.

Factors beyond federal antidiscrimination laws also contributed to the relative improvement of blacks in the 1965–75 period. Princeton economists David Card and Alan Krueger (Krueger served as chief Department of Labor economist during part of the Clinton administration) calculate that about 20 percent of the increase can be attributed to improvements in the quality of elementary and secondary schools attended by blacks in the years immediately prior to the growth in real wages. And blacks were increasingly moving on to higher education. In 1950, 50,000 blacks had graduated from college, most at historically black institutions. By 1960, the number had reached 200,000; by 1970, 470,000, more than half from integrated colleges and universities. Happily, these trends have continued. In 1980, 51 percent of blacks age 25 and over had graduated from high school and 8 percent from college. By 1994, those figures had risen to 73 percent and 13 percent, respectively. For those blacks able to achieve higher education, the rewards have been great. Between 1970 and 1986, for example, black households with incomes above $50,000 increased by 200 percent, a figure that reflected not only an increase in two-spouse working families, but also an upward movement from the middle to the higher income brackets.

Offsetting these trends were the factors responsible for black income stagnation: an economic shift from high wage manufacturing to low wage service jobs; the increased demand for highly skilled labor; the continued deterioration of inner cities and, hence, their lack of attraction for prospective employers; and a shocking increase in black male involvement in crime. But what comes through every credible study of black economic progress during the period is that it was concentrated in the South, that it was due to the adoption of nondiscrimination practices by Southern employers rather than to the voguish assortment of affirmative action and "diversity" programs subsequently forced upon and later embraced by American industry, and, indeed, that it occurred during a period when the legal and administrative tools for affirmative action were, at best, fragmentary.

EEOC did not receive the right to enforce its mandates until 1972, close to the end of the period of black economic progress. The notion of "disparate impact" was unknown until the 1971 Supreme Court decision in *Griggs v. Duke Power.* And voluntary race preference affirmative action programs in the private sector did not receive Supreme Court sanction until the 1979 *Weber* case—by which time black income relative to whites had begun its slide. Moreover, as economist Farrell Bloch tellingly notes in his fine academic study, *Antidiscrimination Law and Minority Employment,* the staffing and budget of both EEOC and OFCCP were at their lowest points during the period of greatest black economic progress, rose precipitously as the black economic condition worsened, and then fell gently but persistently as the black economic situation stagnated. During the 1960s, EEOC never had more than a staff of 579 and a budget of $25 million in constant 1982–84 dollars. This grew to a staff of just over 3,300 and a budget of $159 million in 1981 before tapering off to a staff of 2,700 and a budget of $150 million in 1992, still in 1982–84 dollars. OFCCP too began small before reaching a staff of 1,482 and an operating budget of over $64 million in 1980, again in constant 1982–1984 dollars. In 1992, its staff was 856 and its operating budget just under $40 million. During the period 1980–89, its constant dollar funding was reduced by about 28 percent.

Leonard, the other academician relied on by the Clinton White House to sustain the effectiveness of affirmative action, ignored income data in favor of an approach that compared manpower records of employers covered by OFCCP affirmative action reporting requirements—those with at least fifty employees and government contracts or subcontracts of $50,000 in any particular year—with those not required to report. During the period 1974–80, he found that the growth in minority hiring in covered firms exceeded the growth in uncovered firms by a total of 0.6 percent. After 1980, the difference evaporated, a fact which the Clinton Affirmative Action Review acknowledged, conceding that "available evidence suggests that OFCCP did not have a noticeable impact on the hiring of minority workers by contractor firms in the early and mid-1980s." Both Leonard and the Clinton team attribute this rather devastating indictment of affirmative action policies to unenthusiastic enforcement by OFCCP during the Reagan years. But Krueger, the former top Labor Department economist, offers a somewhat different explanation: "I think that by 1980, most firms had stopped discriminating on the basis of race, whether they were covered or not." And, as early as 1981, economist Richard Freeman observed that "background differences appear to have become a more important impediment than market discrimination to attainment of black–white economic parity among the young."

Bloch's book offers additional explanation as to why affirmative action policies have had such a marginal impact on black employment. For one thing, information regarding available positions, particularly involving smaller companies, often spreads via a "word of mouth network" to which blacks have limited access. Their historically low rates of entrepreneurship reduce one valuable source of employment information. And they may be geographically remote from the facility offering new jobs because, due to high crime rates and other adverse environmental factors, job-creating businesses may prefer not to operate in the inner city. Finally, Bloch suggests that, "in deciding which applicants will become serious job candidates, employers favor initial screening criteria that disproportionately exclude minorities." These screens may include drug testing; a disinclination to consider those who, as adults, ran afoul of the criminal justice system; or an insistence on experience or prior training for the work in question.

Even the modest figures assembled by the Clinton team may, as they acknowledge, overstate the net benefit to minority workers of government-administered affirmative action. If an employer is under federal pressure to hire more minorities and he wants to find those most qualified to fill a vacancy, he will almost certainly recruit most heavily among those who already have similar jobs and are doing them well. Thus, it is reasonable to suppose that much of the difference observed by Leonard between covered and uncovered employers reflected nothing more than a modest migration of minority workers from jobs in the sector that had little to fear from federal oversight to those that had much to fear. Sure enough, government figures show that in 1966, black men were 10 percent less likely than white men to work in firms required to file EEO-1 reports, while by 1980, they were 25 percent more likely to work in such firms. Black women were also 10 percent less likely to work in covered firms in 1966, but by 1980 were 50 percent more likely to do so.

Thus, the White House's first adopted scholar, Heckman, concludes that while antidiscrimination efforts had some early effects on black income in the South, affirmative action has done little or nothing anywhere, including the South; its second scholar, Leonard, depicts nothing more impressive than a modest migration of blacks from small to large employers and government contractors during a period that ended around 1980. In neither case has affirmative action had any quantifiable effect for at least fifteen years, and perhaps as long as twenty. Indeed, in his most recent writing on the subject, Leonard himself laments the evolution of affirmative action from an effort to combat employment discrimination to one whose mission is to combat the results of past discrimination by providing special treatment for minorities on the job, thereby achieving "equality of result rather than equality of opportunity." Leonard believes the reason affirmative action has now stirred so much in the way of political controversy has more to do with "its symbolic importance as a totem of group rights and privileges than with its modest accomplishments to date."

The situation with respect to occupational categories is similar. Bloch constructed Table 1 based upon EEO-1 reports, OFCCP filings, and data from the 1990 census showing rather small differences in the positions achieved by black employees of covered and uncovered establishments, with those in the uncovered establishments actually having higher percentages in technical, sales, professional, and managerial positions.

Table 1. Affirmative Action Does Little to Increase Minority Employment

Occupational category	Federal Contractors	Firms filing EEO-1 Reports	Experienced Labor Force*
	Minorities (%)		
Officials and managers	10.1	10.1	13.1
Professionals	13.5	13.0	15.6
Technicians	18.8	19.0	19.6
Sales workers	18.6	18.8	17.5
Office and clerical workers	24.2	23.1	21.7
Craft workers	17.0	17.5	18.5
Operatives	28.8	28.9	30.3
Laborers	36.1	37.2	31.8
Service workers	40.5	39.4	32.5
Total	**23.1**	**23.0**	**22.3**
	Women (%)		
Officials and managers	25.0	28.1	36.0
Professionals	37.8	48.0	53.4
Technicians	35.4	44.8	44.1
Sales workers	52.5	57.2	53.9
Office and clerical workers	82.5	83.4	77.2
Craft workers	8.8	10.6	7.5
Operatives	32.5	33.4	31.5
Laborers	33.4	34.4	16.4
Service workers	51.0	55.5	58.2
Total	**39.9**	**43.9**	**42.0**

*The "Experienced Labor Force" includes all workers currently employed plus those who have worked within the past five years and are actively seeking employment. The power of the chart is that it shows that for many types of jobs, minorities in the broader labor force appear to be doing as well or better than those protected by federal affirmative action requirements.

There is some evidence that even these figures exaggerate the progress of blacks and other minorities. Economists James P. Smith and Finnis Welch suggest "that a substantial part of the growth in occupational status may be due to job relabeling due to affirmative action requirements." In other words, secretaries become "administrative assistants," bookkeepers become "unit managers," and file clerks become "assistant personnel managers," all with job descriptions and, perhaps, salaries identical to their former incarnations. The changes, of course, have been made to satisfy what the federal affirmative action or equal opportunity officials want the management profile of a nondiscriminating employer to look like.

For years, too, professionals in the field noted the stockpiling of minority managerial talent in personnel departments far removed from departments like finance or production with real influence in the organization. A former senior OFCCP official turned consultant noted matter-of-factly, "You'd be surprised at how many of my clients have African American affirmative action management teams whose principal job is recruiting other African Americans for the affirmative action management team." This practice has to some extent fallen victim to the vagaries of the business cycle and the recent "leaner, meaner" wave of corporate reorganizations. During the economic downturn of the 1990–92 period, blacks employed by the nation's largest companies lost their jobs at a disproportionate rate. According to congressional testimony by former Transportation Secretary William T. Coleman, Jr., a study of 35,000 companies employing more than 40 million workers concluded that blacks lost 59,479 jobs during the period in question, while Asians gained a net of 55,104, Hispanics a net 60,040, and whites a net 71,144. Blacks lost nearly one-third of the blue collar jobs eliminated during the recession and were the only group to lose service worker positions even though there was a substantial net increase of such jobs. The very strong inference is that employees who have been hired to make the numbers look "right," or in the hope that they will acquire the necessary skills on the job, are particularly vulnerable to a shift in business fortunes. This development was anticipated as long ago as the 1970s, when Smith and Welch noted that young college educated blacks were the most immediate beneficiaries of affirmative action as companies competed frantically for them in order to satisfy OFCCP numerical analysis. But as these recruits competed with others on the basis of objective performance, many found themselves frozen in relatively low positions as corporations simply were not able to maintain the "affirmative action bubble" over an indefinite period.

Nor is government employment proving the nondepletable reservoir of job security blacks had expected. At its high point in the late 1980s and early 1990s, some 240,000 blacks found places in the federal government in white collar and managerial positions. Many are now among the 140,000 federal jobs held by blacks that have been eliminated or slated for elimination in the Republican-generated budgetary cutbacks or the "reinventing government" initiative of the Clinton administration.

Despite mountainous evidence that affirmative action doesn't work because it is the wrong medicine for the wrong disease, the Clinton administration continues to suffer from the virus identified by Leonard—the belief that antidiscrimination laws are appropriate vehicles for righting historic wrongs—plus the misguided notion that continuing discriminatory barriers are institutional, pervasive, and debilitating. After running through the economic analysis noted above which largely undermines the efficacy of affirmative action programs, the same White House report then urged their continuation on the basis of the standard raw data on unemployment rates, i.e., that the black economic situation is considerably less favorable than it is for whites, Asians, and others.

Theodore M. Shaw, associate director counsel of the National Association for the Advancement of Colored People (NAACP) Legal Defense Fund, went through the same litany in his March 1995 testimony before the House Subcommittee on Employer–Employee Relations: "African Americans, who constitute 11 percent of the total workforce, made up less than 4 percent of the following occupations as of 1993: lawyers and judges (2.7 percent), dentists (1.9 percent), doctors (3.7 percent), industrial engineers (3.4 percent), engineers (3.7 percent), managers in marketing, advertising, and public relations (3.1 percent)."

True enough, sir, but what is the point? Are qualified black doctors failing to obtain residency appointments or internships? Where are all those black engineers hanging out? Breathes there a law school admissions dean who is not already admitting African American candidates with Law School Admission Tests (LSATs) and grade point averages (GPAs) substantially below rejected white candidates? Yet Shaw's views and those of other civil rights advocacy groups cannot be taken casually.

Shirley Wilcher, head of OFCCP in the Clinton administration, made known early on that she attaches importance to the advice of such organizations in determining the appropriate focus to her ameliorative efforts. For at least four thousand firms each year, those efforts include a formal OFCCP "compliance review." Few firms are selected for review because someone has complained of discrimination. Often an OFCCP computer check may identify a contractor whose percentage of blacks or other minorities appears below others in the area. The agency is particularly on the lookout for firms within growth industries. Thus, in a 1994 "Enforcement Strategy" memorandum, Ms. Wilcher announced she would target "fifty-five compliance reviews for growth industries including health, business, motor freight, warehousing, transportation by air transportation services, auto, electronics, telecommunications, pharmaceutical, employment temporaries, retail, and the finance and insurance industries." Once again, social engineering wears the mask of law enforcement.

The review process begins with a two-page letter generally signed by the district director announcing the review, its time, and location—usually the place of business—and instructing the recipient to submit in advance its Affirmative Action Plan (AAP) together with all relevant employment data. Since any realistic paper projecting future personnel and staffing directions could tell a lot about business and marketing strategies which a company would rather not share with competitors and since all AAP-related material is subject to disclosure under the Freedom of Information Act, many companies are less than candid in what they make available. Any number of prominent attorneys and consultants will concede matter-of-factly that they have clients who routinely prepare two AAPs, one for internal use and the other for disclosure to the OFCCP during a compliance review.

Once they get going, the compliance reviews are nothing if not comprehensive. During the third quarter of 1993, for example, the average time spent on a construction industry audit was 52 hours; on a nonconstruction audit, 141 hours; and on a university audit (bastions of racism all), 427 hours. Small wonder that campus tales proliferate, both real and metaphorical, about efforts to explain why the Slavic Studies opening failed to go to a black or Native American scholar or why tenure was not granted to a minority instructor with zero publications but fascinating classroom oratory.

The procedure is, of course, kafkaesque. If the OFCCP had no intention of finding noncompliance, it would not have investigated in the first place. So it is not surprising that approximately 75 percent of its reviews generate allegations of substantial violation. The contractor then has the options of accepting the proposed remedy, which usually involves back pay for those allegedly discriminated against; creating job or promotion offers, plus some concrete plan for changing the offending practice or procedure; or resisting through an internal OFCCP "trial" presided over by an Administrative Law Judge. The latter course has a few concrete disadvantages. One, of course, is expense. A second is the discomfort of watching accumulated goodwill disappear as the government brands you a racist, a power duly noted in Ms. Wilcher's "Enforcement Strategy" memorandum, which declared, "OFCCP will also use the media as a deterrent by publicizing its enforcement efforts and the penalties and sanctions it has obtained against the worst actors." But the most compelling reason to settle up is time: the period between the initial finding of noncompliance and the ultimate determination of the case inside the agency has been known to stretch to twenty years.

So contractors tend to negotiate settlements. Fighting and compromising over how many new jobs to offer protected minorities or how much back pay to provide has become an almost routine cost of doing business for many contractors. Those costs are not small. A 1980 study undertaken by the Arthur Andersen accounting firm concluded that contractors had expenses attributable to regulation by OFCCP 6.5 percent greater than noncontractors. Today, this regulatory agency, established by executive order, is threatening employers with the loss of federal business unless they hire workers who, without a special training program, are manifestly unqualified for the positions available, and who, even after special training, may well be less qualified than others.

How does a statute, fairly simply worded and purporting only to ban discrimination in employment, evolve into a such a complicated system?

In the case of affirmative action, the answers are:

- First, begin with a plausibly deniable agenda of granting special race preferences to cure the effects of past societal discrimination.
- Second, expand the definition of employment discrimination beyond its plain meaning of intentional bias in hiring, promotion, and termination.
- Third, use the expanded definition to order race-conscious remedies, including numerical quotas, goals, and timetables—traditional enforcement tools—once discrimination has been established.
- Fourth, press sympathetic courts to provide legal cover for racial preferences, both in the public and private sectors, even where no discrimination has been proven or no victims identified.
- Fifth, be alert for new opportunities to "push the envelope" even further, expanding the policy objectives able to support preferential treatment of racial minorities.

How did this come about? Where do its roots lie? In the period just prior to passage of the 1964 Act, the focus of much of the civil rights movement began to shift from breaking the chains of Southern racial segregation to attacking the gross disparities in wealth, housing, and job opportunities nationwide. The old civil rights organizations were challenged as staid, passive, and irrelevant. The voices of Martin Luther King Jr., Roy Wilkins, and Bayard Rustin were often drowned out by those of Malcolm X, Stokely Carmichael, and H. Rap Brown.

Riots in Harlem and Los Angeles foreshadowed later uprisings in Detroit, Newark, Rochester, Washington, D.C., and more than half a dozen other cities. Militant blacks were preaching "Black Power" and proposing "reparations"—payments for past injustice—converting even some moderates to their cause. Urban

League President Whitney Young, for example, called for "a decade of discrimination in favor of Negro youth," while James Farmer of the Committee on Racial Equality (CORE) asked for "some special treatment to overcome the effects of the long special treatment of a negative sort that we have had in the past."

In his classic study, *The Civil Rights Era,* historian Hugh Davis Graham traces how radical black calls for special treatment found a sympathetic audience among some white liberals. They also provided ammunition for opponents of the Civil Rights Act and required supporters to reject in seemingly clear and definitive language any notion of racial preferences. Southern senators led by Sam Ervin of North Carolina and John Tower of Texas asserted that the act would indeed impose quotas and other racial preferences on society. This forced President Kennedy to disown the notion of quotas as compensation for past maltreatment of blacks: "I don't think we can undo the past. In fact, the past is going to be with us for a good many years in uneducated men and women who lost their chance for a decent education. We have to do the best we can now. That is what we are trying to do. I don't think quotas are a good idea. I think it is a mistake to begin to assign quotas on the basis of religion, or race, or color, or nationality. I think we'd get into a good deal of trouble."

The Democrat's "Happy Warrior," Hubert H. Humphrey, was even more emphatic, declaring during debate on the bill, "I will start eating the pages of the law, page by page, if anyone can find a clause that calls for quotas, preferences of racial balance in jobs or education." Senator Clifford Case, the Republican floor manager added, "There is no requirement in Title VII that an employer maintain a racial balance in his workforce. On the contrary, any deliberate attempt to maintain a racial balance, whatever such a balance may be, would involve a violation of Title VII because maintaining such a balance would require an employer to hire or refuse to hire on the basis of race. It must be emphasized that discrimination is prohibited to any individual."

But quotas, goals, and timetables were already part of the standard remedial inventory of the courts in seeking redress for the victims of de jure segregation, particularly with respect to Southern school systems. And wherever the courts, or later, the EEOC, or the OFCCP could find clear evidence of the disparate treatment of blacks and whites in employment, their ability to grant similar relief would become clear. But with the exception of certain Southern industries, such as textiles, it was not easy to find race discrimination in employment blatant enough and sufficiently systemic to invite judicial or administrative cures that would work on a scale big enough to matter. So, a search was begun for a situation where the government could justify a truly ambitious remedy.

The bridge between the 1964 Act and what would become the OFCCP's approach to regulation was the "Philadelphia Plan," which sought to establish employment quotas in the Philadelphia construction trades. The effort was initiated during the Johnson administration and concluded in the Nixon administration through the tough-minded leadership of Secretary of Labor George Shultz.

Philadelphia was a place where virtual segregation was maintained by a small handful of construction craft locals and where heavy federal spending gave Washington substantial clout. Rather than taking labor on directly, the Johnson administration decided to work through federal contractors, requiring the winner of a competitive bid to provide the Labor Department with "manning tables," indicating the percentage of minority workers it planned to employ on the job. If the department found the numbers unsatisfactory, it would begin negotiations for higher ones, the ultimate sanction being recision of the award. Intragovernmental and legal disputes stalled the plan's implementation during the Johnson presidency, but it was revived with gusto by Nixon, Shultz, and Shultz's deputy, Arthur Fletcher. The latter modified the plan by requiring contractors to agree to hire minorities— blacks, Asians, Native Americans, and Spanish-surnamed work- ers—within government-prescribed target ranges prior to receiving the federal contract award. As Fletcher put it, "Visible, measurable goals to correct obvious imbalances are essential."

The fledgling OFCCP went to school on the Philadelphia Plan. In order to put its machinery into high gear, the agency imi- tated Shultz and Fletcher and applied their new approach even to situations where, unlike Philadelphia, there was no evidence of deliberate discrimination either on the part of labor or industry. The result was the agency's "Order Number 4," promulgated in 1971 and still in effect, which, together with implementing reg- ulations, is the regime OFCCP has followed ever since.

The heart of the concept is "underutilization," which OFCCP defines as "having fewer minorities in a particular job category than would reasonably be expected by their availability." Employ- ers discovering they have been underutilizing minorities must come up with a plan including "goals and timetables" to redress the problem. The agency and its apologists have maintained for better than two decades that "goals and timetables" differ from quotas in that their standard is a good faith effort on the part of the employer rather than a rigid numerical straitjacket. But the distinction is largely erased by the OFCCP's own implementing regulations defining minority "availability."

Since 1978, the agency has relied on eight criteria to determine availability: (1) the minority population of the labor area sur- rounding the facility; (2) the size of the minority unemployment force in the labor area surrounding the facility; (3) the percentage of the minority workforce as compared with the total workforce in the immediate labor area; (4) the general availability of minorities having requisite skills in the immediate labor area; (5) the availability of minorities having the requisite skills in the area in which the contractor can reasonably recruit; (6) the availability of promotable and transferable minorities within the contractor's organization; (7) the existence of training institutions capable of training persons in the requisite skills; and (8) the degree of training which the contractor is reasonably able to undertake as a means of making all job classes available to minorities.

Even at a casual glance it is clear that some of the criteria are not even remotely relevant to the issue of availability—for example, general data on population and unemployment rates—while others, such as training, suggest preferential treatment for the protected classes, and still others, such as the concept of "requisite skills," are highly subjective and have, in fact, given rise to decades of debate. Moreover, efforts to estimate the numbers of available minority workers possessing the requisite skills in defined job categories rely upon data which are, at best, crude and imperfect, as are efforts even to define the appropriate population areas. For example, when it comes to construction jobs, both skilled and unskilled, the OFCCP makes the entirely unsupported assumption that available minority workers reflect the percentage of minorities in the population at large.

But, most tellingly, once the agency decides that the contractor has not sufficiently utilized *available* minority talent, it can require the establishment of *goals* and *timetables*. Once it does, a contractor is hardly in a strong position to assert that he cannot meet the goals and timetables because insufficient numbers of minority job candidates are available to meet them because that issue has already been resolved by the agency's finding. For that reason, while allowing for the occasional exception, such as where unanticipated hard times result in drastically curtailed hiring which delays an employer's ability to achieve the minority hiring timetable, most practitioners in the field see goals and timetables as the functional equivalent of quotas.

The OFCCP has gone to extravagant lengths to deny this, to the extent, under Ms. Wilcher, of promulgating an order warning that employers who establish quotas will be charged with violating Title VII. Both the agency and the courts have declared that, unlike a quota, an employer need never hire an unqualified minority candidate to achieve a goal and cannot be subject to sanctions should good faith efforts fail to identify a sufficient number of qualified and available minority applicants to meet its goal. In practice, however, this usually turns out to be a distinction without a difference. Federal Court of Appeals Judge Laurence Silberman, who served as Undersecretary of Labor during the period 1970–73 when many of the "goals and timetables" policies were taking root, has written that policymakers at the time wished to create "a generalized, firm, but gentle pressure to balance the residue of discrimination." Instead, Silberman, Shultz & Company created a monster. As Silberman acknowledged, "I now realize that the distinction we saw between goals and timetables on the one hand, and unconstitutional quotas on the other, was not valid. Our use of numerical standards in pursuit of equal opportunity has led to the very quotas guaranteeing equal results that we initially wished to avoid."

The pithy assessment of neoconservative Irving Kristol also seems apt: "Government officials, corporate human relations' executives, and university presidents loudly protest that quotas are anathema to them, and that they merely have nonspecific goals in mind. It is also true that these people are lying."

■ ■ ■

In an important sense, affirmative action has presented a far more difficult problem for the federal courts than the long line of desegregation cases that followed the historic 1954 *Brown v. Board* decision. The desegregation cases involved official government actions. If a state or local government treated the races differently, the court intervened. Moreover, most of the actions were initiated by such plaintiffs as schoolchildren, voters, or users of public accommodations—the obvious victims of the official discrimination.

When, on the other hand, the Supreme Court has been asked to review affirmative action cases, the issues have been far more subtle. Responding to regulatory or community pressure, an employer may decide to give some form of preference to minority job applicants until such time as a more ethnically balanced workforce is achieved. Often, the beneficiaries have not themselves felt the bite of past discrimination, and the whites passed over for employment, training, or promotion have not themselves received past preference over more qualified minority candidates. If some form of race preference does receive judicial sanction, questions arise as to how long it ought to remain in effect. If, for example, an employer is permitted to consider race a "plus factor" in a community where 25 percent of the population and 10 percent of the available workers for the job in question are black, but where only 2 percent of the employees in that particular job category are black, should the same practice be permitted when the percentage of blacks holding the jobs in question rises to 5 percent, or 10 percent, or 18 percent? And there are even more troublesome questions concerning layoffs. A white male applying for a job or admission to an on-the-job training program may not have expected to be chosen and may be only marginally inconvenienced by being passed over in favor of a black applicant. But the same white male who has been on the job for ten years does legitimately expect to keep his job during a period of cutbacks, at least over someone who has been with the company for only six months.

In a series of important decisions beginning with the 1979 *Weber* case, the Supreme Court developed a number of key principles:

- *United Steelworkers of America AFL-CIO v. Weber* established the proposition that despite the Title VII ban on race discrimination by private employers, an employer may initiate a race-conscious training program designed to "eliminate manifest imbalances in traditionally segregated job categories" and that the beneficiaries may include those who were not personally victimized by past discrimination.

- In *Johnson v. Transportation Agency,* government employers were also granted judicial license to atone for alleged past discrimination, in this instance by hiring a female with slightly lower test scores than a male competitor. The 5–4 Supreme Court decision drew an unusually sharp dissent from Justice Antonin Scalia who charged his colleagues with converting Title VII "from a guarantee that race and sex will *not* be the basis for employment determinations, to a guarantee that it often *will*." Scalia continued: "A statute designed to establish a color-blind and gender-blind workplace has thus been converted into a powerful engine of racism and sexism...."

- But *Wygant v. Jackson Board of Education* clarified the limits of race-consciousness. In it, the Supreme Court rejected either past societal discrimination or the putative need for black role models as sufficiently compelling argument for racial preferences where the issue was the city's attempt to dismiss white teachers while keeping blacks with less seniority.

As the Clinton administration took office, these and related cases had fairly clearly defined the legal status of affirmative action. Both public and private employers were allowed to engage in voluntary race-conscious practices in hiring, training, and promotion even where the intended beneficiaries had not personally been victims of past discrimination, but only to remedy past discriminatory employment or union practices. While past discrimination with respect to the particular jobs in question could justify voluntary race consciousness, general societal discrimination or the desire to cultivate minority role models could not. Further, the rights of innocent white employees could not be unduly trammeled in the process. In no case, for example, during the entire affirmative action era, has the Supreme Court sustained the discriminatory dismissal of whites in order to protect the job status of more recently hired blacks. Finally, while no case decided by the Court sustaining race-consciousness has put a fixed time limit on the practice, even those writing for the majority usually suggest that after, say, ten years, race-conscious employment policies should cease.

The defining moment for the Clinton administration's view of race preferences involved the city of Piscataway, New Jersey, which, in 1989, during the Bush administration, was confronted with budget cuts requiring the dismissal of several teachers. The business education staff at Piscataway High School had to choose between laying off Deborah Williams, a black, and Sharon Taxman, a white, both with equal experience and job ratings. Normally, this would have been decided by the flip of a coin. In this case, though, the Board of Education decided to dismiss Ms. Taxman. As in *Wygant,* there was no documented history of past race discrimination in hiring teachers and, indeed, the high school enjoyed robust black faculty representation. But among the nine teachers in business education, Ms. Williams was the only black.

And, unlike Jackson, Michigan, which had justified its favoritism by claiming the need for black role models, Piscataway used the venerable buzz word "diversity" to justify its action. The Bush Justice Department entered the case on behalf of Ms. Taxman, but when the Clinton administration took over, Deval Patrick, head of the administration's Civil Rights Division, switched sides, an action publicly and explicitly endorsed by President Clinton.

Mr. Patrick would subsequently try to minimize the significance of his decision. In testimony prepared for the House Subcommittee on Employer–Employee Relations, he feigned even-handedness, endorsing the "value of maintaining an integrated faculty.... " But in fact, the faculty at Piscataway High School *was* integrated; only the single small business department was predominantly white. Nor was the issue as narrow as Mr. Patrick and President Clinton maintained. To the contrary, with one audacious stroke, the new Justice Department broke a quarter-century of precedent by asking the federal courts to back the firing of a white employee in the name of affirmative action. For the first time it asked the courts to enshrine faculty "diversity" as lawful ground for government race discrimination, the Fourteenth Amendment notwithstanding. Contrary to all existing case law, it asked the courts to legitimize race preferences where there was no history of discrimination, no manifest racial imbalance, and no traditionally segregated job categories, thereby providing vast new opportunities for race-conscious government intervention.

One suspects that none of this escaped the adroit Mr. Patrick. Nor is it likely to have escaped that former teacher of constitutional law, William Jefferson Clinton.

3

STRANGE BEDFELLOWS

In 1975, a federal trial court in New York City found that Local 28 of the Sheet Metal Workers' International Association had been systematically excluding blacks from membership and from participation in its apprenticeship program. The court ordered the union to revise its admission procedures, end restrictions on the issuance of temporary work permits, and adopt a publicity campaign to make nonwhites aware of employment opportunities through the union. The court further established a 29 percent minority membership target and ordered the union to achieve the figure by 1981 or demonstrate why it couldn't. The union's change of practices was, at best, haphazard and, by 1981, it had come nowhere near meeting the quota mandated by the court. The following year, the court held the union in contempt, not, it suggested, for failing to meet the numerical target, but for not taking all the remedial steps needed to make the target achievable. Now the court ordered a slightly higher percentage quota to be achieved by 1987, and it ordered Local 28 to establish a training fund for minorities that would enable them to become full-fledged skilled craftsmen by the target year. The order was sustained by the Court of Appeals for the Second Circuit and, eventually, by a divided Supreme Court.

The case reached the Supreme Court at a time when Clarence Thomas, now a conservative justice, was running the Equal Employment Opportunity Commission (EEOC). At Thomas's direction, the agency intervened on the side of the union in two critical respects, arguing, first, that it was inappropriate to grant relief to individuals who had not themselves been victims of the illegal discrimination, and, second, that the special training fund ordered by the trial court would violate Title VII of the 1964 Civil Rights Act because it would benefit minorities exclusively. In addition, the union itself challenged the numerical goal established by the court.

On the face of things, it would seem that the case presented the business community with a golden opportunity to join a sympathetic executive branch in erasing some of the more troublesome aspects of the affirmative action regime. Thousands of businesses, for example, need to maintain a costly and time-consuming Affirmative Action Plan (AAP). Employers, moreover, are faced daily with the risk and uncertainty of potential vulnerability—usually in the form of back pay—to people who claim they have been denied employment or promotion on the basis of race, but who have merely failed to pass some screening procedure later found to have a "disparate impact" upon one minority or another.

Sure enough, the National Association of Manufacturers (NAM), which represents most of the nation's largest employers, did file a brief in the case. So did the Equal Employment Advisory Council, an exceptionally influential group in employment law which includes most of the Fortune 300 companies. But both intervened against the union and the Reagan administration, successfully urging the Supreme Court to uphold the trial court's order.

The NAM brief is particularly revealing, first, for its fulsome endorsement of affirmative action: "NAM believes that effective affirmative action plans include outreach, recruitment, counseling, and training activities designed to ensure that qualified minorities and women are considered, for employment opportunities. Goals for minority workforce participation are merely an effective measurement of program success."

Second, like most business organizations that have addressed the subject, NAM sought to articulate a distinction between "goals" and "quotas" with which its members could live. The brief suggested at one point that a goal, like a quota, was a requirement for "a specified racial percentage which must be met by a specified date," but which, unlike a quota, "need not be maintained thereafter." Elsewhere in the brief, a goal was defined as "a numerical objective fixed realistically in terms of the number of vacancies expected and the number of qualified applicants available in the relevant job market." If the employer failed to meet the goal despite good faith efforts, either because fewer vacancies come into being or fewer qualified minorities were available, NAM suggested that no sanctions should apply.

But big business had a far more basic reason for its surrender—self-protection. Under Title VII, it was forbidden to discriminate on the basis of race. But with the prodding of such agencies as EEOC, the Office of Federal Contract Compliance Program (OFCCP) Review, and the Civil Rights Division at Justice, "discrimination" had come to mean far more than the conscious, deliberate exclusion of minorities. Numerical disparities in the number of black employees, for example, could amount to a prima facie case of discrimination, opening up an employer to both individual and class action penalties. The use of selection or promotion tools, such as ability testing or requiring a high school diploma which had a "disparate impact" upon black employees, could also bring on an adverse and costly judgment. But then there was the other side of the coin. Unless protected by the courts, an employer seeking to aid minorities through such race-conscious mechanisms as special recruiting efforts and training programs or simply holding minorities to slightly less demanding qualifications standards, could face legal action from white employees also based on Title VII. In the *Weber* case, in which the Supreme Court had approved a voluntary training program that admitted minorities on a 1:1 basis, Justice Blackmun had warned that to do otherwise would put employers on a "high tightrope without a net beneath them." Now, NAM argued, "[p]ermitting voluntary affirmative action programs allows employers to avoid the 'high tightrope,' and is fully consistent with the well-established principle under Title VII [and Executive Order 11246] that voluntary compliance is the preferred means of eliminating employment discrimination."

With their success in the *Weber* and *Local 28* cases, corporate America could now preemptively defend itself against many minority-initiated discrimination suits by developing voluntary affirmative action programs without fear of legal action from whites.

The big corporate sector had in fact long since come to the rescue of affirmative action or its principal agency enforcer, the OFCCP. Early in his term as attorney general during the second Reagan administration, Edwin Meese moved to junk Lyndon Johnson's Executive Order 11246, which had institutionalized affirmative action in the contracting community and created the OFCCP as enforcer. Meese had good support at Justice and a fair amount on Donald Regan's White House staff, and he had made certain that Labor Secretary William Brock, a firm supporter of affirmative action, was out of the loop until the effort was well advanced. But he underestimated the speed with which Brock could mobilize opposition to the plan from the corporate sector. With the Fortune 300 types phoning their friends in the administration, Ronald Reagan learned of Meese's plan and moved to postpone decision on the matter. Meese himself was warned that an effort to eliminate the order by executive fiat could provoke the Democratic Congress to legislate even more rigid instructions, and the matter was dropped.

When affirmative action began to come under serious challenge following the elections of 1994, again it was the largest U.S. corporations and their Washington agents who came most quickly to the rescue. The Equal Employment Advisory Council rushed into print a memo charging that much contemporary criticism "is based on ignorance or misunderstanding" of affirmative action. A generation of litigation and bureaucratic dogmatism notwithstanding, nothing in any of these programs "requires a contractor to place an unqualified person in a job." And are goals and timetables the functional equivalent of quotas? Certainly not. But of course, "it is assumed that over time an employer's workforce will reflect approximately the same race and gender profile as the labor pool from which the workers are being selected."

Individual business leaders also spoke out. Edwin L. Artzt, chairman and CEO of Procter and Gamble, assured the president, Congress, and the states that "the principles of affirmative action are right." John L. Hulck, chairman of MERCK, said, "We will continue goals and timetables no matter what the government does." And Mary E. Herbert, diversity director of Allied Signal, added a touch of political correctness with, "We go above and beyond compliance, and if there are changes in Washington, we won't stop or slow down. Ideas are not the monopoly of white Anglo-Saxon male Protestants."

The defense by Fortune 300 companies of affirmative action in general and OFCCP regulation in particular is calculated in part, as we have seen, to erect a "litigation shield" against charges of discrimination by whites. But there are other reasons as well. First, while affirmative action may be one of the costs of doing business for the big fellows—like complying with the Occupational Safety and Health Administration (OSHA) or environmental laws—it is no threat to their existence and can even be viewed as raising the entry barrier to potential competitors, the little guys. In the late 1980s, the struggling Puerto Rico Safety Equipment Corporation was nearly driven out of business, even though 100 percent of its employees were minorities, because it lacked the resources to satisfy OFCCP's appetite for paperwork. But General Motors will not go belly-up for tardiness in filing its Affirmative Action Plan.

The same applies to the related area of minority set-asides in government contracting. Joe Henry, the Columbus, Ohio, house painter whose lawsuit has received national attention, can be told that the Ohio State University dorms which he has been painting for twenty years will henceforth be handled by a minority contractor. But there are no African American airplane manufacturers ready to capture Boeing's share of the market. Nor are Brown and Root and Bechtel—each, like Boeing, large enough to have its own affirmative action programs for subcontractors—likely to lose much business because the Pentagon tries to allocate at least 5 percent of its contracts to minorities. But white regional construction contractors, dependent for their livelihoods on military work, wonder where their next job will come from after being told that all construction work on a big army or air force base has been "sheltered" for minorities for the entire year. A more honest way of putting it would have been, "No whites need apply."

At another level, the corporate commitment to affirmative action cannot be termed totally cynical. Today's CEOs were college students in the 1950s, 1960s, and 1970s. The civil rights battles, the urban riots, the assassinations of Martin Luther King Jr., and the Kennedy brothers, Vietnam, and the feminist movement have all had a hand in shaping their outlook. Most regard racism as an outrage. More than two-thirds consistently respond positively to surveys by *Fortune* magazine regarding the wisdom of affirmative action, though concededly the term covers a broad array of corporate activities. Three-quarters say they would continue with some form of affirmative action even if government regulation were to evaporate.

Illustrative is the case of Xerox whose CEO, Joseph C. Wilson, underwent a period of deep introspection following race riots in Rochester, New York, the company's home base, in the mid-sixties. Wilson, well known in the business community for his progressive approach to organized labor, had never consciously discriminated against another human being, but had never made any special effort to recruit, train, or promote blacks either. Few Xerox executives at any level were black. The company's sales force included not a single black. Wilson made a deliberate decision to change that. In 1969, he recognized a new intracompany group calling itself the Bay Area Black Employees, the first of a number of caucus groups, which, according to company literature, "have served as critics, partners, helpers, adversaries, and whistle-blowers to assure that management never lost sight of its commitment to offer equal opportunity to all Xerox people." A Harvard Business School case history of the company's ethnic policy noted that the caucuses did as much to enhance the effort of black members as they did to raise the consciousness of the company in dealing with minority employees. According to Harvard, "[i]ndividuals would be held accountable for their performance to their peers in the black caucus group." The aim was to "create a pool of qualified, successful black employees who could rise up through management ranks."

In 1984, Xerox linked the compensation and advancement of department managers to their achievement of diversity, and by 1995, according to company records, 45 of 251 Xerox vice presidents and directors were members of minority groups, 10 of 41 corporate officers were women or minorities, 14 percent of the company workforce was black, and 7 percent were Hispanics. Says the manager of corporate employment, Theodore Payne, "Relative numbers. That's the hard business, that's what most people don't like to deal with, but we do that all the time." Not surprisingly, Xerox now boasts caucuses representing Hispanics, women, senior citizens, and gays and lesbians in addition to blacks.

Increasingly, corporate officers speak of their commitment to diversity in the workforce and corporate hierarchy. Louis V. Gerstner, Jr., CEO of IBM, says that his company's competitiveness "will be enhanced through a workforce which reflects the growing diversity of the external labor force, and the growing diversity of our customers." And Robert E. Allen, chairman and CEO of AT&T, says his company's "diversity strategy" is a "competitive advantage...."

Soaring tributes to the unique contribution of each race and ethnic group aside, demographics are at the heart of the diversity movement. According to most projections, by the turn of the century only about a quarter of those entering the labor force each year will be white males. And most larger firms sell to a variety of domestic ethnic markets. Most too are concerned with reputation; the last thing a CEO wants to deal with are a few dozen minority pickets outside his gate accusing his company of racism. Add to that the number of American companies with manufacturing facilities in Asia and Latin America, those who import foreign made goods and those who market their product globally, and the virtue of ethnically mixed work, sales, and management forces is clear. "Diversity is not the solution, it is the condition," says Washington consultant Charles Mann.

The efforts to conform the corporate environment to this brave new world sometimes court journalistic fun. In, "The Diversity Industry," appearing in *The New Republic,* 5 July 1993, writer Heather MacDonald amusingly, and frighteningly, chronicled how corporations have hired "diversity consultants" who, through "diversity awareness" and "valuing differences," purport to teach firms how to "manage" the transition to an improved "diversity profile." In what was truly a tale of corporate culture deconstructionism run amok, Ms. MacDonald described a situation where affirmative action is trashed as an effort to impose WASP values on "nontraditional" employees, where equal treatment is unfair because "fairness equals treating people appropriately" rather than equally, and where, in the words of one consultant, "If minorities do not meet existing employment criteria, then corporations need to expand the definition of qualifications," which means placing less weight on "math, science, and engineering credentials" because they may be "considerably biased." Many of the "awareness sessions," in fact, led to brutal confrontations as consultants urged participants to put their biases on display. At one university session, an attractive, well-dressed female professor broke into tears after being attacked by the discussion leaders for being a member of the "privileged white elite."

"When diversity first hit the radar screen about 10 years ago there was a lot of that touchy, feely, study your navel stuff," recalls Jeffrey A. Norris, president of the Equal Employment Advisory Council. "But there has been a tremendous evolution. Now when corporations speak of diversity, they are talking about having appropriate representation from members of different groups present and participating when decisions are made. It's been transferred from a social policy to a line on the chart of where and how authority flows. The thinking is that the decision is likely to be better than if it is made simply by a group of white guys who all went to the same colleges sitting around a table."

Diversity programs have suffered at many companies due to the downsizing practices of the 1990s, and their advantages remain more testimonial than documented. A small number of well-known corporations—Hoechot Celanese, Avon, AT&T, Xerox, IBM, and Levi Strauss make most lists—remain publicly and privately committed to diversity programs. Others confide privately that they are not finding minorities able to move up to senior management positions in the hoped-for numbers. To some extent, the situation is similar to the quest for black academic talent by the higher education community: the top corporations, like the top schools, can grab their share of the minority "stars." But the pool of topflight minority talent remains distressingly thin. And the overall numbers are often cited by minority advocates as proof positive of corporate (or academic) racism, when in fact they fail even to support a prima facie case of racial discrimination.

Leonard Biermann, a Washington consultant who as the long-time senior civil servant with OFCCP logged more time as acting director than anyone else has as director, agrees. "You're seeing less and less of that exotic 'let it all hang out' diversity stuff," he says. "Almost everyone who tried it found it did more harm than good. The big guys now look at diversity as a corporate asset, not an exercise in group therapy or applied sociology."

The combination of a social conscience on racial issues, a perceived need to protect voluntary affirmative action efforts from legal assault, and a commitment to diversity based on "bottom line" considerations provided the Fortune 300 companies with an inexhaustible supply of goodwill toward OFCCP, but the agency, particularly during the Clinton presidency, has just about exhausted it. Because in word and deed it shares the two fatal flaws of the civil rights bureaucracy: first, a belief that racial discrimination is as rampant as ever, though perhaps more subtle and better disguised, and, second, a devotion to punitive regulatory mechanisms—the crudest possible devices for social engineering—to achieve equal outcomes rather than equal opportunities. In the case of the Clinton OFCCP, these flaws, combined with a genuine lack of feel of the way business actually works, have led to the greatest loss of corporate support for the agency in its history.

One of the most common corporate complaints is that the agency requires a "workforce analysis" reflecting its own primitive notions of how business is organized. "Consider some of the changes that have occurred since the early 1970s and then consider that the mentality of OFCCP has failed to keep pace with any of them," argues Larry Lorber, who ran the agency during the Ford administration. He and others speak of the earlier period as the days of "warm body hiring"—when there were huge numbers of unskilled but well-paying jobs because companies in such industries as steel, paper, automobiles, and communications had grown into fat oligopolists; when job applicants normally showed up at the plant gate; when workers in heavy industry tended to stay with the same firm for much if not all of their working lives; when the service sector of the economy was a small fraction of what it is today; and when terms like downsizing, outsourcing, hostile takeovers, and the Internet were still in the future. According to Lorber, "A worker today changes jobs seven times during his working life, which means the fact that he is no longer with you doesn't mean you have discriminated against him." Lorber continues, "In 1970 a paper mill had fifty workers on the floor; today it has one fellow working a computer, four robots, and two guys with poles standing by if things get clogged up. A secretary in 1970 operated an IBM 'Selectric';

today she uses a word processor, which means she must be computer smart. To hire a worker in 1970, you looked for someone who was healthy. Now you need someone with a fair amount of technical knowledge, good judgment, the capacity to grow. OFCCP recognizes none of this change."

The purpose of OFCCP's workforce analysis is to take a look at the vertical array of a company's employees, along with race and gender information, so that the agency can determine whether there is any illegal discrimination. But the particulars required by OFCCP for each and every supervisor may or may not reflect the way decisions are made in a particular company. In June 1995 congressional testimony, Jeffrey A. Norris, president of the Equal Employment Advisory Committee (EEAC), the pro-affirmative action Fortune 300 group, complained, "Recently, I saw a workforce analysis for a medium-sized establishment that was over 500 pages long and contained numerous departments in which there was only one person," he recalled. "It is impossible to perform any meaningful analysis when the workforce is fractured into so many small pieces."

OFCCP also requires covered employers to have a written Affirmative Action Plan at each one of their establishments, the theory being that if the unit is small enough, even an inconsequential deviation from matching local minority availability will suffice to generate a goal and timetable remedy. The result is the proliferation of Affirmative Action Plans for every one of a company's offices or outlets even though personnel decisions may all be made at the district or division level. In the case of such industries as branch banking or insurance, which may involve hundreds of offices dispersed over a broad geographic area, the OFCCP approach borders on the absurd.

Companies and their representatives can cite any number of cases with respect to which the Clinton OFCCP has manifested its fixation with the past. The agency began proceedings against a large Georgia paper mill, claiming it had passed over black applicants as qualified as whites who had been hired. As a remedy, the agency sought a consent decree by virtue of which the company would identify the least qualified white hired within the past two years and agree to hire every black no less qualified who applied for a vacancy during the next five years. The company eventually signed a consent decree but without the destructive provision. "We would have taken that to the Supreme Court if we had to," claims the company's Washington, D.C., lawyer. "At a time when every successful company in the country is trying to upgrade its staff, it is perverse to demand that we downgrade ours."

The issue of who is a job applicant, a popular subject of debate during the Paleozoic era of affirmative action, has resurfaced in the 1990s, thanks to the OFCCP's Ms. Wilcher and her colleagues. The question is important, since one of the statistical studies assessing discriminatory behavior involves the rejection rates of minority applicants by similarly situated employers.

For that reason, employers have long and happily regarded it as settled that someone achieves applicant status only after meeting threshold qualifications and taking such concrete steps as appearing for a job interview or taking a test for the company to consider. For that reason, a considerable number of employers, including many well-known companies, have been unpleasantly surprised to hear OFCCP argue that anyone contacting a company for a job must be considered an applicant. Astonishingly, this approach penalizes the best known companies and those with the most progressive reputations in the minority communities since they are precisely the ones that receive the largest number of unsolicited "applications." Also disadvantaged are those companies that have expended the greatest effort in targeting pools of minority manpower, again because such efforts tend to generate large numbers of "applications" from both qualified and unqualified individuals. And the OFCCP's definitions will, of course, expand with the speed of new technology. In one situation an inquiry regarding potential employment reached one company by way of the Internet. OFCCP promptly proclaimed that "surfer" was "an applicant," a perversity with potentially mind-boggling consequences.

One of the nation's largest and most respected credit card companies found itself doing battle with OFCCP over the question of "minimal qualifications," described by a number of sources as the agency's "hot issue of the nineties." The company demands that, to be considered for training as customer service agents, applicants demonstrate their ability with word processors, some basic math skills, as well as reading, transposing, and entering the sort of material familiar to any credit card holder. To OFCCP, this represents a formula for rejecting minority applicants, and it is insisting that applicants demonstrate only sufficient qualifications to enable them to be trained up to the level necessary to enter the company's regular training program. In effect, the agency is insisting that as the price to avoid citation for discriminating on the basis of race, this employer, and many others, undertake at their own expense a program in which new employees are "trained to train."

At this point the game is no longer nondiscrimination or outreach but social engineering writ large, with employers expected to cure deficiencies in the qualifications of applicants that have nothing whatsoever to do with any prior conduct of the business community. And like other efforts at social engineering, the training gambit, grounded in the belief that ability differences will "fade out with experience," is bound to be exposed as the fools' gold that it is. Psychologist Linda Gottfredson of the University of Delaware has written tellingly that only if less-qualified workers are

provided with some compensatory advantage over the more qualified ones will the performance gap between them close. When
both are afforded the opportunity for additional training and
education, the gap between them is more likely to widen. "Eventually, as they too acquire experience," she wrote, "brighter
workers out-perform equally well-trained or experienced, but less
bright, counterparts."

■   ■   ■

OFCCP, moreover, is not the only agency straining at the outer
limits of its legal authority, and perhaps going beyond, to impose
its notion of social justice on employers. The Federal Communications Commission has used its power to ensure that broadcast
diversity is wedged into virtually every employment decision a
broadcaster makes, at times employing fines, at times threatening
license renewal to impose its vision of equality. Beginning in the
1970s, the commission required stations with as few as five
employees to hire minorities at 50 percent of their representation
in the local labor pool. Later, stations had to fill their top positions at a 25 percent minority/women rate. The standard was
changed to 50:50 in 1980.

In 1987, Reagan appointees were finally able to get the commission to drop the quota game in favor of a "best efforts"
standard. This produced steady progress as minorities went from
16.8 percent of all broadcast employees and 10.9 percent of officials and managers in 1988 to 18.2 percent and 12.5 percent,
respectively, in 1992. For women, the comparable figures were
38.3 percent of all positions and 31.2 percent of managers in 1988,
with 39.5 percent and 33.8 percent the comparable 1992 figures.

The Clinton appointees worked both substantive and procedural changes. The hard 50:50 rule was reimposed. In addition,
licensees have to prove that they now "recruit... so as to attract"

adequate pools of minorities and women to fill at least 66 percent of all openings. Stations not meeting the commission's ethnic mix standards must provide elaborate information on how each job is filled, including the numbers of applicants for the position, the sex, race, and/or national origin of each, along with similar information on each applicant interviewed and the successful candidate. Additional information must be provided on the referral source for each applicant and the number of referrals received from each source.

Examples of egregious injustice abound. One station was fined for laxity even though it had hired minorities at a rate equal to 100 percent of their participation in the local labor pool. A station run by a church was fined in part for giving preferences to students at the local seminary. Another station, although it exceeded the 66 percent standard, was fined because not enough of its new employees were Hispanic.

Data compiled by the Texas Association of Broadcasters show that the annual cost of complying with these standards in the typical metro area broadcasting outlet runs to $37,400. A group of ninety-eight broadcast licensees commenting on the procedures complained, "Like the sorcerer's apprentice who could not stop bringing water to a flooded room, Commission EEO enforcement has become a rote mechanical process disconnected from its original useful purposes."

4

MERIT TESTING AND RACE

Merit certification and job testing are yet other issues where the rhetoric of the Clinton administration and its policies have diverged sharply, perhaps with disastrous future consequences. No administration in recent times has been more vocal about the need for excellence, none has issued more fervent appeals for training and skills development, none has so conspicuously made global competition a core foreign policy concern—and none has done more to sabotage all of these through a relentless assault upon objective job selection criteria.

At times conflicting policies pour out of the same cabinet department. No one worked harder than Secretary of Labor Robert Reich to establish a National Skills Standard Board under the Goals 2000: Educate America Act. The hope was that the board would encourage voluntary worker participation to establish high standards for various trades and workplace competence leading to certification of individual workers. Reich assumed that employers would prefer to hire people with certified skills and that they would subsidize employee training in order to upgrade the quality of their workforce.

But key players inside the department, including Ms. Wilcher and Assistant Secretary Bernard Anderson, reflecting the view of the civil rights lobby, were concerned that the certification process would work to the disadvantage of minorities since they would not fare as well as others on objective examinations. So they drafted legislation that instructed the board to "avoid disparate impact" on minorities. The final bill, changed but only marginally improved, provides: "The endorsement or absence of an endorsement by the National Board of a skill standard, or assessment and certification system... shall not be used in any action or proceeding to establish that the use of skill standard or assessment and certification system conforms or does not conform to the requirements of civil rights law."

In other words, Reich, whose admiration for the German practice of skill certification is legendary, has wound up instead with a game of Russian roulette. As James C. Sharf of HRStrategies has written, "[t]he act thus encourages the use of national skill standards while at the same time allowing employers to be sued for using them because of their likely adverse impact." Aware of their vulnerability—they would be potentially liable if individuals of diverse race or ethnicity performed differently after training— employers would be slow to sponsor the training programs necessary to make the project succeed. Instead, they would conduct business as usual—today, employers in the United States invest only about 2 percent of their total compensation costs in worker training, half the Japanese rate.

Like the issues of quotas and reverse discrimination, the question of merit testing antedates passage of the Civil Rights Act of 1964 and was, in fact, one of the more contentious matters dealt with in the act. More than any other it is responsible for replacing intent with results in adjudicating discrimination claims. It has been the subject of major Supreme Court decisions and was the driving force behind enactment of the Civil Rights Act of 1991.

Testing is a social flashpoint issue because it involves the chronic failure of blacks and Hispanics to score as well as whites and Asians in standardized assessments of cognitive ability. The relevance of such tests to future job performance, and the more general applicability of test results and their utility in terms of dollars and cents, have been clarified by the leading industrial psychologists of the era. Yet the tests are consistently denigrated by civil rights administrators who frankly concede that they simply cannot accept the truth.

Testing has emerged as the one area of affirmative action where big business has to some extent fought to retain at least some freedom of action, a clear indication of its vital importance in terms of efficiency, productivity, and money. It has been chewed and digested, analyzed and regressed, square rooted and standardly deviated. It has been cursed, praised, ventilated, litigated, mutilated, and masticated. It is at once the superhighway to future equality and the one-lane bridge on which bedrock notions of America, the meritocracy, and America, the land of social justice, collide.

Long before the modern civil rights movement, most employers agreed that a job applicant who could read and write, comprehend simple narrative paragraphs, reason clearly, and perform basic mathematical tasks—particularly police, firemen, and others involved with the public safety—would use good judgment in certain situations and probably make a better employee than one who could not. By 1963, 90 percent of the nation's employers maintained testing programs for white collar, clerical, and, in many cases, supervisory, production, and even assembly line jobs.

But that year, a black man from Illinois named Leon Myart was rejected for a job by the Motorola Corporation on the basis of his performance on a short multiple-choice general ability test and he filed a grievance with the Illinois Fair Employment Commission (FEC). The FEC hearing examiner held the test unfair to "culturally deprived and disadvantaged groups" because it failed to account for "inequalities and differences in the environment." The examiner ordered Motorola to hire Myart and to stop administering the test.

The order caused a furor among the state's employers since it literally meant that an applicant for a librarian job could not be tested for literacy nor a would-be bookkeeper for the ability to add and subtract. Their concern quickly spread throughout the business community where 80 percent to 90 percent of employers used testing to determine admission to various training or apprenticeship programs, for pay increases or promotion, or in selecting executives. In Congress, which was then debating what would become of the Civil Rights Act of 1964, opponents of the act used the ruling in their arsenal of arguments against it. That failing, the leading Republican opponent, Senator John Tower of Texas, added language protecting the right of employers to administer tests. Sec. 703(h) provided that it would be lawful for an employer "to give and to act upon the results of any *professionally developed* ability test provided that such test, its administration or action upon the results is not designed, intended or used to discriminate because of race... " (emphasis added).

In an interpretive memorandum, Senate floor leaders Joe Clark and Clifford Case wrote: "There is no requirement in Title VII that employers abandon bona fide qualification tests where, because of differences in background and education, members of some groups are able to perform better on these tests than members of other groups. An employer may set his qualifications as high as he likes, he may test to determine which applicants have these qualifications, and he may hire, assign, and promote on the basis of test performance."

Notwithstanding any of this, the Equal Employment Opportunity Commission (EEOC) in 1966 issued guidelines declaring that when a test or other selection device resulted in a proportionately lower selection rate of minorities, the employer or employment agency administering it would be found guilty of discrimination unless it could "validate" the test in accordance with procedures set forth by the agency. These validation procedures, borrowed from standards published by the American Psychological Association (APA) and intended to apply to laboratory or clinical rather than employment situations, proved to be so exacting that for more than a decade no challenged employer was ever able to meet them. APA would subsequently expressly declare its guidelines inappropriate to the employment testing context, but it was routinely ignored by the government.

By administrative fiat, EEOC thus achieved several goals important to those who saw the Civil Rights Act as a vehicle for social rather than mere legal justice. Through the doctrine of disparate impact, it had removed intent as a necessary ingredient in both administrative and legal matters involving alleged employer discrimination. This paved the way for the sort of outcomes-oriented enforcement that is today central to the administration of civil rights laws. In addition, it established numbers as the central yardstick by which compliance with the act would be judged. It had also undermined the notion of merit and objectivity in the belief that these classic democratic values were less reliable than race-conscious preferences in addressing the economic needs of minorities. And it got its hooks deeply into the question of testing and applicant qualifications which would dominate employer discrimination law for a generation. In the definitive two-volume study,

Ability Testing, published in 1982 by the National Academy of Science, the academy's National Research Council (NRC) stated, "There is some irony that an agency with no intrinsic interest in tests has come to be the arbiter of what constitutes technical adequacy." The NRC recommended that "the validity of a testing process should not be compromised in an effort to shape the distribution of the workforce," and called upon federal and state authorities "to provide employers with a range of legally defensible decision rules to guide their use of test results so that the effect of differential performance can be mitigated without destroying the utility of testing." Employers still wait.

The issue of adverse minority impact and testing came to the Supreme Court in the 1971 case of *Griggs v. Duke Power Co.*, and the Court unanimously held that tests which create a "disparate impact" upon minorities cannot be used by prospective employers unless they can be shown to relate to job performance and are justified by "business necessity." *Griggs* is perhaps the most important and cited case in the post-1964 history of affirmative action. Written by the avuncular, moderate, intensely patriotic, and fair-minded Chief Justice Warren E. Burger, it could also stand as a sort of model for the adage that "tough cases make bad law."

Duke Power had a history of rampant discrimination against blacks, hiring them prior to the act only as laborers working outside the plant itself. With passage of the 1964 Act, it opened all jobs to blacks. And there were no allegations that its practice of requiring a high school diploma plus competitive scores on general intelligence and cognitive ability tests for the inside jobs was the product of discriminatory intent. But blacks performed notoriously less well than whites on these tests, a fact Burger attributed to their "inferior education." And their rates of high school graduation were only about one-third those of whites. Thus, few won jobs inside the plant.

Justice Burger agreed with the EEOC that Duke Power had not established that the skills it sought to measure were relevant to those needed to perform the work satisfactorily. Therefore, with no showing of "business necessity," the company could not establish conditions that served as "built-in headwinds" for minorities.

Griggs and its progeny trampled through the corporate community like a herd of runaway elephants. Challenges and responses became formularized. The complaining party first established the fact of disparate impact. The company would respond by seeking to show the test was job related and required by business necessity, a difficult task in light of the EEOC guidelines. If challenged further, the company would try to demonstrate that no alternative method could provide the required caliber of employee. But this need to prove a negative proved fatal even to the few employers who had successfully defended the challenged instrument. At the same time, neither EEOC nor its sister enforcement agency, OFCCP (Office of Federal Contract Compliance Program) Review, ever developed a working model that would pass muster for employers to follow since their goal was to bury testing, not to praise—or ease—it.

During the 1970s, among other reasons, tests were thrown out for failure to conduct a study to determine whether they were as valid for black as for white applicants; for inadequate analysis of what the job entailed; for using invalidated cut-off scores; for not establishing that ranking applicants on the basis of test scores translated into identical rankings on the job; for insufficient proof that the qualities tested were the same as those needed to succeed on the job; and for failing to try hard enough to find an alternative means of judging job applicants, which would have less adverse impact on minorities.

EEOC policy had the desired effect, at least in the early years. Whereas in the mid-sixties, 90 percent of the nation's employers administered tests for at least certain jobs, the figure had declined to less than 45 percent by the mid-seventies.

■　■　■

The Chinese tested civil servants in the twelfth century, and the British began making appointments to their civil service on the basis of competitive exams in the mid-nineteenth century. In her textbook, *Psychological Testing*, Anne Anastasi noted that what we think of as ability or intelligence testing had its origins in the late 1800s with a community of European experimental psychologists who, partly through work with the retarded, began the systematic measurement of such functions as "muscular strength, speed of movement, sensitivity to pain, keenness of vision and hearing, weight discrimination, reaction time, memory, and the like," in the belief that "a measure of intellectual functions could be obtained through tests of sensory discrimination and reaction time."

But the French psychologist Alfred Benet critiqued this focus on response to sensory stimuli, urging that more attention be paid to such intellectual functions as "memory, imagination, attention, comprehension, suggestibility, aesthetic appreciation, and many others." In 1904, Benet was appointed to the Commission for the Study of Retarded Children, which provided him with an enormous clinical base for his studies. Two years later, working with his commission colleague Thomas Simon, he developed a test of thirty questions organized in ascending order of difficulty which he administered to a control group of fifty normal children aged three to eleven years. A second scale expanded the age range to three to thirteen years and the size of the control group to ninety. This time, all questions answered correctly by 80 percent to 90 percent of the normal three-year-olds were placed under category "3" on the "Benet-Simon" scale, those passed by the same percentage of normal four-year-olds were placed in category "4," and so on. Thus, a child passing the test for, say, a ten-year-old was said to have achieved that "mental level."

In 1916, psychology professor L. M. Terman of Stanford University expanded the Benet-Simon scale to include adult categories and expressed the score of test takers on the "Stanford-Benet Scale" as a percentage of their chronological age (adults never aged), terming the result their "intelligence quotient," or IQ. A ten-year-old who answered questions at the level of a normal twelve-year-old would have an IQ of 120; one who answered questions at the level of a nine-and-one-half-year-old would have an IQ of 95, and so on.

Employment and ability testing was widely adopted in U.S. government and business. The 1881 assassination of President Garfield by a bitterly frustrated office seeker capped a period of growing disenchantment with the half-century-old spoils system and triggered passage of the first Civil Service Act. Soon, 10 percent of federal jobs were being filled through competitive examination. The percentage grew to 60 percent by 1908, and the practice was emulated by many of the larger and more progressive states and cities.

This was also a period of rapid industrialization and corporate fascination with the ideas of Frederick W. Taylor of Bethlehem Steel, the "father of scientific management." Taylor's published time and motion studies of the worker "Schmidt" and others earned him a permanent niche in the annals of business academia. The emerging science of ability testing met both the corporate and educational exigencies of the day. A huge influx of immigrants threatened to overwhelm the nascent public school system, and industry had to contend with high turnover, serious absenteeism, frightening accident rates, and the growing militancy and radicalism of a labor movement bulging with immigrants.

While today's generation glibly speaks of its "racial and ethnic diversity," a Senate committee in 1908 reported that 72 percent of New York City schoolchildren had fathers born abroad; that for most, English was a second language; and that the figure was close to 50 percent in many other major cities. In 1870, there had been eighty thousand students in American high schools, nearly all of them in private schools, and most, college bound; by 1910, there were one million high school students in the country, 90 percent of them in public schools, the vast majority headed for the workforce. There was thus an urgent need to rationalize the selection and assignment process in both industry and education, to match the man with the job and the student with the appropriate course of study, to sort out the contributions each could be expected to make to his company and his community, and to identify those unfit for employment or further general education.

There was, in short, a need to make order from chaos.

On the education side, reformers by the turn of the century were grumbling that the performance of students in areas like spelling and arithmetic had declined precipitately. As would again happen nine decades later, many advocated standardized tests to improve their schooling. In 1911, the National Education Association established its Committee of Tests and Standards of Efficiency, and at Columbia University, Professor Edward Thorndyke developed tests for achievement in arithmetic, handwriting, spelling, drawing, reading, and language ability. These and other efforts were received with such enthusiasm by school systems that they soon entered a period referred to by one commentator as "an orgy of tabulation." On the corporate side, by 1915, tests for twenty types of work had been developed, and such companies as American Tobacco, National Lead, Western Electric, and Metropolitan Life were using them to select employees.

In World War I, the military, faced with the sudden need to transform a small peacetime shell into a large fighting army, used testing to assign its draftees. Thousands of military units had to be fashioned out of a population of draftees composed largely of immigrants and sons of immigrants about whose intelligence, skills, and psychology the generals knew precious little. For assistance, the army turned to many of the nation's leading academic experimental psychologists. Several became officers while others joined a Committee for Psychology organized by Professor Robert M. Yerkes of Harvard, president of the American Psychological Association, which in turn set up a Committee on Classification of Personnel that worked in the office of Adjutant General H. P. McCain. Quickly, they saw the need for tests which were standardized, could be graded quickly, and could be administered to large groups rather than individually. They developed what became known as the army's "Alpha" test, a "paper-and-pencil" exam consisting of multiple choice and true or false questions which could be scored with a key. It was modeled on many of the prewar intelligence tests, measuring grammar, vocabulary, arithmetic, "common sense," and general knowledge. The army found, however, that so many of its draftees either failed to speak English or were functionally illiterate that a "Beta" test had to be designed using pictures and diagrams. Altogether, nearly two million soldiers were tested over a period of less than eighteen months.

At the request of the National Academy of Science, Yerkes and his colleagues undertook a massive postwar analysis of the results of the army testing program based on a sample of more than 160,000 tests. They reached two important conclusions, the first of which survived, with important modifications, while the second, which had a profound impact on public policy, was disowned within a decade, even by many of its authors, as scientifically flawed. First, they observed stunning differences in intelligence among men in different occupations, suggesting that tests of general intelligence were the most appropriate selection technique for any given position. That conclusion has not proved to be too far off base, although the experts of the period did not allow adequately for the contribution of education—and hence wealth—to high test scores.

Second, the authors found a wide variation in scores linked to national origin, the highest scores belonging to native-born whites, followed by recruits from Northern and Western Europe, the lowest from Eastern and Southern Europe. The scores of blacks were particularly low. Like many of the foreign-born, most blacks took the Beta examinations. These findings were picked up by nativists and eugenicists who argued that immigrants from the low countries of Europe were polluting the American gene pool. Among the most prominent adherents of this view was Carl Bingham, later the architect of the College Entrance Examinations who, in his 1923 book, *Study of American Intelligence,* advanced a theory of racial determinism of intelligence.

The matter did not end there. The initial interpretation of the Yerkes data was subjected to years of critical reassessment by psychologists, most of whom concluded that the tests did not sufficiently control for such factors as familiarity with English, education, and the home environment to support its conclusions with respect to differential group intelligence. Indeed, only seven years later, Bingham himself would conduct a review of more recent test findings "which show that comparative studies of various national and racial groups cannot be made with existing tests, and which show, in particular, that one of the most pretentious of these comparative racial studies—the writer's own—was without foundation." But the damage had been done. In 1924, Congress enacted the National Origins Act which imposed immigrant nationality quotas based upon the presence of each national group in the country prior to 1890, when the large influx from Eastern and Southern Europe began.

It should be evident even from this brief account of the early years of ability testing that the subject received intense, prolonged, and fastidious scrutiny from many of the nation's preeminent academic specialists in the field of human psychology as well as by human resource managers in industry and senior military and civilian personnel officials in the government. As early errors and fallacies were revealed, techniques were modified to correct them. Vast resources were poured into a study of which abilities would translate into a high probability of performing successfully on any given job and how those abilities could most fairly and accurately be measured. Tens of millions of job applicants were tested over the years, as were generations of soldiers and officers. Highly sophisticated clinical tests were performed in the field, as in the prolonged 1920s study of workers at the Western Electric Company's Hawthorne Works, experiments that would lead an entire school of industrial sociologists to conclude that "social relations within the workplace were more important than individual aptitudes or indeed skills, in determining performance on the job and productivity." Thousands of articles and academic papers and scores of books addressed testing as it related to personnel selection, nearly all asserting that hiring was an art as much as a science and that testing was one among many tools that helped those responsible for hiring to make better choices. "[E]ach decision to accept or reject a job applicant is actually a prediction—based on a varying mixture of information and hunch—that the candidate will or won't succeed on the job," warned one industry handbook of the early 1960s.

To appreciate how testing actually came to be used as a tool in job selection, compare it to a professional football scouting combine which every year tests the speed, strength, leaping ability, flexibility, and endurance of thousands of college athletes, as well as their height, weight, body fat, and other physiological characteristics, and the specialized skills of punters, kickers, and passers. The standard or criterion by which success for each position is judged differs from position to position and so, therefore, are the particular skills or physical characteristics judged to be important. And, of course, the combines make no attempt to quantify such intangible factors as character, integrity, leadership, and commitment which often separate the stars from the pedestrian performers. Every year, some number of first round draft selections—based largely on the scouting combine reports—fail to make any impact on their teams, while a handful of low round picks or even free agents perform splendidly. Still, the work of the combines is considered valuable, and teams do, in fact, pay big bucks to obtain the information because it improves the odds.

The developers of employment tests go through a similar process. They begin with a job analysis which defines the knowledge, skills, and abilities necessary to perform the job well, as well as the standard or criterion by which success for the job in question is measured. The emphasis should be on those things that distinguish this job from other jobs and on those aspects of performance that distinguish most sharply the good workers from the bad ones. It may be producing so many units per hour or work which is error-free. It may be the amount of sales, regular attendance, the ability to supervise others, the likelihood of success in completing a training program, or simply the ratings of superiors.

Next, the test makers will develop an assortment of questions, the correct answers to which correlate with the applicant's predictive success in achieving the criterion established. If the test is a good one, the higher the applicant's percentile, the more likely he or she is to meet the criterion, once employed. If it is not, the correlation between performance on the test and on the job will be low; in the worst cases, it may even be negative. If there is a perfect correlation between performance on the test and success in achieving the criterion, the "validity coefficient" is expressed as 1.0. If the relationship is perfectly inverse, it is –1.0. A validity coefficient— the relationship between the test score and the criterion measure—of .50 is regarded in testing and industry circles as extremely valuable; even one of .30 is considered useful. That is because a validity coefficient of .50 is likely to translate into a better than 75 percent chance that an applicant in the top 20 percentiles will be among the top 50 percent of performers on the job while one in the bottom 20 percentiles may have only about a 20 percent chance of being among the top 50 percent.

Another way of understanding the probabilities involved has been suggested by industrial psychologists Robert A. Gordon, Mary A. Lewis, and Ann M. Quigley. If a gambler tried to predict the outcome of a coin toss by tossing another coin first, the first coin would be right half the time and wrong half the time for a validity correlation of 0. But if a "magic" coin were invented that produced a .30 correlation with the second coin, the person owning the "magic" coin would win 65 percent of the flips. If the validity coefficient were .50, the lucky owner would win 75 percent of the flips. That is both good gambling and good business.

Again, we are talking about improving the odds—bettering the efficiency of the hiring process in an imperfect world where it is not possible to retain every job applicant for a period long enough to determine whether he or she performs well enough to merit a permanent position relative to some other applicant. Even the most zealous defender of tests does not overstate their predictive value, given the limitations of testing itself. A simple ability test cannot measure the same sorts of intangibles that our football scout was unable to measure with his scales, yardstick, and stopwatch, that is, commitment, creativity, integrity, leadership, and good emotional and physical health. Thus, *Selecting and Inducting Employees*, one of the standard managerial handbooks of the 1950s warns, "*Low scores are more significant in predicting failure on the job than are high scores in predicting success"* (emphasis in original). In short, there is no perfect instrument of testing.

Yet in respect to what the ability tests can and do measure, they have become better and better. Publishers of tests—there are more than five hundred major ones in the United States—understand the importance of "reliability," that the test consistently measures what it purports to measure. They are familiar with the kinds of multiple choice questions that explore an applicant's verbal reasoning, numerical ability, abstract reasoning, clerical speed and accuracy, mechanical reasoning, sense of space relations, spelling, and language usage. The literature is thick with advice for test developers and consumers on the importance, for example, of structuring the test so that the test taker moves from simpler to more difficult questions, thereby allowing him or her to gain a degree of confidence and avoid squandering time early in the exam. They are also advised that a particular question which is answered correctly by 50 percent of the test takers is generally more useful than one passed by either a very low percentage or a very high one since it separates a greater number of the applicants from one another.

Interestingly, criterion validity is only one of three types of measuring devices. To the extent that, say, a typing test presents a sample of the actual work that might be done on the job, it is said to have "content" validity. A test designed to measure a specific trait (one of our coaches says, "Bring me a guy who is six foot five inches, 250 pounds, and who runs the 40 in 4.7 seconds or less") is described as having "construct" validity. In most, but not all, circumstances criterion validity is believed to be the most reliable.

More than nine million servicemen and -women were tested during the Second World War. The military was careful to assure the nation that the Army General Classification Test "made no pretense of measuring native intelligence," but instead provided only "a rough indication of trainableness." Yet the army exam ranked test takers into one of five categories, from "slow" to "very rapid" learner and was the principal basis of assigning all but a relative handful of draftees. In addition, a variation of the College Entrance Examination was administered to officer candidates; another highly successful testing program—which included psychiatric interviews—was maintained throughout the war; and the Office of Strategic Services (OSS) set up batteries of tests for clandestine intelligence agents that took three days to administer and included not only psychiatric interviews, but situational test assessments performed under simulated operational conditions. The OSS procedure furnished a model for more than one thousand corporate "assessment centers," established within a decade of the war's end, to screen executive position candidates.

Two other points should be made with respect to testing in the days immediately preceding the civil rights era. First, while distinctions can be made between IQ testing and the sort of ability tests being developed for use in the employment context, there is considerable overlap, and few involved with testing would deny that an applicant with a higher level of "cognitive ability," or the g factor, has a significant advantage over one with less. But, of course, the advantage is not limited to obtaining high scores on tests. Assuming the tests are reasonably valid, the applicant who did better on the test would be more likely to perform better on the job.

Second, once test makers had learned how to remove from their instruments the cultural, educational, and language biases which had "polluted" the results during and immediately after the First World War, ability testing was widely regarded as a democratic egalitarian procedure that leveled the playing field for those of modest or immigrant backgrounds. The NRC study recalls that in the 1950s, "testing seemed a liberating tool that could circumvent the privileges of birth and wealth to open the doors of opportunity to Americans of all kinds."

Professionals also wondered on the basis of several surveys whether tests prepared for jobs at one company or plant were "situationally specific," i.e., had little or no applicability to apparently similar jobs at other plants. Again on the basis of surveys, there seemed to be wide differences regarding the utility of tests: did the differences they were able to quantify among individuals translate into differences on the job that had a real dollars-and-cents impact upon the employer? Was there a point of diminishing returns where a particular individual might be "too bright" for the position for which he or she had applied? And was the improvement in performance linear, where better performance on the job extended all the way up the percentiles, or was there so little difference between increments that above some cutoff score, differences on the tests translated into little or nothing any employer would care about?

■　■　■

Many of these issues would be incorporated into the more emotional debate over the impact of testing on employment opportunities for blacks, but it was only after the EEOC and, later, the OFCCP, determined to destroy the practice of testing because of its disparate impact that the tests came under fire as alleged tools of racism.

With the legal leverage afforded them by the *Griggs* decision, EEOC and OFCCP routinely refused to accept the validity or applicability of standardized tests. Employers had to prove that the tests were valid for every job at each location. At the same time, the agencies were at their most bullish in challenging "underutilization" of minorities, and in a way that amounted to little more than a quota system. In the circular logic of the day, the tests contributed to "underutilization through their disparate impact on minorities." The bureaucratic "take no prisoners" campaign brought on a resurgence of theories about tests and minorities that amounted to little more than scientific quackery. It was suggested, for example, that they had "differential validity"—that they had predictive value for whites, but not for blacks—or that they were "unfair" in the technical sense of underpredicting black performance simply because "blacks don't test well." Both theories would fail to survive scientific scrutiny in the 1970s and 1980s.

Small companies soon found they could afford neither the elaborate validation ritual demanded of tests nor the years of litigation needed to rebut the charges against them. They abandoned testing wholesale. Even many larger companies put their testing operations on hold. By the mid-1970s tests were administered only by companies employing about 42 percent of the nation's workers. Again, this was no accident, but the precise result intended by the regulatory agencies. In one of the most revealing comments of the entire period, David L. Rose, chief of the Employment Section of the Civil Rights Division at Justice, bragged in a 1976 interview with *Labor Law Daily,* "Under the present EEOC guidelines, few employers are able to show the validity of any of their selection procedures, and the risk of their being held unlawful is high. Since not only tests but also all other procedures must be validated, the thrust of the present guidelines is to place almost all test users in a posture of noncompliance; to give great discretion to enforcement personnel to determine who should be prosecuted; and to set aside objective procedures in favor of numerical hiring."

Then the results started to come in, and they were truly jolting to the business community. Many companies that had abandoned ability testing began to notice declines in the quality of work in critical areas ranging from productivity to quality control, from absenteeism to the frequency of accidents on the job. The time was ripe for someone to tie all the evidence together, to challenge the factual and intellectual underpinnings of the EEOC approach, and to explore whether in pursuit of its own social agenda, the agency and its collaborators had not been engaging in some very shoddy science.

Enter Frank L. Schmidt and John E. Hunter, two industrial psychologists who first met while professors at Michigan State University and who, a quarter century later, would jointly win the most prestigious award in their field, the Distinguished Scientific Award for the Application of Psychology. During the late 1970s and early 1980s, Schmidt also served as a senior consultant to the U.S. Office of Personnel Management (OPM), the successor to the Civil Service Commission.

The great breakthrough achieved by Schmidt and Hunter was to apply a new statistical technique known as meta-analysis to hundreds of previous studies measuring the validity of general aptitude tests as predictors of future job performance, not only for the particular position for which the test was being administered, but to a far greater universe of positions requiring many or all of the same cognitive abilities. Meta-analysis permitted the data from hundreds of previous studies to be combined and subjected to more sophisticated analysis, which in turn reduced erroneous interpretation based on poor sampling techniques or reliance on idiosyncratic studies. The results of the combined data were statistically more reliable than any previous individual sample.

Schmidt and Hunter found that earlier studies, which had suggested a narrow applicability, had been distorted by poor methodology. In some cases, for example, the size of the sample was simply too small to provide statistically reliable results; in others, the range of those in the sample had been artificially narrowed to the point where the study failed to measure the importance of the variable being tested. If, for example, a sampling is limited to professors of nuclear physics at Ivy League universities, the results might well suggest that there is no discernible relationship between IQ and academic success. Of course, those with lesser IQs are weeded out long before becoming Ivy League nuclear physicists. Similarly, in our example of the football scouting project, comparing the performances only of those players surviving both the final cut and training camp could lead to erroneous conclusions regarding the link between size, speed, strength, and other objectively measured abilities and game performance, since those who failed to make one of the teams were necessarily excluded from the sample and an entire universe of smaller, slower, weaker human beings never reported for tryouts.

In a series of papers published over the course of more than twenty years, beginning in the early 1970s, Schmidt and Hunter (and others) used the meta-analysis technique, in effect, to validate the results of tests that, viewed in isolation, were not sufficiently significant statistically to reflect much beyond chance occurrence. In the process, the two established to the satisfaction of a preponderance of the scientific community that well-constructed standardized tests had broad applicability to a wide range of jobs. The importance of this "validity generalization" is difficult to overstate. It persuasively rebuts challenges that a particular test impacts disproportionately on minorities by providing a rationale entirely consistent with the "business necessity" standard laid down by *Griggs*: the tests are highly predictive of who will and who will not succeed on the job. James C. Sharf of HRStrategies put it this way: *"If adverse impact based upon Griggs is the general presumption of employment discrimination, validity generalization becomes the general rebuttal"* (emphasis in original).

In their work, Schmidt and Hunter established, or rather, reestablished certain propositions which have once again become part of the common wisdom of the profession:

- First, measures of general cognitive ability are substantially correlated to success on the job in virtually every situation that has been competently measured.
- Second, while measures of cognitive ability predict performance in training programs better than performance on the job, success in training programs is itself highly correlated to success on the job.
- Third, the more complex the job, the better the general aptitude measures of cognitive ability predict performance.
- Fourth, increases in job performance from improved selection validity can have a profound effect upon productivity. In 1986, while Schmidt was still with OPM, he, Hunter, and two OPM colleagues published a paper estimating that selecting government white collar employees by valid measures of cognitive ability rather than such nontest procedures as education and experience, would generate $600 million in increased productivity each year, $8 billion over the median thirteen-year government career of white collar workers. The increased productivity could allow government to reduce new white collar hires by 20,044 per year, or 9 percent. Years earlier, Schmidt and Hunter had postulated similar results for the private sector, but those studies were based on statistical projections rather than the empirical evidence to which Schmidt had access through OPM. Their study also came at an interesting moment. For many years, applicants for government white collar jobs had been given the

Professional and Administrative Career Examination (PACE) which was essentially a test of general intelligence. In 1980, 9.5 percent of the government's PACE hires were black or Hispanic. Civil rights organizations then challenged PACE in the courts, claiming disparate impact, and under consent decrees, both the Carter and Reagan administrations agreed to stop using the test. A far more narrowly tailored (far less predictive) job-related PACE test was substituted and by 1986—the year of the Schmidt-Hunter Study—it had produced a black and Hispanic hiring representation of 27.4 percent.

■ Fifth, the relationship between ability as measured on competency tests and job performance is linear; it continues along an upward regression slope at all levels of measured ability.

■ Sixth, it is not possible to establish a minimum cut-off score, deeming everyone above it "qualified" for a particular job, without compromising performance severely. This is due partly to the linear relationship just described and also because the minimum scores attained by some who eventually succeed at the job are so low—emphasizing that important qualities related to job performance cannot be measured on standard ability tests—that the overall quality of the workforce would be lowered materially.

In the process of developing their concept of validity generalization, Schmidt and Hunter exploded a number of myths, some held by a segment of the scientific community before the civil rights era, others deliberately promulgated in the wake of the 1964 Act. One myth refuted was the notion that a competently developed general ability test was valid only for the particular job, plant, or locality for which it was administered. To the contrary, the evidence is now overwhelming and overwhelmingly accepted that correctly produced tests have great general validity.

Second was the theory, or myth, of "subgroup validity differences," which held that employment tests of cognitive abilities were inappropriate for blacks, Hispanics, and other minorities and that differences in scores were caused by defects in the test rather than genuine differences in developed group abilities. Some adherents of this theory argued that the tests were valid for whites but invalid for minorities—presumably for reasons of cultural bias—while others held that they were predictive for all groups but far more predictive for whites. Adherents of both positions based their case on statistical studies which suggested either the absence of any correlation or the existence of a very small correlation between minority test scores and their performance on the job. But Schmidt, and many other psychologists and statisticians working independently, demonstrated that the theory of "subgroup validity differences" rested upon poor sampling techniques and that when appropriate methodology was employed the difference in correlation between test scores and job performance between whites and minorities was no greater than could be expected to occur by chance.

A related theory, also voguish during the late 1960s and early 1970s, was that, regardless of their validity, the tests were "unfair" in that they tended to "underpredict" minority job performance. But a number of subsequent studies debunked this theory too, finding in each case that lower test scores among minorities accurately predicted lower job performance, just as with whites, regardless of whether the job performance was measured by such subjective means as job ratings by a superior, or objective means, such as job samples. As Schmidt later wrote:

"The cumulative research on test fairness shows that the average ability and cognitive skill differences between groups are directly reflected in job performance, indicating that they are not artifacts. The differences are *not* created by the tests, but are preexisting, and thus the problem is not a defect or deficiency in the tests." Or, as the *Civil Service Journal* observed in the early 1980s, "A test can fairly and accurately provide equal opportunity for individuals to demonstrate ability to perform a job. What the psychological measurement cannot do is provide a valid procedure that assures equal probability of success for members of groups based on characteristics unrelated to performance ability, when real ability levels differ among members of the group."

The work of Schmidt and Hunter finally disabused those who thought that a lowering of standards to accommodate minorities would concentrate the ensuing lowered productivity in the cluster of minorities so hired. The two psychologists noted that since minorities account for only about 15 percent of the labor force, lowering standards meant that large numbers of less-qualified whites got through the same door and contributed the lion's share of the productivity drop.

Nor did Schmidt and Hunter pull any punches when it came to specific companies. They pointed to the case of General Electric (GE), which, in the early 1970s dropped all job aptitude tests in order to "get the government off its back" by hiring more minorities. But the company found that a large percentage of these people—minorities and others—so hired were not promotable. "GE had merely transferred the adverse impact from the hiring stage to the promotion stage," concluded Schmidt and Hunter. The company soon resumed testing via an outside consulting firm, a practice now widely copied.

And when U.S. Steel dramatically lowered its standards, it found markedly lower "mastery" scores in its training program, far higher flunk-out and drop-out rates, increased training time needed for those who did make it through, and lower average ratings of later job performance. Schmidt and Hunter concluded: "A major reason for the marked decline in U.S. productivity growth in the last few years is the decline in the accuracy with which employers have been sorting people into jobs. And this decline in accuracy is caused by substantial reductions in the use of valid job aptitude tests."

In the early 1970s, V. Jon Bentz was head of Psychological Research and Services for Sears & Roebuck, a company which had long been in the forefront in the use of tests for prospective employees and more complex assessment procedures for executives and senior management. After EEOC published its revised guidelines in 1972, Bentz conducted a study of test results at Sears which showed that while blacks as a group tended to do less well than whites on the test, those who scored high enough to be selected had job performance ratings as high as their white colleagues. Nonetheless, fearing that Sears might be charged with illegal discrimination, Bentz decided to "race norm" the tests, judging blacks only against other blacks and hiring from the top percentiles of each race. At the time, black executives with the company vehemently objected to the institutionalization of lower or "double standards" for blacks, fearing it would institutionalize "second-class citizenship" for future black employees. But because of the implied government ultimatum, Bentz overruled their objections and implemented the new procedure.

"In the long run our black personnel executives were correct, and I was wrong," Bentz later wrote. "Poorer scorers performed poorly in the long run, causing problems which were perpetuated. A side effect was the breaking down of administrative discipline. For years we had exercised excellent control over the selection process. When we formalized dual selection standards, administrators began to feel that if we 'officially fudged a bit here,' why not a bit there. The long-term effect (in a highly decentralized, geographically dispersed organization) was a breakdown in the use of selection procedures and standards."

Almost all Schmidt and Hunter's contentions have found overwhelming support among economists, industrial psychologists, consultants, and CEOs. And corporations, as they came to appreciate what harm the affirmative action regulatory regime had wrought, gradually returned to testing, often, like GE, outsourcing the work and insisting in advance on proper validation of the tests.

The regulators too became aware of the mounting evidence of test validity. But if their principal concern had been productivity, they would have gone to work at Commerce, not at the EEOC or OFCCP. "There is not any way in which black people tomorrow as a group are going to, no matter what kind of test you give them, score the same way white people score," Eleanor Holmes Norton complained while chairman of Jimmy Carter's EEOC. "And I can't live with that. I think employers can. And I think test validation gives them an A-1 out. Because if you validate your tests you don't have to worry about the exclusion of minorities and women any longer...."

Norton and her successors at both agencies continued to make life difficult for those using tests. As veteran test developer Frank W. Erwin, a former assistant to the Johnson administration's secretary of labor, W. Willard Wirtz, has noted, "The thermometers are still here, only they're better and they're more defensible. The thermometer breakers are still here, too, still hanging on to selected court cases and rejected theories, and still thinking that getting rid of thermometers will warm up cold rooms."

For companies, the trick became to use well-validated tests to the greatest extent possible while playing the numbers game aggressively enough to keep affirmative action wolves from the door. Ted Carron was the head personnel man for the Ethyl Corporation, which employed about 15,000 people at facilities in a number of locations including Houston; Detroit; Baton Rouge; and Orangeburg, South Carolina. He watched as the director of the Houston plant succumbed to pressure from federal regulators to drop the company's testing program, substituting an aggressive interview process in its place.

As a result, productivity dropped and the accident rate zoomed. The director was transferred and his replacement promptly resumed testing. Carron noted that the petroleum products industry could be hazardous with an ever-present danger of fire and explosion as well as air and water pollution. "If you don't have a properly trained labor force you can be a danger to yourself and your community," he says. Carron also turned to outsourcing for the development of Ethyl's testing program. His consultant: Professor Frank Schmidt.

Carron was not blind to the need to increase the potential pool of black employees and managers, recalling, "We beat the bushes in the black churches, with their fraternal organizations, with the historically black colleges and universities. We really had to test the hell out of them in the South to find quality black employees and at the same time I had to educate our managers to work with them because a number of them had grown up here during the years of segregation and had a limited view of what blacks were capable of doing."

Carron would set a fairly high cutoff score for his tests. "Then I would take the highest scoring white, the highest scoring black, and alternate that way till I ran out of blacks above the cutoff point. Then the rest of my hires would be whites above the line. It didn't bother me that some of the blacks hired had lower scores than any of the whites or that some whites with higher scores than some of the blacks were not offered jobs. To me the key was the cutoff score. We got good employees."

Other corporate executives who may not have worked as hard as Carron in expanding the black applicant pool adopted the race-norming selection method, which, as described above, involves segregating the blacks or other minority applicants, ranking each test taker by percentile within his or her racial group, and then hiring the top percentiles until all places are taken. The technique was adopted by the Department of Labor's U.S. Employment Service for use by state employment services with the General Aptitude Test Battery. Very simply, what this meant was that a private employer seeking referrals of available personnel together with their scores on objective aptitude exams from their state employment office was provided instead with a list which consciously and deliberately misrepresented the standings of black and other preferred minority test takers by reporting their percentiles only in the context of other preferred minorities taking the exam. From all available evidence, most of those private sector employers who learned of the practice either ignored it, or, in many instances, adopted the race-norming procedure in their own recruitment and hiring.

The widespread use of race norming became generally known when Congress studied testing while writing the Civil Rights Act of 1991, and conservative columnists and others jumped on the practice as an indication of the extent to which elementary notions of equal opportunity had been corrupted by the drive for equality of result. Pressure from the right led to the banning of race norming in the 1991 act, although in other respects, the act underlined the demand for equal results.

The ban, as we shall see, led to a race by business to develop other ways of accomplishing the same thing. What many critics had failed to understand was that for the corporate or federal supervisor, race norming had been an almost classic exercise in damage control. If you simply lower your standards, you get a lousy work-force, white and minority. But if you race norm, your white selectees are all above the line you set while your minorities are the best available. Disparate impact is eliminated, the civil rights enforcers are happy, and economic damage is limited. In fact the only thing that suffers is an abstraction called integrity of process.

The principal purpose of the 1991 act was to codify the *Griggs* disparate impact standards imposed by the Burger Court, which had not previously been endorsed per se by Congress and which had suffered modest judicial erosion in a few recent cases. The act's combination of a strict disparate impact standard and the abolition of the race-norming damage control mechanism has led to a burst of testing creativity among corporate America—much of it as closely guarded as a new formula to "get the dirt out," some of it highly promising, much of it intellectually corrupt.

Cognitive ability is one and probably the single most valid pre-dictor of success in a variety of jobs and positions, but it is a way for employers to improve the odds of selecting a qualified employee. It is *not* definitive and is only the best *single* indicator known to industrial psychologists.

And while cognitive ability is certainly important, so are many other traits. Richard J. Herrnstein and Charles Murray correctly noted in *The Bell Curve* that smart secretaries and even busboys may have a decided edge in on-the-job performance over those with more modest cognitive ability. But their g is wasted if the busboy has a tendency to punch out headwaiters or smoke dope, or if the secretary spends most of each day surreptitiously work-ing on her first novel.

Similarly, all other things being equal, a smart salesman has an advantage over a less smart one and a smart sergeant could save your platoon while a dumb one could bring it to ruin. But all other things are rarely equal. If the smart salesman is an introvert compared with the one with a shade less cognitive ability, or if the smart sergeant wets his pants when the bullets start to fly while the less smart one holds the line, suddenly a few extra points on the g exam mean very little.

Perhaps the foremost pioneers in exploring job predictors that might complement tests of cognitive ability are Laetta M. Hough and Marvin D. Dunnette of Personnel Decisions Research Institute in St. Paul, Minnesota. In one of the more massive projects of its kind ever documented, Hough and Dunnette studied three thousand operators at two hundred hydroelectric, fossil fuel, and nuclear power plants representing seventy different companies. They tested for cognitive ability, but also used a series of biographical—and personality—type questions to weed out those who were hostile toward authority, irresponsible and impulsive, emotionally unstable, incompetent, or afflicted with some form of psychopathology. The four criteria against which operators were judged were emotional stability, operations competence, problem-solving ability, and overall performance.

In 1986 dollars, Hough and Dunnette found that high scorers on the combined tests working as nuclear control room operators could save their companies $112,000 per year compared with low scorers, while those who were simply plant operators could save $21,000 per year. While the figures at fossil and hydroelectric plants were somewhat lower, they estimated that two hundred employees hired strictly according to the test results could save their companies about $49 million per year. The tests were valid for all operators, regardless of age, race, or sex. And, "[t]hough scores on the cognitive measures showed evidence of adverse impact, no adverse impact was shown for the noncognitive biographical and personality measures."

Like tests of cognitive ability, the search for desirable personality traits (assuming they can be identified with precision for the position in question) and the hope of identifying undesirable ones go back to the earliest days of testing. Columbia's Professor Edward Thorndyke, during the first three decades of the current century, sought from his interview subjects examples from childhood and adolescence which could shed light on their mature personalities. Harvard's William Whyte, author in 1956 of *The Organization Man*, thought the practice of trying to glean personality insights from attitudinal questions sufficiently intrusive to warrant his writing an essay instructing test takers on how to "cheat" on such questions.

But the science of exam construction and administration has since advanced to the point where Hough and others are certain that intentional distortions can be screened and true character ascertained. Hough has constructed nine personality traits which all of us have in differing quantities and which are desirable in differing quantities for different jobs:

1. Affiliation (socialization)
2. Potency (impact, influence, and energy displayed)
3. Achievement (competence in one's work)
4. Dependability (conscientiousness)
5. Adjustment (emotional stability, stress tolerance)
6. Agreeableness
7. Intelligence
8. Rugged individualism (masculine, decisive, action-oriented, independent, unsentimental)
9. Locus of control (belief that there are consequences associated with behavior and that people control what happens to them through their own actions)

Again, different positions have different personality requirements. In Hough's analysis, executive performance correlates with potency and achievement, but far less with dependability, adjustment, and agreeableness. Service-oriented work correlates highly with emotional stability, agreeableness, and conscientiousness. Good sales personnel have high correlations with potency, intelligence, and agreeableness, but less with adjustment, and their correlation with dependability is negative.

Schmidt and Hunter have themselves been involved in developing job selection criteria to complement simple reliance on cognitive skills. They and others have gotten good results with certain "biodata" and "integrity" (dependability) standards which basically search for desired personality traits in would-be employees and then determine whether job applicants possess them. Schmidt believes that by combining these techniques with cognitive ability tests, employers can obtain better validity while reducing disparate impact substantially. "If you were to run a cognitive ability test for 100 vacancies and had 100 black applicants and 100 white applicants, statistically, you would probably wind up hiring 85 whites and 15 blacks. But if you combined that with tests measuring integrity—our technical name for dependability—really conscientiousness, you would wind up with 65 whites and 35 blacks, and you would have the superior group of employees. So you are a winner, both in terms of efficiency and social justice."

Mary L. Tenopyr of AT&T, one of the quiet giants in the testing field, has in recent papers described several other ways in which—prodded by a numbers-oriented bureaucracy—testers are trying to replace race norming with other forms of damage control. They include:

- Banding, which takes the top test score and creates a zone below it within which the testers assume that little substantive difference exists among candidates and declare that all falling within the zone are "equal." The band can either be stationary, or it can "slide" downward as candidates within it are selected. It has the virtue of controlling damage about as well as race norming, but its legality is suspect. The practice was held lawful by one federal circuit court of appeals, but only in the context of a public employment consent decree in which the city of San Francisco was seeking to redress past discrimination in hiring police officers. Banding undertaken by either public or private employers with no recent history of discrimination to reduce or eradicate different scores between ethnic or racial groups raises far more difficult questions and could well be judged illegal.

- Adjusting upward the scores of minority candidates, thus making race a "plus" factor, a method arguably (but doubtfully) approved by the Supreme Court in the famous *Bakke* case.

- Substituting work "portfolios" and/or oral interviews for tests.

- Permitting minorities longer periods to complete their tests, or allowing them to take the identical test on successive days.

- Adjusting the test content to accommodate minority performance, such as eliminating questions on which they do relatively poorly.

The Clinton administration meanwhile has continued efforts to keep the disparate impact standard sacrosanct. OFCCP forced the Seicor Corporation of Hickory, North Carolina, into junking the well-validated "Employee Aptitude Survey," developed by Psychological Services, Inc. of Glendale, California, and offering nearly $175,000 in back pay to 752 women and minorities whom the company failed to hire "because of their low scores on a test which had not been properly validated and was not job-related."

The president, in his fulsome endorsement of affirmative action, assured the nation that nothing on his agenda would lead to "unqualified" candidates getting jobs, contracts, or university admissions. The term, as we have seen, is among the most elastic in all of society, so indefinite that it has yet to find its way into any defining case or statute. Is a worker who is $12,000 per year less productive than one with an identical job "qualified"? What about a student who can "muddle through" with a C average, but contributes little to the academic environment and has no graduate or professional school potential? Must an employer hire any minority who is "qualified," or can he set standards high enough to attract the best?

In theory and in the letter of the law, the federal government has given one message. In practice, it has given quite another.

5

THE RED AND THE BLUE

Perhaps the last great battlefields in the thirty-year war over testing are the nation's police and fire departments. Many of the disputes have been going on for decades. The typical situation began with a fire department, like Chicago's, which practiced blatant discrimination, declining to hire blacks and Hispanics, or later, assigning them to segregated firehouses, or giving police exams that eliminated minorities at rates the Justice Department and civil rights community found intolerable.

Confronted with a lawsuit initiated either by a minority activist organization with Justice Department support or by Justice alone, the jurisdiction would likely wind up signing a consent decree which would include minority recruitment efforts and numerical employment targets together with some commitment to address concerns with the validity of any test administered. The court would, meanwhile, retain supervisory jurisdiction over the matter.

Depending upon the action actually taken by the police or fire department, the next round would either be initiated by the original plaintiff or plaintiffs complaining that the hiring procedures were still unfair or by representatives of the white firefighters or police officers claiming that the procedures now favored minorities, thereby denying them their rights under the Equal Protection Clause of the Fourteenth Amendment.

In Birmingham, for example, the city's first black mayor, Richard Arrington, signed a consent decree in 1981 which committed the fire department to hire and promote blacks and whites on a one-for-one basis. No one could deny that some form of relief was needed for blacks who had long been excluded from work at a department more famous in the 1960s for using its fire hoses against civil rights demonstrators than fires. But the remedy imposed was both crude and open-ended. In an August 1995 report on the history of the dispute, the *New York Times* recalled the year 1983 when eighty-nine whites and nine blacks passed a lieutenant's examination. Of that group, two whites and three blacks received the promotion. "The city picked the whites who ranked first and second then passed over seventy-six other whites to promote the three highest-scoring black candidates."

There followed nearly a decade and a half of growing bitterness within the department. Firefighters divided along racial lines. There was little contact between the two groups even at the station house. Morale suffered. In 1994, a federal appellate court held the original consent decree was unconstitutionally broad. It wrote, "We can imagine nothing less conducive to eliminating the vestiges of past discrimination than a government separating its employees into two categories, black and white, and allocating a rigid, inflexible number of promotions to each group, year in and year out."

It can be argued that fifteen years after the initial decree so few blacks applying for jobs or promotions have suffered from discrimination that the practice of hiring by merit ought to be restored immediately and comprehensively. The problem is that when that happens the percentage of successful black competitors usually sinks to levels that many people find unacceptable. So the attack by the federal civil rights establishment turns to the instrument blamed for the problem, the test itself.

Nassau County, New York, a sprawling Long Island suburb, first came to Justice's attention in 1976 when it administered a written exam prepared by New York State for use by hundreds of its subdivisions in hiring police officers. The exam, which focused heavily on math and reading comprehension skills, was given to 3,411 whites and 232 blacks. Nearly 64 percent of the whites taking the exam passed. The pass rate for blacks was just over 21 percent. Only 1 among the top 126 qualifiers was black.

In addition, the county required new officers to have completed at least two years of college, a requirement that eliminated all surviving black candidates save one who, along with 149 whites, was eventually offered a place on the force.

Justice took the county to court in a 1977 lawsuit, claiming that both the exam and the college requirement had a disparate impact on minorities, that the exam had not been properly validated and that there was no manifest connection between attending college and performing acceptably as a police officer.

After five years of litigation, Nassau County signed a consent degree with what was by now the Reagan Justice Department, waiving the college requirement, junking the exam, pledging to recruit actively in the minority communities with the goal of obtaining blacks and Hispanics in proportion to their place in the qualified labor force, offering a "second chance" to all minorities rejected on the basis of the exam or the college requirement, and setting aside $975,000 to compensate those "wrongfully" rejected. But a second exam, administered in 1983, produced similar results and Justice pressed its case. The county retained consultants to develop yet a third exam.

This one was administered in December 1987. Its documented validity was superior to its predecessors, but the adverse impact was nearly as great. Once again, Justice refused to accept the results and the case went back to court, this time accompanied by a parade of expert witnesses enlisted by the two sides.

In May 1990, the parties signed yet another consent decree. This time the United States and Nassau County agreed to undertake "a joint project to design, develop and validate a new instrument for use by the County in the selection of candidates for appointment to the rank of Police Officer...." Until such time as the new test could be administered, the county was permitted to hire officers on the basis of those portions of the 1987 exam whose validities were not challenged.

The new exam was developed by David Jones, president of the Detroit-based consulting firm HRStrategies. In addition to bio-data material, it included written questions and answers on job-related literature the applicants had been permitted to take home to study for several weeks and a large "video section" in which candidates responded to questions about material presented to them in the form of slides, graphs, and motion pictures.

More than 25,000 applicants took the exam which was administered in two locations, the Nassau Coliseum and Madison Square Garden. The passing rates for whites and Hispanics were statistically equal. Blacks passed at a rate 77 percent as great as whites. The Justice Department informed Nassau County it accepted the results of the exam it had helped design, and eighteen years of litigation came to an end.

"Through 18 years and four presidents the message from the Justice Department was clearly that there was no way in Hell they would ever sign onto an exam that had an adverse impact on blacks and Hispanics," says James Sharf. "What we finally came up with was more than satisfactory if you assume a cop will never have to write a coherent sentence or interpret what someone else has written. But I don't think anyone who lives in Washington could ever make that assumption."

The police department of the nation's Capital has a notorious record for seeing felony charges dismissed because of police incompetence in filling out arrest reports and related records. A study conducted by the *Washington Post* for the year 1994 showed that of 309 murder charges filed in D.C. Superior Court, 228 had been resolved by 5 January 1996. But only 1 in 9 had resulted in a conviction for first degree murder, 4 in 10 resulted in no conviction at all, and 58—what the paper termed, "a disturbing number"—were dismissed prior to indictment. According to the paper, "Prosecutors cite sloppy police work that fails to keep on top of witnesses and corroborating evidence."

This should not be surprising given that recruiting standards have been so lax for so many years that courses in remedial reading are part and parcel of the police recruit training program. In 1994, the *Post* ran a series of articles reporting that more than two hundred D.C. officers had been arrested on charges ranging from shoplifting to murder; many of those two hundred had been recruited in the 1989–90 period when hiring standards went into complete remission. In October 1995, Carl T. Rowan, Jr., distinguished black commentator and nationally syndicated columnist, complained in a *Post* article, "The police department has virtually no objective means by which to rate the efficiency of its officers, or to tie their performance to promotions." It is, he might have added, the logical product of a local political environment hospitable to the seeds of testing destruction planted by the Equal Employment Opportunity Commission (EEOC) and the Office of Federal Contract Compliance Program (OFCCP) Review. And like so many other instances of misapplied compassion, its intended beneficiary—the minority community—is instead the most victimized of all, since members of that community are the most dependent on police protection.

The Nassau County litigation was costly, time consuming, and arguably perverse, but compared with Chicago, the impact on police business and morale was slight. Since 1976, when the Seventh Circuit Court of Appeals affirmed a decree requiring the Chicago police force to abide by a 40 percent hiring and promotion quota, the city has been embroiled in litigation. For two decades now, any time the city had to make a hiring or promotion decision, its officials knew the most predictable result would be fresh litigation by whites or blacks claiming their rights had been trampled and seeking relief under the Equal Protection Clause.

Understandably, perhaps, its solution has been to avoid hiring or promoting anybody unless absolutely necessary. As *Newsweek* noted, the city's 1994 sergeant exam was the first since 1985; that year's lieutenants' exam was the first since 1987. With hiring held to a minimum, the department has had to pay its officers overtime for the thousands of extra work hours. No fewer than forty-nine recorded decisions have resulted from that initial decree. So many intervening plaintiffs and defendants have argued about every aspect of the decree's implementation that the same circuit court that affirmed the quota in the 1970s likened the suit in 1989 to the never-ending equity actions ridiculed by Dickens in *The Bleak House.*

The following year, the presiding judge noted that the case had persisted through five presidencies, adding, "If this case had been filed when the Constitution was adopted, we would be nearing the end of Thomas Jefferson's stay in the White House, the Alien and Sedition Acts would have come and gone, the Louisiana Purchase would have been completed.... Chicago's police force has been under judicial control almost as long as the interval between Pearl Harbor and the Kennedy administration." In addition, the court noted, "No one knows how many parties there are; recently, we dismissed one aspect of the case in which the lawyer seemed to have lost his clients—and no one noticed!"

The case began in 1973 when Renault Robinson, a twenty-six-year-old black police officer, formed the Afro American (later, African American) Patrolman's League and, with the cooperation of the Justice Department, sued the city for discriminatory hiring and promotion on its police force. At the time, the relevant racial compositions were:

	White	*Black*	*Hispanic*
City	60%	33%	7%
Force	83%	16%	1%

The hiring exam was multiple choice. A passing score was 62.5 percent. Whites passed at a rate of 67 percent, blacks at 33 percent, and Hispanics at 32 percent. Robinson launched a similar complaint against promotion procedures both on the basis of the multiple choice exam and the efficiency and seniority ratings used. When the city offered no evidence of the procedures' validity, the court enjoined use of the exams and ordered the hiring quota. Chicago's late mayor, Richard Daley, called the decision "abhorrent to all Americans."

Implementation of the quota caused a surge in racial tension on the force. White officers, whose only offense was having passed an exam that many minorities flunked, found themselves bumped as many as three hundred spaces down the promotion roster. They began taunting the blacks who made errors, calling them "quota sergeants" to their faces. Various parties began intervening in the lawsuit left and right. Ultimately, the quota remained in place and the city was forced to develop and administer a new set of exams.

Alas, the new exams created an even greater racial disparity than the original ones. To get Washington off its back, the city dumped whites who had passed the exam off the new roster, thereby creating a new batch of litigants who joined their comrades from the 1973 debacle. The method employed to exclude whites who had passed the exam is buried in the mountains of litigation. Most likely it involved some form of race norming, whereby blacks competed against each other for a specified percentage of the sought-after places. Two other possibilities: white officers may simply have been told with no documentation that they failed to meet the total score needed for promotion, a method used by the Chicago Fire Department to meet its racial quotas. Or, as happened in one documented case, whites may have been given low ratings on the subjective parts of the exam, which were then given far greater weight than was customary relative to the written test.

Other cases, reported by the *Washington Post*, included Sergeant John Apel, who in 1985 was summarily dropped from 360 to 750 on the promotion list simply because he was white, and Ron Shogren, whose test score placed him seventeenth in line for promotion, but who was dropped 1,500 places to make room for a minority.

Whites continued to sue, sometimes with positive results. In 1986, six white officers who were transferred out of the Office of Municipal Investigations in an effort to increase black representation were awarded $4.3 million by a jury of seven whites and one black.

In 1987, the city sought for the third time to create a diversity-friendly exam in an effort to promote five hundred patrol officers. Minority sergeants were consulted about the knowledge, skills, and abilities important to their position, and the city used the information to create a kinder, gentler, minority-friendly exam. When the results were in, however, the break-down was as follows:

	White	Black	Hispanic
Candidates (%)	67	27	6
Percentage of total pool who passed	83	13.2	3.6

Under the going so-called "80 percent rule," which declares presumptively invalid any exam in which minorities fail to pass at a rate at least equal to 80 percent of white passing rates, the exam could not pass muster. So the city made some adjustments to support what it called "racial standardization," a euphemism for quota implementation, declaring, "The city does not believe that minute differences in scores reflect meaningful differences in a candidate's ability to perform the complex and sensitive job of police sergeant."

Following "racial standardization," the department refused to promote eighty-four white officers who had passed the exam, while seventy-two blacks and twelve Hispanics who did not were awarded the rank of sergeant.

Just as the department was yielding to new pressures from His-panics and women to increase their quotas, the federal district court was about to declare that enough was enough. In a 1988 decision, the court stated, "We realize that the gender, racial, and ethnic mix of sergeants does not fully reflect the patrol officer mix.... Quotas are an anathema to those who are bypassed as a result of them. They have been the most vexatious remedy in this litigation. In our judgment, they should be terminated."

By the early 1990s, Chicago's fear of promotion exams had left it desperate for new sergeants. The mayor, wishing to avoid further litigation, sought to create an absolutely fair test of demonstrable validity and paid independent consultants $5 million to create and administer such an exam.

The latest instrument was administered to 4,700 officers in March 1994. The city had decided to promote 114 new sergeants. With minorities now composing 37 percent of the force, the city felt it could promote directly from the lists of those doing well on the exam. But the top 114 scorers on the test included 109 whites and 5 minorities of which only 1 was a black male. Defending the promotions in a column appearing in the *Chicago Sun Times*, Mayor Daley said, "In the past thirty years, there has never been a smooth and painless promotions process that has not triggered a lawsuit, either from minorities charging unfairness or whites charging reverse discrimination. The city always gets sued every time promotions are made. That is why the last police sergeants exam was in 1985, and the results were not posted until 1988."

Minorities were furious. First they charged the results were racially biased, then that white officers had been given copies of the exam to study at home, an allegation for which no proof was offered. Late in 1994, 192 black and Hispanic officers sued to enjoin the city from using the exam results in making promotion decisions. They asked for damages of $10,000 each on the grounds that they had been "humiliated" by the implication that they had not studied hard enough.

A few months later, it was time to promote 54 sergeants to lieutenant, and all were made from the test rankings. Only 3 minorities made the cut. Of the top 175 scores on the lieutenant's exam, only 13 were minorities. Then, in a surprise move, Police Superintendent Matt Rodriguez, with Daley's blessing, made an additional 13 "merit-based" promotions. Eight of the 13 went to minorities. White officers went to court, and a federal judge immediately agreed that the promotions violated the 1991 Civil Rights

Act, which includes a bar against race norming. The merit promotions were dropped. And the 54 designated promotions from the exam list proceeded.

The Fraternal Order of Police refused to endorse Daley's 1995 reelection bid. So did the African American Police League. Fraternal Order President Bill Nolan complained, "Whether Daley tries to call it merit or race, it's illegal either way." African American Police League President Patricia Hill replied that "[y]ou still have fifty-two whites promoted to lieutenant. So how is that affirmative action?" And Daley complained, "You can't win or lose."

As of late 1994, the *New York Times* reported Chicago's police force was 24.9 percent black compared with a black city population of 39.1 percent. Los Angeles has a force which is 14.1 percent black to go with its 14 percent black population. Detroit's police force is 58.3 percent black, for a 78.7 percent black population; Philadelphia, 28.7 percent for a 39.9 percent black population; and New York, a partial exception to growing minority representation in its force, has 11.4 percent blacks for a population which is 28.7 percent black. Female and Hispanic representation is increasing, but there are fewer black males on the force than there were 20 years ago, a commentary more on the horrific problems afflicting young black males in the city than on any racial discrimination practiced by police recruiters. In 1993, a massive effort by New York City to stimulate minority interest in police careers drew just over 50,000 candidates, only 43 percent of them white, to take that summer's qualifying exam. Of the 37,500 who passed, only about 12,000 were black or Hispanic. In all of the major cities the higher police ranks are dominated by whites who continue to pass qualifying exams in far higher percentages than blacks or Hispanics.

Experts differ on the contribution proportional representation of minorities on police forces could make to fighting crime and making inner cities safer. The weight of opinion is that as long as there are enough minority police to serve as ambassadors to the minority communities and to work as undercover agents, training, experience, intelligence, integrity, and good judgment are far more important than skin pigmentation. But Patrick Murphy, the New York City Police commissioner a generation ago, disagrees. He recently told the *New York Times*, "All the training, all the good supervision in the world cannot make up for the life experiences of a black officer in understanding the life and culture of the people in the black community."

Slowly, the remedies imposed by courts years ago are being complied with. Sometimes, as with Chicago, the city, in order to end the court's jurisdiction, enters a consent decree agreeing to apply an assortment of affirmative action measures well into the future. On other occasions, as with Cleveland, the agreed-upon balance on the force having been achieved, the court effectively declares the case over and permits the city to resume hiring police officers (or firefighters) on the basis of objective tests. That may trigger another cycle of litigation beginning with claims of disparate impact. Or perhaps a process of resegregation will begin again, slowly at first, but gaining steam as minorities become discouraged from taking the competitive exam. Or perhaps, with the right kind of aggressive intervention against the sort of neighborhood, home, and family environment that shapes the experience of so many inner-city blacks, and the right kind of black leadership, future competitive exams will find minority candidates ready, willing, and able to compete on more even terms.

6

RACE AND UNIVERSITY ADMISSIONS

It is April 1995 in Ithaca, New York. The computer has just printed out the list of 224 names accepted for admission to the Cornell University School of Industrial and Labor Relations (I&LR) for the fall 1995 semester, and Richard Wagner, the dean of admissions, is looking it over. He is a tall, distinguished man with white hair, a Vermont Yankee who thinks the work that he has done getting blacks, Hispanics, and Mexicans into the I&LR school may one day get him into heaven. But now as he stares at a copy of this list, his eyes show concern, perhaps a little sadness. "In terms of affirmative action, this is going to be a bad year," he warns. "We can offer only a few under EOP [the Equal Opportunity Program]. And there is intense competition for the ones that don't need EOP to get in."

Wagner hands the list to a visitor and begins to explain the letters under the heading, "Ethnicity." "A" is American Indian. "B" is black. "C" is Hispanic—that is, any Central or South American who is not of Mexican ancestry or a Puerto Rican national. "D" is Asian—that counts as a minority but not an underrepresented minority. "E" is Puerto Rican. "F" is Caucasian. "G" is Mexican American. "J" is foreign. And "N" is not reported—applicants are not required to disclose their ethnicity, though Wagner is not above making an educated guess.

About three-quarters of the way across the page is a column marked "Academic Index" (AI). Wagner explains that it is derived by taking the average of an applicant's highest math and verbal Scholastic Aptitude Test (SAT) scores, the average of his three highest achievement SAT scores, and his percentile class rank. Each of those three figures—combined math and verbal SAT, achievement SAT, class rank—is then translated into points, 20 points reflecting the low end of the spectrum, 80 points, the high end. The three scores are then added to produce the "Academic Index." The lowest possible AI is 60, and the highest is 240. The highest score among those accepted for admission to the Class of '99 was 228; the lowest, 161.

That score, 161, could translate into 440 on the verbal SAT, 580 on the math, 400 to 480 on the achievement tests, and a 3.3 high school grade point average (GPA), putting an applicant in the top 25 percent to 30 percent of his class. "I'll let you in on a little secret," Wagner continues. "This year the eight Ivy League presidents decided to make 161 the cut-off for athletes—anyone lower than that can only be admitted to an Ivy League school by the vote of a special review committee. So we decided to make it our affirmative action cut-off as well."

Wagner begins reviewing the list. He stops at a Jewish name in the top cluster. "This young man is from a high school in Long Island. Three of the top five in his graduating class applied to the I&LR school."

Did the other two get in?

"No. We can't have that kind of concentration; it has nothing to do with affirmative action."

Would you say that if they were minorities?

"I'll cross that bridge when I come to it. Right now I have trouble finding three from the same city."

The eighth name on the list has a Spanish surname. "This is my pride and joy," says Wagner. "Mexican. Her folks are migrant laborers from California. And look at that Academic Index—218! Can you imagine that! She's also been accepted at Stanford. I'm holding my breath."

That is a big problem for Cornell and many other schools. The top black high school graduates get into Harvard, Yale, Princeton, Stanford, and Duke on their own, just like any outstanding student. Then these schools move down a rung, accepting minority students who, in most cases, would not make the school if they were white. That, in a nutshell, is how affirmative action in the service of university "diversity" works. But it leaves the I&LR school, a giant in its field, and many other fine colleges and universities with many minority students who, were they white or Asian, would be heading for Boston University, Syracuse, or Ohio State—fine schools all, but not the nation's most selective.

The migrant workers' daughter was not counted as an Equal Opportunity Program admission, having gotten in strictly on merit.

Four places below her on Wagner's list is another Mexican American girl about whom he is nearly as excited, and eighteen places further down, a Hispanic boy; both clearly merit admissions. Then the pickings become slim. The first black, a young woman, is the 124th name to appear on the list, but still with a solid Academic Index of 194. Below her name, although there is an occasional "underrepresented minority," the list gets only a sprinkling of "Bs," "Cs," "Es," and "Gs" until near the bottom of the fourth and final page. Of the bottom thirteen names, one is Caucasian and one, Asian. The rest are EOP admissions.

But of the 224 names on the list, only 10 are black, half the 1994 total. The reason is a math course that was added to the curriculum at the insistence of the faculty. Pre-calculus was considered a good introduction to the sort of advanced statistics courses now required for anyone interested in personnel administration, labor economics, or an academic career. But when the 1994 freshmen were placed in a "pre-cal" course in the liberal arts school, more than half of those admitted under I&LR's affirmative action program received grades no higher than D, and more than a third flunked outright. So the faculty snatched at least part of Wagner's discretionary authority from him, imposing a rule that regardless of race or any other credentials, no student would be accepted who failed to score at least 500 on the math portion of the SAT.

"That devastated our affirmative action program," says Wagner, who calls the faculty's action "an example of a self-perpetuating white male culture."

"And," he sighs, "it's so unnecessary."

He has more paper to show, a list of the thirty-three EOP students selected for the classes graduating in 1992 through 1998. So far, two have been dismissed for academic reasons, and three others dropped out for reasons that may or may not have had anything to do with academics. "This year our graduation rate will be 100 percent—100 percent! And look at this." He points to the name of a black member of the Class of '95—SATs: 330 verbal, 390 math. "Consider what this kid's life would be like without EOP and what it will be like because we gave her a chance. Now, is there anything else you want to know?"

Yes, what about those two Jewish kids from Long Island who didn't make the cut?

"Ah, they'll be fine."

Those two kids were in good company. The twelve-page list of all applicant dispositions shows many Caucasians who had been rejected with SAT scores above 1200, even 1300, while the minority applicants with much lower scores were being accepted or placed on the waiting list.

"A white kid who doesn't get in with 1200 or 1300 SATs invariably has some other problem, like mediocre class standing," explains David B. Lipsky, the school's able dean. "The most-qualified white students would have been accepted in our day [Class of '61], and they would be accepted today. The only difference is that today you have more borderline whites losing out to [the] beneficiaries of affirmative action programs."

Professor John Bishop was the leading faculty advocate for raising the floor on the math SATs, the main reason why the I&LR school wound up with a numerically small group of minority students compared with groups in recent years, but a group that also could be the most academically competitive in the school's history.

Bishop's position is consistent with his long-held view as a labor economist that it is wrong and self-defeating to make it difficult for employers to test the verbal and math reasoning processes of potential employees. He is fond of telling whoever will listen that 70 percent of the nation's population will never get a college degree, but that their education and training, as much as that of the elite, will determine future productivity. In 1991, he told the House Labor Committee that "employers need to be told by people in authority that they are acting in the national interest when they seek out and reward those who have higher level academic skills."

The SATs, which measure developed verbal and mathematical comprehension and reasoning skills in a context similar to what the student will encounter in college, are regarded as good predictors of how well a student will perform during his or her first year of higher education. No college or university in the country regards them as infallible and none admits its entire freshman class based upon a mechanical application of SAT and a high school GPA. But with vast differences in the quality of public and private high schools, and with considerable differences in the high school curricula among applicants, the SATs are regarded as a good check on the GPA. At many of the nation's most selective colleges and universities—say, the top twenty-five universities and the top twenty-five liberal arts colleges—for most students a combined SAT score of 1200 out of 1600 is close to mandatory for admission, and in the even more rarified atmosphere of the most elite schools, scores of 1300 and above are close to essential. Below the top one hundred schools, a combined score of 800 or even lower is far from uncommon.

In 1976, the first year for which a direct comparison of the races is available, the combined black score on the SATs was 686 and the score for whites was 944, a gap of 258 points. Since then, blacks have raised their combined score to 744, while, in 1995, the combined white score was 946, a gap of 202 points. On the face of it, the black gain of 58 points is impressive. But as noted by the *Journal of Blacks in Higher Education* (*JBHE*), an extremely valuable source on academic questions involving race at U.S. colleges and universities, nearly all the gain occurred during the 1976–85 period, perhaps because of improvements in black educational preparation during the civil rights and Great Society eras. *JBHE* notes: "Over the past eight years, black scores have increased by only seven points whereas whites scores have increased by 11 points. Since 1991 the gap between black and white scores has grown each year." It is instructive to consider some of the reasons suggested by *JBHE* for this most recent setback, in addition to deteriorating educational conditions and security at many inner-city schools:

- Tackling serious academic pursuits has become "uncool" in recent years, with the result that blacks who get good grades are disparaged among their peers for "acting white."
- "The steady disappearance of the two-parent families," particularly in black communities.
- The "back to basics" educational movement among whites which has brought renewed focus on reading, writing, math, and science; by contrast, school reform movements in inner cities "are increasingly teaching black students to feel good about themselves instead of concentrating on teaching them reading and mathematics."
- "Increasing emphasis on Afrocentric studies in predominantly black schools has reduced study in core math and reading programs that are vital to good scores on the SAT."

In its Autumn 1995 issue, *JBHE* presented the results of previously unpublished data it had obtained from The College Board comparing the SAT credentials of blacks and whites based on that year's SAT results as might be required by one of the most selective schools conducting a color-blind admissions policy. For the year, only 649 black students, or 0.6 percent, scored 650 or higher on the verbal SAT, while 28,000 white students, or 4.2 percent, broke the 650 verbal line. *"Thus whites were 7 times as likely as blacks to score above 650 on the verbal SAT"* (emphasis in original).

On the math SAT, 2,050 blacks, or 1 percent, scored above 650, while 90,000 whites, or 13 percent, exceeded 650. A more complete breakdown of SAT scores by race is depicted in Table 2.

Table 2. SAT Scores Differ Widely by Race

Percentage of 1995 Test Takers in Each Ethnic Group Who Scored Within Given Range

SAT Score	VERBAL SAT		MATH SAT	
	White (%)	Black (%)	White (%)	Black (%)
750 to 800	0.1	0.0	1.4	0.1
700 to 749	1.2	0.2	4.4	0.5
650 to 699	2.9	0.4	7.6	1.4
600 to 649	5.4	1.1	10.3	2.6
550 to 599	9.1	2.5	11.5	3.8
500 to 549	12.3	4.5	14.3	6.8
450 to 499	17.5	8.8	14.3	10.2
400 to 449	19.4	14.5	14.1	15.1
350 to 399	15.4	18.6	11.1	19.0
300 to 349	10.1	20.8	7.8	23.9
250 to 299	4.9	16.2	2.8	13.1
200 to 249	1.9	12.3	0.5	3.5

Source: The College Board.

JBHE offered this analysis: "There are approximately 45,000 places for entering freshmen at the nation's highest-ranked universities. At the present time, about 3,000 of these places are held by African Americans. If the huge racial gap in SAT scores continues to prevail and these institutions make their admissions decisions without regard to race, blacks will be able to win only 2 percent of these positions. As indicated by their share of the top-scoring SAT, the number of entering black freshmen at the nation's top-ranked institutions would drop to 900."

That is not considered acceptable by most educators. To President Nan Keohane of Duke University, for example, it would mean "returning to what the university was when you could watch 'Ozzie and Harriet' on your black-and-white 12-inch TV screen, and buy a DeSoto at your local car dealership.

I would hope that anyone who is drawn to the reimagined vision of Duke would think carefully about the consequences of this preference."

The universal response of academia has been to relax admissions standards for blacks and other favored minorities. School admissions offices differ only in the degree to which they grant this preferential treatment, not to whether they grant it. The policy is reflected both in the comparative ratio of acceptances to applications and the gap in credentials between whites and blacks. Table 3 presents the results of *JBHE*'s survey on the admission of black students relative to others among the most selective universities for the year 1995. Table 4 presents the same with respect to the nation's leading liberal arts colleges. As blank spaces indicate, not all institutions were willing to provide complete data.

The admissions procedures produce black freshmen with decidedly lower combined SATs than white freshmen, even at the nation's leading private universities which attract by far the most qualified applicants of both races. Table 5 lists the figures for 1992.

Many academicians claim that the tendency of the prestige institutions to enroll blacks who lack top academic credentials produces a "mismatch," which cascades all the way down the academic ladder, with blacks forced to compete at schools a notch or two above where their talents should have landed them. The black who is a marginal student at Stanford, Rice, or Dartmouth, it is argued, could be a substantial academic presence at, say, Cal Santa Barbara, Texas A&M, or Boston College, all strong institutions. At least threshold support for the proposition that black students who clearly belong in college would, in many cases, be better off at a slightly less demanding institution can be found in a 1994 National Collegiate Athletic Association survey of six-year graduation rates at the nation's 301 schools that play Division 1

Table 3. Higher Percentage of Black Applicants

Institution	All Applicants	Total Students Accepted	Overall % Acceptance Rate
Harvard	17,847	2,106	11.8
Princeton	14,311	2,010	14.0
Yale	12,617	2,397	19.0
MIT	7,888	2,133	26.8
Stanford	15,390	2,907	18.8
Duke	14,437	4,124	28.6
CalTech	1,893	511	27.0
Dartmouth	10,006	2,370	23.7
Columbia	8,714	2,042	23.4
U. of Chicago	5,846	3,177	54.3
Brown	13,898	2,792	20.1
Rice	6,780	1,730	25.5
U. of Pennsylvania	15,073	4,960	32.9
Northwestern	12,926	5,200	40.2
Cornell	20,599	7,004	34.0
Emory	9,504	4,420	46.5
U. of Virginia	17,895	6,546	36.6
Vanderbilt	8,879	5,152	58.0
Notre Dame	9,999	3,700	37.0
Washington	9,379	5,285	56.3
U. of Michigan	19,208	12,984	67.6
Johns Hopkins	7,875	3,383	42.9
U. of Ca., Berk.	22,780	8,767	38.4
Carnegie Melon	10,310	5,634	54.6
Georgetown	12,835	2,849	22.2

* As rated by *U.S. News & World Report*. Colleges are listed in rank order.
** Declined to provide statistics.

Accepted by Top Universities* for the Fall of 1995

Black Applicants	Blacks Accepted	Black Acceptance Rate	Black % of Freshman Class
**	215	**	9.3
**	**	**	9.0
**	**	**	7.4
322	138	39.8	6.1
**	278	**	8.3
**	**	**	7.7
29	10	34.5	0.0
**	177	**	6.4
**	**	**	8.9
358	138	38.5	2.8
730	253	34.7	7.3
288	149	51.7	10.0
938	**	**	6.7
568	**	**	6.1
950	371	39.1	4.3
1,054	562	53.3	9.0
1,490	807	54.2	12.5
448	179	39.9	4.0
295	187	63.4	3.8
714	346	48.5	3.8
1,498	1,103	73.6	11.2
513	**	**	5.6
1,204	614	50.9	6.5
484	310	64.0	4.7
986	285	28.9	7.2

Source: *JBHE* survey of college and university admissions offices.

	All	Total Students	Acceptance
Institution	Applicants	Accepted	Rate %

Table 4. Top Liberal Arts Schools

Institution	All Applicants	Total Students Accepted	Acceptance Rate %
Amherst	4,836	930	19.2
Williams*			
Swarthmore	3,524	1,212	34.4
Wellesley	3,411	1,344	39.4
Pomona	3,586	1,230	34.3
Bowdoin	4,122	1,253	30.4
Haverford	2,718	985	36.2
Davidson	3,059	1,051	34.4
Wesleyan	5,501	1,946	35.4
Carleton	2,854	1,441	50.5
Middlebury	3,818	1,367	35.9
Claremont	2,174	882	40.5
Smith	3,333	1,624	48.7
Bryn Mawr	1,719	999	58.1
Wash. and Lee	3,446	1,074	31.2
Vassar*			
Grinnell	2,163	1,446	66.9
Colgate	6,005	2,235	37.2
Oberlin	3,728	2,691	72.2
Colorado	3,426	1,875	54.7
Bates	3,505	1,287	36.7
Trinity	3,150	1,750	55.5
Colby	4,216	1,604	38.0
Holy Cross	3,526	1,772	50.1
Bucknell	6,597	3,641	55.2

* Declined to provide statistics to *JBHE* research department.

Follow Suit, Fall of 1995

Black Applicants	Blacks Accepted	Black Acceptance Rate %	Black % of Freshman Class
180	92	51.1	6.9
202	80	39.6	4.2
222	112	50.4	7.3
113	73	64.6	3.5
84	59	70.2	3.1
112	54	48.2	4.1
95	34	35.8	3.9
439	197	44.9	8.5
76	51	67.1	3.2
108	74	68.5	3.9
83	41	49.4	3.1
235	88	37.4	4.1
104	53	51.0	3.5
72	33	45.8	3.6
87	43	49.4	3.8
174	72	41.4	3.7
225	188	83.5	8.0
58	40	69.0	2.7
88	45	51.1	1.3
189	109	57.7	4.5
75	39	52.0	1.2
89	43	48.3	2.3
123	93	75.6	2.4

Source: *JBHE* survey of college and university admissions offices.

athletic schedules. At those schools, which tend to be among the more challenging schools academically, the study showed that 57 percent of white students matriculate within six years, but only 34 percent of blacks do. At the larger state universities, which within any given system also tend to be more challenging, the same pattern applies, as shown in Table 6.

Table 5. Black Freshmen at Elite Colleges Have Lower SAT Scores

Institution	Gap Between Blacks' and Whites' SAT Scores
Harvard	95
Princeton	150
Duke	184
Dartmouth	218
Columbia	82
Brown	150
Rice	271
Pennsylvania	150
Cornell	162
Stanford	171
Johns Hopkins	155

At the prestige universities, the adage is that it is far tougher to get in than to stay in. Still, in many cases the differences are substantial.

There is no easy answer as to why matriculation rates differ so sharply from school to school. Some have developed intervention systems that include guidance, social support, and mentoring that seem to work, particularly where—as at the University of Virginia—black advisors and administrators encourage students to form bonds within the larger community. Others provide a nurturing environment for the entire student body that benefits majority and minority students alike. But the maintenance of admissions standards cannot be overlooked. *JBHE*

Table 6. At Large State Universities More Blacks Than Whites Fail to Graduate Within Six Years

Institution	White Rate (%)	Black Rate (%)	Difference (%)
Mississippi	49	48	1
Alabama	55	49	6
South Carolina	62	56	6
Georgia	60	48	12
Arkansas	39	26	13
Kentucky	50	37	13
Oklahoma	44	31	13
Tennessee	52	39	13
Arizona	49	33	16
Delaware	71	53	18
LSU	38	20	18
Florida	61	42	19
Texas	63	44	19
West Virginia	55	36	19
Wisconsin	69	48	21
Maryland	62	40	22
Missouri	58	36	22
North Carolina	83	59	24
Colorado	65	39	26
Iowa	62	36	26
Kansas	57	30	27
Minnesota	40	13	27
Illinois	81	53	28
Ohio State	56	28	28
Massachusetts	67	38	29
Nebraska	51	21	30
Penn State	79	49	30
Rutgers	78	48	30
Indiana	64	34	30
U. of Washington	67	25	42

notes, for example, that Mississippi, Alabama, and several other schools, principally in the South, maintain a fixed SAT cutoff point below which they simply will not accept students. The journal reports that "only the most highly qualified black students in the particular state are admitted to the predominantly white institutions."

Tenured black faculty is another problem. Considering the commitment schools have shown to accepting minority students with marginal credentials, it is somewhat surprising that, despite a good deal of federal pressure to hire black faculty and any number of public commitments to do the same on the part of university leaders, the number of tenured black faculty at prominent institutions remains very low. Table 7 lists figures for the academic year 1991.

Dean Lipsky of the I&LR School at Cornell describes the faculty situation this way: "There is no question but that we have clearly weighed race in making some faculty hires and thus have made some risky ones. But tenure decisions are made by tenured faculty. And my observation is that tenured faculty are thinking in terms of a thirty- or forty-year decision and are far more reluctant to take risks for purposes of racial diversity. And that's where the numbers come back to haunt us and we find ourselves in litigation. The charge is made that the percentage of blacks earning tenure is too low. But the reason is that colleges and universities are more flexible in bringing them onto the faculty than in making tenure decisions."

The field is small to begin with. In 1991, blacks accounted for 3.8 percent of the doctorates earned nationwide by U.S. citizens and less than 5 percent of all master's degrees. In 1992, blacks earned a total of four Ph.D.s in mathematics. In 1993, the following doctoral degrees were earned by blacks: humanities, 112; social sciences, 90; psychology, 119; natural sciences, 133; engineering, 80.

Even if all of these young degree-holders shunned lucrative business careers, electing academia instead, the numbers would

Table 7. Top Schools Still Have Few Black Professors
(Includes full and associate professors)

Institution	Total Tenured	Black Tenured	Tenured Black Faculty (%)
Brown	409	11	2.7
Harvard	785	20	2.5
Dartmouth	284	7	2.5
U. of Virginia	929	22	2.4
U. of Ca., Berk.	1,185	27	2.3
UCLA	1,260	28	2.2
Tufts	279	6	2.2
Georgetown	459	10	2.2
SUNY-Binghamton	292	6	2.1
Ga. Inst. of Technology	427	9	2.1
Emory	588	12	2.0
Duke	850	17	2.0
Cornell	1,131	23	2.0
U. of Ca., San Diego	659	13	2.0
Boston	333	6	1.8
U. of Ca., Davis	1,038	18	1.7
Northwestern	812	13	1.6
Tulane	449	7	1.6
New York	998	15	1.5
Boston	517	8	1.5
Brandeis	226	3	1.3
Johns Hopkins	238	3	1.3
MIT	619	8	1.3
U. of Ca., Irvine	542	7	1.3
U. of Wisconsin	1,719	21	1.2
Carnegie Melon	302	2	0.7
Vanderbilt	701	5	0.7
Lehigh	261	1	0.4
Rensselaer Polytechnic	273	1	0.4
Total for Group	**18,565**	**329**	**1.8**

Source: U.S. Department of Labor, 1991

still make it tough on schools anxious to increase their share of blacks on track for tenure. What occurs instead is a "bidding war" for qualified African American academicians. Jon Westling, provost at Boston University, estimates that qualified black academicians in such critical fields as law, engineering, and the natural sciences earn an average 10 percent "premium" for their services. When a real star, such as Harvard's Henry Louis Gates, comes along, he is treated like a .350 hitter who has just entered his period of free agency. Far more often, militant black student demands for more tenured black faculty eventually wear down administrators who, by now, have a handy repository for black scholars of little repute: African American studies.

No less an African studies scholar than Phillip Curtin of the University of Wisconsin has complained in writing about the pyramiding of black academicians in such programs. Confronted with questions about the practice, university administrators tend to wring their hands, smile resignedly, and say, "Well, what do you want us to do? You know the pressure we are under." More than a generation ago, the young black economist Thomas Sowell, now a senior fellow at Stanford's Hoover Institution, alerted his colleagues to the trend: "The speed and thoroughness with which white administrators have accepted and embraced black separatist demands at some colleges has surprised many people who did not realize what a godsend this separatism is to an administrator who is caught in the crossfire between angry faculty members alarmed about academic standards and militants demanding body count."

The premium salaries and puffed up African American studies departments lift some of the burden of meeting minority faculty hiring goals. But were it not for the expedient of employing foreign-born scholars, many of the nation's top academic institutions would find themselves in a perennial war with the Labor

Department's Office of Federal Contract Compliance Program (OFCCP) Review, which oversees national compliance with affirmative action mandates among those businesses and institutions contracting with the federal government. Although statistics on the subject are hard to come by, James S. Robb of the Social Contract Press reports on one survey by Stanford University which found that more than half its ethnic faculty members were foreign born, and the University of Michigan reported that 56.1 percent of its Asian American faculty members were noncitizens, as were 23.3 percent of its Hispanic faculty members and 18.8 percent of its black faculty members. And with Asians who are not U.S. citizens exceeding those who are by a factor of as much as 10:1 among doctoral and postdoctoral students in the hard sciences, it is fair to assume that the results of affirmative action programs in these areas are also generously padded.

■ ■ ■

Accepting blacks with substantially lower academic credentials than whites who are rejected, is, of course, a form of race discrimination—particularly for one of the spurned whites. And the legal foundation for such action is, at best, problematical. The Equal Protection Clause of the Fourteenth Amendment requires states to treat all races equally unless a compelling state interest indicates otherwise. In the 130 years since the amendment was adopted, the only state interest found sufficiently compelling was the need to remedy past official discrimination, a standard still relevant in a handful of southern and border state situations, but nowhere else. Further, Title VI of the Civil Rights Act of 1964, as amended, extends equal protection standards to colleges and universities receiving federal grants, a tent sufficiently big to house all but a handful of lesser institutions.

The one occasion taken by the Supreme Court to assess the

legality of racially skewed admissions policies was the milestone
1978 case, *Regents of University of California v. Bakke.* The
Medical School at the University of California at Davis, established in 1968, had compensated for the paucity of blacks and
Hispanics able to meet its entrance requirements by designating
sixteen places in each class of one hundred for them. In 1973, a
white applicant named Alan Bakke applied for admission and was
rejected. The following year, following a second rejection, he
sued, claiming the minority quota program violated his rights
under the Equal Protection Clause of the Fourteenth Amendment as well as Title VI of the Civil Rights Act of 1964. In 1974,
this is the way Bakke stacked up against the average minority candidate admitted under the quota program in the categories of
science grade point average, overall grade point average, verbal,
quantitative, science, and general information:

	SGPA	*OGPA*	*Verbal*	*Quantitative*	*Science*	*Gen. Inf.*
Bakke	3.44	3.46	96	94	97	72
Minority	2.42	2.62	34	30	37	18

Bakke prevailed in the state courts, and when the Supreme
Court granted review, every lawyer, politician, civil rights advocate, and journalist knew that a seminal decision on the question
of so-called "reverse discrimination" was in the works and all
expected that the Court's words would be pored over for years by
scholars, commentators, and other courts, not only in the education context but in employment and other related areas.

Unfortunately, the Court divided in such a way as to deprive
the nation of a majority reasoning on key elements of the decision. Four Justices, led by Justice Stevens, concluded that Bakke
should prevail under the statutory language of Title VI, thereby
finding it unnecessary to consider the constitutional questions

involved. A second group of four argued that racial classifications intended to help groups which have long suffered discrimination met the required strict judicial standard as did California's interest in curing chronic minority underrepresentation in the medical profession. Although Justice Brennan wrote that section of the argument, the separate words of Justice Marshall still stand as among the more stirring judicial recitations of America's mistreatment of blacks and perhaps the most effective defense of group rights ever delivered from the bench:

> It is unnecessary in twentieth-century America to have individual Negroes demonstrate that they have been victims of racial discrimination; the racism of our society has been so pervasive that none, regardless of wealth or position, has managed to escape its impact. The experience of Negroes in America has been different in kind, not just degree, from that of other ethnic groups. It is not merely the history of slavery alone but also that a whole people were marked as inferior by the law. And that mark has endured. The dream of America as the great melting pot has not been realized for the Negro; because of his skin color he never even made it into the pot.

That left it up to Powell. And the tall Virginia patrician saw the case in a manner different from both other blocs. To a point, he shared the reasoning of the four justices who held that the quota was an affront to Bakke's rights and could not be justified by the fact that blacks in general had suffered past deprivations, writing, "We have never approved a classification that aids persons perceived as members of relatively victimized groups at the expense of other innocent individuals in the absence of judicial, legislative, or administrative findings of constitutional or statutory violations."

But Powell regarded the issue as a conflict not between majority and minority rights, but rather between Bakke's statutory and constitutional right to equal protection and the First Amendment right of the university to decide for itself what was taught, how it was taught, who taught it, and who was admitted as a student. He had no difficulty disposing of the claim that government had the right to discriminate in a "benign" fashion; there was nothing benign about bestowing special rights upon minorities which were unavailable to citizens of the majority race. "The guarantee of equal protection cannot mean one thing when applied to one individual and something else when applied to a person of another color. If both are not accorded the same protection then it is not equal." Also, "preferential programs may only reinforce common stereotypes holding that certain groups are unable to achieve success without special protection based on a factor having no relationship to individual worth." And, "there is a measure of inequity in forcing innocent persons in respondent's position to bear the burdens of redressing grievances not of their making."

The rigid quota system, which effectively had excluded Bakke from consideration for sixteen of the one hundred seats in the class, had to be struck down.

But Powell, joined by the Brennan bloc which had dissented from the opinion ordering Bakke admitted, also reversed that portion of the state court ruling which had held that race can never be a consideration in university admission, and this part of his ruling would be seized on by practitioners in university admissions. Race, said Powell, cannot be the only factor recommending a candidate for admission, but a state institution's quest for student diversity is also entitled to some First Amendment protection. "In such an admissions program," said Powell, "race or ethnic background may be deemed a 'plus' in a particular applicant's file, yet it does not insulate the individual from comparison with all other candidates for the available seats."

The *Bakke* case was vitally important to colleges and universities, both public and private. All were under varying degrees of pressure to admit more minorities despite their failure to achieve anywhere near parity on standardized tests and objective admissions criteria, and all wanted as much legal leeway as possible to move in that direction. Harvard's Archibald Cox, the former solicitor general, argued the case for the University of California, and Harvard submitted its own amicus brief together with a copy of the *Harvard College Admissions Program*. Powell quoted the *Program* at length in his opinion and included the entire document as an appendix. Clearly, he wanted it to be used as a guide in helping institutions of higher learning to define the extent to which their legitimate First Amendment interest in diversity could offset the Equal Protection mandates of Title VI or the Fourteenth Amendment.

The Harvard document noted the long-standing school tradition of seeking students of diverse talents, backgrounds, and geographic origins. More recently, in the quest for diversity, "the race of an applicant may tip the balance in his favor just as geographic origin or a life spent on a farm may tip the balance in other candidates' cases. A farm boy from Idaho can bring something to Harvard College that a Bostonian cannot offer. Similarly, a black student can usually bring something that a white person cannot offer."

There is something offensively disingenuous about the document's wording, just as there is in the argument repeated time and again by affirmative action apologists that goes, "Well, for years, athletes, sons of alumni, Saudi princes, tuba players, and hog-growing Kansans have gotten a plus for being what they are. Why not blacks?" There are several answers:

- First, none of these practices appear to be placing qualified blacks at a disadvantage. The problem is not that high achieving black students are being denied places at elite colleges and universities but rather that too many of those admitted match the academic credentials of their fellow students.

- Second, to the extent blacks already fall in any of these categories they have shared the plus factor with others.

- Third, there is little if any evidence that sons and daughters of alumni have, as a group, academic credentials even slightly below the norm. At Harvard, for example, where the black versus white SAT gap is among the most narrow as any prestige school in the country, 95 points, those who receive special consideration as relatives of alumni average just 35 points below their peers. There are, moreover, no special orientations at colleges and universities for children of alumni, no "support groups," no separate dorms, no group remediation. And while athletes, tuba players, sons of Saudi princes, and others may or may not require special help, all are expected to contribute substantially to the school because of their individual talents or circumstances, not merely because of the color of their skin.

- Fourth, race has always been a special and volatile classification. The nation did not fight a civil war, undertake reconstruction, and wage a fierce political struggle for civil rights in the South because farm boys from Kansas, Nebraska, or Idaho were stigmatized, enslaved, intimidated, abused, and segregated. Rather, these struggles were launched because at least half the white people in this society found intolerable what the other half were doing to the Negro. The nation could not endure permanently half slave and half free, nor could it emerge from the war against Nazism to lead the free world in battle against totalitarian communism so long as racial divisions were codified in law and enforced by the police power of several states.

And more than any other in the arsenal, the great weapon that was used to break down the walls of segregation was the battering ram of equality before the law. Let merit, not race, prevail, was the cry. Let us judge one another, as Martin Luther King Jr., prayed his sons would be judged, "not by the color of their skin but by the content of their character." So when the principle of equality before the law is today attacked, when it is put under siege by forces that have anointed themselves as spokesmen for the disadvantaged and gather under the proud banner of civil rights, and when it is glibly dismissed by politically fashionable academicians who exalt instead the golden calf called "diversity" as though it were some bedrock constitutional principle, it is worth recalling that the edifice of civil rights was built upon the rock of legal equality and that the principle of equal protection provides the most enduring and credible shelter against future abuse.

Justice Powell recognized that the principle of "equal protection" should not be wounded by his commitment to academic freedom. His liberal use of the Harvard document was intended to emphasize the limited yet vital First Amendment role diversity might play in shaping a university's admissions policy. He recalled Justice Frankfurter's admonition, "A boundary line is none the worse for being narrow," continuing, "and a court would not assume that a university, professing to employ a facially nondiscriminatory admissions policy, would operate it as a cover for the functional equivalent of a quota system."

Contrary to Justice Powell's clear intention, far from providing a narrow zone wherein university discretion to achieve greater diversity by making race a small "plus factor" could operate, his words were treated by many state institutions as a license to admit as many minorities as they wished regardless of relative credentials, so long as the magic word *"diversity"* was thrown into the mix. The practice is reflected both in the wide divergence of SAT scores between whites and blacks and also in those specific situations which have come to light via lawsuit or state oversight.

Law school admission policies at the University of Texas, for example, received a perhaps unwelcome vetting in *Hopwood v. Texas*, a suit brought by four rejected white applicants. Texas, of course, with its long history of de jure racial discrimination, had invited decades of federal scrutiny and litigation. By the mid-1980s, it was under intense pressure from Clarence Thomas, who then headed the Office of Civil Rights (OCR) in the Reagan Department of Education, to produce a plan for admitting blacks and Hispanics to each and every state university graduate school in approximate proportion to their percentage of graduates from the state's undergraduate institutions. When Texas took its time, OCR pushed its own plan, which the state finally accepted and which included a provision that "admissions officers will consider each candidate's entire record and will admit black and Hispanic students who demonstrate potential for success but who do not necessarily meet all the traditional admission requirements."

We next encounter the Texas Law School in the year 1992, by which time it has established a separate subcommittee to review minority applicants, is applying different "presumptive acceptance" and "presumptive rejection" standards to them in terms of their college GPAs and Law School Admission Test (LSAT) scores, and is placing those who do not gain immediate admission on a separate priority waiting list.

Given this background, it is almost incidental that the "presumptive rejection" grade for whites was higher than the "presumptive acceptance" grade for blacks and Hispanics, or that, of the forty-one blacks and fifty-five Hispanics admitted in 1992, at most nine blacks and eighteen Hispanics would have been admitted had common standards been applied. Nor does it much matter that the school stumbled all over itself trying to explain whether the practice of race preferences was needed to redress past discrimination, to bring more minority lawyers into Texas, or to enhance diversity at the law school. (What is the diversity value of thirty-two blacks and thirty-seven Hispanics who would not be at the school but for their ethnicity, compared with nine blacks and eighteen Hispanics who can hold their heads high knowing they have earned their places at the school on merit?)

What does matter is that the situation resulted from what may be called the three deadly sins of affirmative action, excesses that over time are defensible neither legally nor politically:

- First, preference which springs from membership in an ethnic group that had suffered past discrimination rather than redress for discrimination they have suffered as individuals.
- Second, numerical targets that are the functional equivalent of quotas.
- Third, a lowering of objective race-neutral standards in order to achieve the established quotas simply because these standards have a disparate impact upon the favored groups.

When the case reached the Fifth Circuit Court of Appeals in March 1996, the court concluded that in offering diversity as a justification for racial preferences Justice Powell had never spoken for anyone but himself (not entirely true) and, further, that his standard should be discarded as embracing more constitutional mischief than value. "Finally, the classification of persons on the basis of race for the purpose of diversity frustrates, rather than facilitates, the goals of equal protection." It was fine for a school, in a quest for diversity or other attributes, to favor athletes, cello players, children of alumni, or those who had overcome disadvantaged childhoods or whose backgrounds suggested a social conscience appropriate to the profession. But, "[t]o foster such diversity, state universities and law schools and other governmental entities must scrutinize applicants individually, rather than resorting to the dangerous proxy of race."

In the spring of 1995, despite the urging of the Clinton Justice Department, the Supreme Court declined to review a Fourth Circuit decision in *Podberesky v. Kirwan* which threw out the University of Maryland's Banneker scholarship program. It was a racially exclusive scholarship for which blacks from any part of the country were eligible with the awards based on merit, not need. The very description of the program suggests, in the words of the late Senator Sam Ervin, "more constitutional infirmities than a hound dog has fleas." Under its terms, the son or daughter of a black millionaire from Atlanta could win a Maryland scholarship for which an impoverished Mexican American from Baltimore was racially ineligible (the successful plaintiff was in fact Hispanic). Out-of-state blacks could never have been among the most harmed victims of any past discrimination by the state of Maryland even during the university's de jure or de facto segregation periods. The "remedy" could hardly have been less narrowly tailored to achieve any legitimate state purpose. And, with luck, the program would terminate a moment or two before the Second Coming.

The practice came under challenge from the Bush administration in an unlikely way. Organizers of the Fiesta Bowl, seeking to blunt black protest that they were holding their game in a state which, at the time, failed to honor Martin Luther King Jr.'s, birthday as a holiday, announced the intention to award two scholarships per year to blacks, in Dr. King's name, at each school participating in the contest. That provoked Michael L. Williams, the assistant secretary of Education for Civil Rights, to write the Fiesta Bowl organizers, declaring that their scholarships would be illegal. For his effort, Williams was branded by moviemaker Spike Lee as "an Uncle Tom handkerchief-head Negro," who should, as Lee told a *Playboy* interviewer, "be beat with a 'Louisville Slugger' in an alley."

In court, the state's defense of the program proved less than edifying, employing the sort of constitutional gibberish long rejected by the judiciary: The scholarship was designed to cure the university's poor reputation in the African American community, to provide campus "role models" for other blacks, and to address the problem of low black retention and graduation rates.

Following their loss in the courts, officials at the University of Maryland and elsewhere set about to discover how to continue providing race-based scholarships without technically violating the court's ruling. From the Department of Education came the following advice: Offer scholarships authorized by Congress, a theory that probably died with the *Adarand* decision. Or, offer scholarships to overcome past discrimination, if you can prove it. Or, offer scholarships to improve campus diversity. In point of fact, university officials, Maryland political leaders, civil rights activists, and even Deval Patrick, head of the Civil Rights Division at the Clinton Justice Department, ought solemnly and silently to thank the court for tossing out the Banneker program because somewhere, sometime, somebody running for office would have highlighted it as a reflection of wanton race prejudice against everyone but blacks. And then all the breast-beating about racism and

"Willie Horton politics" and the use of "wedge issues" designed to divide us would have rung hollow. When you stand in a court of law and argue with a straight face that a person's race alone makes him or her eligible for a state scholarship, you no longer have the "clean hands" needed to beat back the demagogue.

■   ■   ■

During the Reconstruction years, a number of Northern religious groups founded educational institutions in the South, whose purpose was to begin educating the recently freed slaves. Most of the new schools were exclusively for blacks; a handful were integrated. Among those admitting both blacks and whites was Berea College in Kentucky. Young men of both races studied there by choice until 1908 when the state passed a law requiring the rigid segregation of the races in all institutions of learning. From then until the post-*Brown v. Board* era, Berea was totally white. One of the young men who graduated from Berea Medical School during its segregated period was John Sturgel. Sturgel, a pathologist, went on to practice in Virginia and teach at the University of Virginia Medical School. Today, he is its dean of admissions.

A soft-spoken man with the inner serenity of one who has survived three coronary attacks, Sturgel describes the affirmative action program at the University of Virginia Medical School as "something that works." Sixteen percent of the school is black. They are, in Sturgel's words, "evenly distributed with other students in terms of class rank." In two of the past three years, the top student in the graduating class was black.

The only thing that hasn't worked, according to Sturgel, is an experimental program encouraged and substantially financed by the federal government in which ten minorities with marginal credentials were conditionally accepted but required to take an entire summer's worth of remedial work. On the average, two of the ten dropped out before class started; the remainder were "having more difficulty" getting passing grades in their medical courses.

Virginia has some advantages. A premier medical school in an area of gracious living where, even during the years of enforced segregation, there was an underlying civility between the races, it has now become a "hot" school, high on the list of preferences for both whites and blacks. It is also part of a great state university whose faculty and administration—both black and white—are unabashed in their love and devotion to the place and tireless in their efforts to proselytize potential scholars. For the fall of 1995, the medical school received 5,435 applications—12 percent from minorities—for an eventual class of 139 which would include twenty-two minority students.

With this kind of pool, Virginia, while making some allowance for race, has a heavy concentration of students—both white and black—with high GPAs and high Medical College Admissions Tests (MCAT).

But few medical schools are in Virginia's category. During the era of affirmative action and race preference, many have reached down to select minorities with low GPAs and low MCATs or with mixed credentials. Throughout the period, one thing has been consistent: at any level of credentials, a black or Hispanic student will have an easier time winning acceptance to medical school than will a white or Asian student with similar credentials. According to a study published in the November 1992 issue of *Academic Medicine,* minorities with low GPAs and low MCATs will in most years find a medical school that will accept them about 30 percent of the time; whites with similar credentials will get in about 15 percent of the time. For those with low GPAs and high MCATs, about 75 percent of minorities will find a medical school willing to take them, as opposed to less than half of the white applicants. Minorities with low MCATs and high GPAs get into medical school about 55 percent of the time; for whites, the figure is about 35 percent.

The extent to which minority medical school applicants are favored over whites was acknowledged in the Spring 1995 *JBHE*: "In 1994, the average grade point average for blacks accepted to medical school was 3.05 compared to 3.50 for whites. The average GPA for admitted blacks was actually below the average GPA for whites who were rejected for admission. Similarly, average scores on the MCAT for black men who were admitted to medical school were below the average scores for white men who were denied admission."

Given the preferential admissions policies, it is not surprising that blacks perform more poorly in medical school and on the critical National Board of Medical Examiners tests. The October 1994 issue of *Academic Medicine* reported on a massive survey of student performance in medical school from 1976 through 1988. As pressures to increase the number of minorities in medical school accelerated, the performance of those in medical school reflected the relaxed standards. According to the report, "[t]he proportion of 1976 black-American matriculants graduating in four years was 72.2; that of 1988 matriculants dropped to 51.6. For whites, the comparable figures were 94 in 1976 and 72 in 1988."

The report notes that many of the superior students had lower four-year graduation rates due to an increased propensity to take on special research projects. But for most of the minorities, "graduation has been delayed for remediation of academic difficulty or slowing of the pace of education to overcome handicaps in academic preparation and learning skills."

Regarding performance on the National Board exams, according to the 7 September 1994 *Journal of the American Medical Association,* on the 1988 exam, "pass rates were 88 for whites,

84 for Asians, 66 for Hispanics, and 49 for blacks." The mean score for black females was 369; for black males, 392; for white females, 467; and for white males, 499.

As might have been expected the study found a high correlation between the performance on the boards and early scores and grades on MCAT and various science courses.

Getting into medical school is, of course, highly competitive. Affirmative action is the operative national admissions policy; the motto of medical schools these days is "3000 by 2000," three thousand new minority medical school students by the year 2000. As it is applied, the policy routinely denies admission to more qualified whites and Asians and provides admission to less qualified blacks and Hispanics. The evidence is overwhelming that this gap carries over into performance in medical school and on the qualifying exam to become a doctor. As early as 1976 Professor Bernard Davis of Harvard Medical School published a critique of Harvard's practices in the *New England Journal of Medicine* in which he chronicled the erosion of standards at Harvard following the school's decision to reserve 20 percent of each medical school class for minorities. First, required science courses were dropped when it became clear that minorities fared poorly in them. Next, a pass–fail grading system replaced the traditional letter grades. Then simply passing the national medical boards was determined to be adequate for satisfactory performance at Harvard. When minorities failed in disproportionate numbers they were given five opportunities to pass, and when this proved insufficient, the provision was waived altogether.

The conclusion is inescapable: due to the institution of race preferences, this country is sending out doctors who are substantially less qualified than those who would be starting the practice of medicine were race preferences to be abandoned. Repeat, this society, which keeps potentially useful drugs off the market until they are tested for a near eternity, which bans carcinogens that must be eaten by the pound to produce harm—*this society consciously and deliberately graduates doctors who are less qualified to treat the sick than would be the case if admissions to medical school were based purely on ability and not on race.* If that were not the case, then a compelling argument could be made for junking GPAs, MCATs, and Medical Examination Boards altogether as cruel and irrelevant distractions.

Given the growing legal and political threats to race-based admissions policies coupled with the strong desire on the part of many to help those who need help the most, any number of commentators have urged a transition to preference programs based on class, not race. Why dote on the wealthy black student from Atlanta, the argument goes, when the poor white kid from Appalachia requires assistance more urgently? If the standard is disadvantage, let the colleges and universities administer their admissions policies on that basis and that basis alone. Certainly enough blacks would be helped by such a policy to make it worthwhile without building any number of potential showstoppers into the program.

Unfortunately, the approach fails for several reasons:

- First, there are many more poor whites than poor blacks, and many poor Hispanics and poor Asians as well.
- Second, the poor whites not only do substantially better than poor blacks on standardized tests such as the SAT, they do about as well as blacks from upper-income families.
- Third, to the extent that the calls for "need, not race" urge the admission of substantial numbers of less qualified applicants, you are still discriminating against the

more qualified and you are still burdening the system with categories of students who may require special help just to get by and who may never be outstanding prospects for graduate work no matter how much help they get.

■ Fourth, most of the elite private universities already have "need blind" admissions policies by virtue of which applicants are admitted without regard to their ability to finance their education and are assured of sufficient help to complete four years of education. Arbitrarily expanding the number of such students could place substantial additional burdens on institutions of higher learning which are already feeling the bite of state and federal funding cutbacks.

Writing in the Summer 1995 issue of *JBHE*, Robert Bruce Salter noted that there are 2.5 whites with family incomes under $30,000 for every black at that level. In 1994, of the more than 100,000 blacks who took the SAT, only 538 from families with incomes under $30,000 scored above 600 on the verbal portion of the test and 1,185 scored over 600 on the math portion. For whites with family incomes under $30,000, the comparable numbers were 6,627, exceeding 600 on the verbal exam and 17,248 in math. Thus, low-income whites with a combined score of 1,200 outnumbered low-income blacks by a factor of thirteen to one.

The fallacy of using class instead of race as the educational arbiter was detected by Andrew Hacker in his 1992 book, *Two Nations*. Reviewing SAT performance for the year 1990, Hacker came up with the following average combined verbal and math scores for blacks and whites at different income levels:

Family Income	Black SAT Scores	White SAT Scores
$10,000 to $29,999	704	879
$30,000 to $49,999	751	908
$50,000 to $69,999	790	947
$70,000 and over	854	998

Asians, of course, do better than either whites or blacks on the SAT. And many are recent arrivals from poor families. Salter warns that in a color-blind admissions system, "High-achieving Asian students from these lower-income families would garner many places at the nation's most prestigious universities which previously had been reserved for blacks."

As indicated, to a considerable extent, U.S. institutions of higher education, particularly the most selective ones, have long had "affirmative action" programs based on class, not race, in the form of "need-blind" admission policies. Through a combination of "Pell grants"—federally funded assistance to needy students— state and private scholarships, loans, and guaranteed part-time employment, the schools can assure any rising freshman that he will not have to quit school for want of funds.

In an era of tightening academic budgets, these programs could well be threatened due to the expense of race preference policies. Whereas 34 percent of all white students and 44.4 percent of Asian Americans require some financial assistance to make it through college, the figures are 86.7 percent for blacks, 67.9 percent for Hispanics, and 73.1 percent for Native Americans.

When more of these students are admitted under affirmative action programs, costs for the university go up. If tuition is raised to cover the higher costs, subsidies to economically deprived students must go up again, meaning the university loses a fair chunk of its higher tuition right off the top. With shrinking federal loan subsidies and other financial problems, affirmative action costs are today only a relatively minor source of university economic woes, but they are a potentially soft target. Ron Ehrenberg, a Cornell vice president, predicts, "The day is not too far off when, if we want to maintain diversity programs at their current ambitious level, we may have to have a category of applications called, 'Admit/Deny,' meaning the student is welcome to come here, but we have no money to provide for his needs." Ehrenberg believes, "That could trigger a real backlash against affirmative action."

Perhaps that process is already beginning. While many prestige universities have continued aggressive affirmative action admissions programs, others have leveled off or cut back materially. The result appears to be a declining enrollment of blacks, at least at many of the nation's premier schools, but with those blacks who do attend doing reasonably well in relationship to whites in matriculating within a six-year period. (See Table 8.)

Table 8. Black Enrollment in Some Prestige Schools Dropping, 1980–1992

Institution	Percent Black Enrollment 1980	Percent Black Enrollment 1992	Percent Change
Brown	6.2	5.8	−6.5
U. of Chicago	4.1	3.7	−9.8
Stanford	6.1	5.2	−14.8
Columbia	6.2	5.0	−19.4
Cornell	5.0	4.0	−20.0
Northwestern	8.2	6.1	−25.6
Princeton	7.5	5.3	−29.3
Dartmouth	7.7	5.4	−29.9
MIT	5.4	3.5	−35.2

A majority of these schools now have six-year black graduation rates in the high 80 and low 90 percentages. Producing a black student body which is more closely aligned with the whites' academically may be one good reason for colleges and universities to temper their numbers game with a healthy dose of attention to the sort of academic, social, and political environment they would like on campus once the numbers are achieved. Another reason was well stated by *JBHE*: "These huge differences in SAT scores tend to threaten the continuance of affirmative action since many courts supporting racial preferences in education have done so in the belief that race is being taken into account by admissions officers only when other academic and standardized credentials are relatively equal."

Christopher R. Montgomery grew up in a lower-middle-class black neighborhood in Washington, D.C. His dad works as a supervisor at the motor pool at the Department of Transportation; his mother, in the stacks at the Library of Congress. Although divorced, both parents have remained on good terms, and both played strong roles in Chris's upbringing, inspiring him to stay out of trouble and "stick with the books," and paying for a good Catholic high school in the District. Chris was accepted at Cornell University on merit—a good GPA, strong positive recommendations from his teachers, and combined SATs over 1200. He majored in sociology. Upon graduation with the Class of '95, he went to work for a management consulting firm headquartered in Northern Virginia.

During his senior year, Montgomery wrote a term paper for his Sociology 491 course entitled *Race or Reason: An Analysis of the Value of Affirmative Action*. In it he argues that affirmative action involving modest race preferences is a reasonable price to pay in order to bring blacks into fields where, due to past societal discrimination, they are underrepresented. He says the same is true with respect to university admissions. "Affirmative action does not guarantee that women and minorities have a place at the table, they still must constantly prove themselves by overachieving and staying on top. Discussions of 'lowering standards' and 'giving away opportunities to the unqualified' ignore the fact that affirmative action does not help minorities take exams, study, or graduate."

Montgomery argues that diversity is both academically important and socially just and that, particularly with respect to publicly funded state institutions, "meager representation" of minorities as a product of strict reliance on high school GPAs and SATs would be a "woefully inadequate" social response to generations of discrimination.

Chris Montgomery makes some fair points. The boozing WASP frat boys of our grandfathers' generation lost something when their Ivy League schools limited Jewish enrollment to 2 percent—by any objective standard, many times that number should have been, and, eventually were admitted—and those who matriculated in the 1950s and early 1960s would have had a more rounded college experience had they had more blacks and Hispanics as classmates. Our public institutions have the duty to provide the advantages of higher education to those qualified. And one could argue that study at the nation's premier institutions of higher learning is so enriching that it would be good were it to permeate, if only by osmosis, all strata of our society.

But the underlying plea of Montgomery's paper is misdirected. Among the entire community of conservative scholars and administrators almost no one advocates a mechanical admissions process that is blind to the virtue of character, the tenacity of purpose, and the commitment to achievement reflected in those who have overcome economic or cultural disadvantage to excel at the secondary school level and who wish to succeed in higher education. Few in their hearts do not make race a "plus factor" or "tie breaker" when appraising candidates of equal or approximately equal academic credentials. The exultation of Dean Richard Wagner over "my pride and joy" beats within a thousand academic breasts when a truly superior minority student chooses to attend their institutions. Admissions deans and other administrators the nation over attest that deciding whom to admit and whom to reject is, at the margins, "both a science and an art," and almost everyone who has ever been involved with the process has his or her own favorite account of the "diamond in the rough" who barely got in and then astonished all with a glowing academic record.

But when race itself becomes a mechanical process, when the quest for statistical parity is exalted above all else, when finely nuanced exceptions to the constitutional norm of equal treatment under the law are abused and cheapened to the point of non-recognition, the healthy flexibility many would gladly embrace is shattered and defenders of this nation's core values move, as they must, to the attack. And what will likely emerge from the process, as is already happening in college after college and state after state, are student bodies that include fewer "mismatches," minorities whose academic capabilities equip them for fine schools but not the nation's finest. Would such a process miss too many "diamonds in the rough"? Probably not. A late bloomer can make himself known at Boston University as easily as at Harvard, perhaps more easily. And if study at Harvard or any of the nation's other great colleges and universities is important to this particular individual, he will find it far simpler to transfer to a premier institution after showing his mettle at a slightly lesser one.

The way to deal with the Chris Montgomerys of this nation is to judge them not by the color of their skin, but by the content of their character. In the long run, they will be better for it. And so shall we.

7

"THREE HOURS TO LIVE"

In April 1969, more than one hundred black students occupied Willard Straight Hall, the student union building at Cornell University, in protest against mild reprimands issued to three black students growing out of their involvement in other campus incidents. Mistakenly fearing an armed attack from whites, they were able to smuggle weapons and ammunition into the building, which they held until the crisis was over and they had bargained successfully for recision of the reprimands and other relief. The faculty at first resisted the capitulation by university administrators, but, under severe pressure from students and others, reversed itself a few days later and acceded to the settlement. The move provoked great bitterness, particularly in the government and history departments where antirecision sentiment ran strong. Because of the incident, the president of Cornell was forced to resign, several prominent professors left the university, one committed suicide, and the character of race relations on campus was permanently altered.

In later years, campus minorities and those in sympathy with their more radical agendas would see the Straight takeover as the rays of a morning sun piercing the long, dark night, while other Cornellians would regard the incident as a metaphor for the transition of American universities from the passions and emotions of the civil rights era to the jaded world of affirmative action. Neither side would dispute it was a signal event in the life of their university.

■ ■ ■

Affirmative action at colleges and universities did not, of course, emerge full bloom in the 1980s and 1990s. It was the product of conscious and deliberate policy choices by university administrators a generation ago, a potent medicine, they thought, for the racial sickness of the times. When the medicine produced violent shudders in the patient and manifestly failed to cure the disease, the response was to increase the dosage rather than change the prescription. And nowhere was the shudder more violent, the cure less evident, and the after-effects more lingering than at Cornell, in Ithaca, New York.

Back in the early 1960s, Cornell would typically have only a few dozen blacks in its student body, small in number but integrated socially, academically, and politically. In 1963, President James F. Perkins organized the Committee on Special Education Projects (COSEP). Its mission was to "recommend and initiate programs through which Cornell could make a larger contribution to the education of qualified students who have been disadvantaged by their cultural, economic, and educational environments."

COSEP found few blacks qualified for the Ivy League who were in fact not already in the Ivy League. So it recommended admission of what a 1969 Trustees Report on Campus Unrest described as "students whose credentials will appear marginal or worse by the usual Cornell Admissions standards but who otherwise give strong evidence of being able to compete at Cornell."

Exactly what sort of "strong evidence" COSEP had in mind was not described at the time. To this day the search for minorities whose superior academic potential is reflected neither in high school GPAs nor SATs remains something of the Holy Grail of the affirmative action movement. Nonetheless, 37 blacks entered Cornell under the COSEP program in 1965, 49 in 1966, 67 in 1967, 49 in 1968, and 107 in 1969. By the spring of 1969, there were more than 300 black undergraduates on the Cornell campus, most from the COSEP program.

Perkins quickly ran into trouble on several fronts. Having never announced his program or even informed the faculty as a whole about it, professors were taken aback when suddenly substantial numbers of students appeared in their courses who were neither prepared for class nor able to keep up with the work. Informally, however, the word spread that it would be unwise to flunk these students however marginal their performance.

Second, as the committee later reported, "[a]lumni, and particularly alumni secondary school interviewers, became incensed when good white students from their local schools were not offered admission to Cornell but black students with much less impressive records were."

Finally, while the administrators had imagined the blacks would be anxious to integrate and assume their rightful place on campus and in American society, the blacks themselves seemed to feel their rightful place was in the vanguard of a movement dedicated to transforming what they viewed as a racist academic institution in a racist social order to something vaguely more just. Compared with the ghetto or even the South, the place lacked a sense of community, the blacks contended. "Ithaca itself," said one, "is an alien environment for black students from an urban area. It's too pastoral, it's too idyllic for them." Another thought they were expected to act "like trained monkeys to showcase themselves for these white boys who were going to go out and control the world, but with a higher sensitivity toward black people."

As time passed, "the blacks became more and more vitally involved in separation and staying within the black community," even though traditionally white fraternities and sororities actively sought their membership. Moreover, "blacks who wanted to remain outside this separatist movement found themselves shut out by the militant blacks and subject to derision by, and pressures from, them."

On Thanksgiving weekend, 1968, Howard University hosted a summit meeting of black student leaders from around the country, including Cornell. Out of it arose demands at dozens of schools not only for black studies programs and departments but for separate black schools within the larger university. The Cornell blacks returned to Ithaca and began demanding and then demonstrating for an autonomous black college, on one occasion storming a podium where Perkins himself was speaking.

During a December campus demonstration, three blacks were apprehended brandishing toy weapons. And one cold winter morning in early 1969 Perkins found his Day Hall administrative office surrounded by black demonstrators. A decent, liberal man, the president feared his tormentors might suffer a chill and phoned out for coffee and doughnuts as a warmer-upper. Seeing the delivery truck pull up, the demonstrators assumed the refreshments were for those inside the building, surrounded the delivery man, and appropriated his wares.

In a separate incident, a visiting Catholic priest and economics professor, Father Michael McPhelin, was accused of racism in his lectures. When he declined to permit black students to deliver their own economics lecture, McPhelin was physically prevented from conducting his class by black students who demanded his dismissal. Professors at Cornell began to fear that the university's definition of civil rights no longer embraced academic freedom.

Early in 1969, the trustees approved an African studies center and allocated $240,000 for the first year of its operations. Some blacks interpreted the move as weakness and stupidity, one later confiding, "I don't think there's a question that black studies are essentially opposed to the interests of white society and I don't see why the society, unless we dupe them into doing it, should subsidize its own destruction."

Despite their gains, some of the blacks faced disciplinary proceedings growing out of the toy weapons incident and the classroom harassment of Father McPhelin. The judiciary code had been written nearly two years earlier by Alan Sindler, a government professor. Sindler had been helped by Tom Jones, a black student from a comfortable family who had been president of his freshman class and who briefly served as head of the Conduct Board. Nonetheless, the Afro-American Students (AAS) claimed the board was part of the racist structure of a racist university and therefore had no authority over them.

On Friday, April 18, the board cleared two students involved in the McPhelin incident and issued mild reprimands to three others involved with the toy weapons. That evening a cross was burned on the lawn of the Wari House, an off-campus female dorm for participants in the COSEP program. The culprit has never been found, and many have long suspected that militant blacks themselves set the blaze. At 5:30 A.M., between fifty and one hundred unarmed blacks, led by AAS President Ed Whitfield, took over Willard Straight Hall. A magnificent old Gothic building resting atop "Libe Slope," "the Straight," along with the bell tower of Olin Library is the informal campus monument, the postcard picture that says, "Cornell." In addition to the student union, the building also accommodated a handful of rooms so that visitors could lodge right on campus. April 18 being the start of "parents weekend," many of those expelled from the building by the blacks were visiting sons and daughters at the school and had been awaiting a welcoming address by President Perkins scheduled for later in the morning. Under the circumstances, Perkins would cancel the address which had been entitled, "The Stability of the University."

A few hours after the seizure, a group of white fraternity boys from Delta Upsilon entered the building through ground level windows and sought to end the siege. The blacks beat them off. One of the black combatants later complained, "If I'd been allowed to, I probably would have killed the little fat sucker that I was, I was beating up on, because I wanted to kick his guts out."

Throughout the day, Perkins and other key administration players—Vice Provost W. Keith Kennedy; Robert D. Miller, dean of the faculty; Steven Muller, vice president for public affairs; and Provost Dale Corson, who had returned from New York City— sought to get a handle on the crisis. Kennedy had been in touch with Whitfield inside the building. Bedrock black demands included recision of the Conduct Board citations and nonretaliation for any activities involving the takeover.

The student body in general seemed sympathetic to the blacks. Students for a Democratic Society (SDS) were already demonstrating their support outside the Straight, and even the Interfraternity Council passed a mildly supportive resolution on the key recision question.

At 10:30 P.M., a campus policeman reported seeing guns being carried into those holding the Straight. The report was accurate. The blacks had taken two-way radios inside in order to maintain contact with campus supporters and "scouts." Earlier in the day, reports from these sources indicated that whites were taking target practice in the deep gorges that bracket the campus. Later, word came that eight carloads of armed whites were preparing to storm the Straight. As a "defensive" measure the occupiers ordered weapons brought in. Leaders inside the building considered, but rejected, a proposal to burn down the Straight.

By this point, the issue had become a national cause célèbre. Network television crews and a battery of national reporters were on the scene. Miller, the faculty dean, and Vice Povost Kennedy were the point men for dealing with the students. Miller knew that any resolution would require sanction by the entire faculty. In fact, several professors had already called, imploring against capitulation, some even threatening to quit if Perkins yielded. The most prominent among them was Clinton Rossiter, chairman of the government department, nationally renowned expert on the presidency, and a devoted Cornellian (Class of '39).

Shortly before 5 P.M. on Saturday, Dean Miller and Whitfield, the black leader, reached a final agreement, cleared in advance with President Perkins and Corson, the provost. Miller pledged to recommend recision to the full faculty and to resign if they refused to accept his recommendation. The deal included a university promise to secure civil representation for the blacks in any action growing out of the takeover of the Straight, to provide twenty-four-hour protection for the Wari House—the residence for black women—and to investigate police conduct with respect both to the attack and the penetration of the Straight by the Delta Upsilon fraternity boys.

The Afro-American Students group pledged only to end the occupation of the Straight and to cooperate in framing a new judicial code. In what Miller viewed as a "minor" concession, the blacks were allowed to carry their guns out of the Straight and march with them to the Black Studies headquarters on Wait Avenue, about half a mile away, before disarming.

With the deal now finalized, one hundred blacks emerged from

Willard Straight Hall, many with guns raised, some with ammunition belts fastened. Kennedy, Miller, and Muller (the Public Relations chief) shuffled about uncomfortably on the steps behind them, aware that many would view the scene as a symbol of university weakness in the face of pressure from student militants, but satisfied that they had averted serious injury or loss of life, and confident their accord would be ratified by the faculty. To underline who had won and who had caved in, Eric Evans, one of the key Afro-American Students leaders, read a statement threatening that failure by Cornell to implement its side of the bargain "may force us to again confront the university in some manner." Then, as cameras rolled or clicked, the blacks marched off, one later recalling, "To me the brotherhood was beautiful when he [Whitfield] came out the door with his gun. He should have pulled the trigger and shot the guy shooting the camera for whites."

Perkins forever cemented his reputation as the perfect liberal foil for the radicals of his era with his conduct over the next twenty-four hours. Early on Monday, a bit tardily, he announced a ban on guns on campus. He also declared a "situation of emergency," a term whose implications he failed to define, announced that anyone taking over a building for "coercive purposes" would be suspended, and convened a "convocation" for 3 P.M. at Barton Hall, the huge Gothic-style armory.

Nearly ten thousand attended the gathering, but Perkins incredibly failed to discuss the Straight takeover, the choices presented, or the issues involved, merely calling upon those affiliated with the university to act as "humane men" in the days ahead. Perkins then drifted over to Bailey Hall, a rotunda-shaped university landmark, where the faculty meeting had convened at 4:40 P.M. Faculty Dean Miller shortly thereafter introduced his resolution approving the agreement with the Afro-American Students. After four hours of vigorous debate, the clear sentiment was that to yield in the face of illegal conduct and threats of worse was to court disaster as an institution of learning. Participants in the session recall in particular an eloquent defense of academic freedom offered by Clinton Rossiter.

Unable to convince the faculty, Perkins eventually decided to join them, introducing a seven-point substitute resolution. While expressing sympathy "for the problems of the black students in adjusting themselves to life at Cornell," the resolution went on to say:

> The Faculty condemns the seizure of Willard Straight Hall; the Faculty condemns the carrying and use of weapons by anyone except those officially responsible for maintaining law and order on the campus; the presence of arms and the seizure of Willard Straight Hall make it impossible for the Faculty to agree at this meeting to dismiss the penalties imposed on the three students.

The Faculty Council was directed to meet with the Afro-American Students group the following day to explore ways of resolving the crisis. At the conclusion of the meeting, Miller announced he had "vacated" his position as dean of faculty, in order to "keep my act of faith" with the AAS.

On Tuesday, the blacks refused to meet with the Faculty Council and there were rumblings all day that further militant action would be taken. SDS returned to Barton Hall and mobilized an evening gathering of six thousand students in support of the black demands. Tom Jones of AAS gave a long radio interview at 6 P.M., directly threatening violence to a total of seven administrators and professors—including Perkins and Rossiter—unless the Faculty Council convened by 9 P.M. to approve recision, declaring, "Cornell has three hours to live."

The *Cornell Alumni News,* in a special 1969 edition devoted entirely to the event, reported that Jones would repeat the threat for a later Barton Hall audience: "Now the pigs are going to die too…. We are moving tonight. Cornell has until 9 to live. It is now 3 minutes after 8." Several of those personally threatened by Jones took refuge with their families in local motels that evening, one under an assumed name.

But the tactics of the Afro-American Students already had the university in full-fledged retreat. Save for the history and government departments, which overwhelmingly wanted to hold firm, individual faculty groups had been meeting throughout the day to urge surrender. By early Tuesday evening, the Faculty Council itself was ready to throw in the towel and scheduled a meeting for 1:30 P.M. Wednesday to make it official. Philosophy Professor Max Black told the students in Barton Hall, "We hear you, we care, we are trying to understand you and want together with you to do something." Promptly at the appointed time of 1:30 P.M., the faculty overwhelmingly reversed itself and endorsed the Miller–Whitfield agreement.

Perkins waited until after the faculty vote before returning to the Hall where, flanked by David Burak of SDS and key black leader Eric Evans, he announced that the recision package had been approved. As the decibel level reached deafening proportions, Perkins, like a triumphant general, waved his arms in return salute to a crowd of ten thousand who were in fact hailing his abject capitulation.

But fifteen professors from the government department and eight from history would have none of it. Before the initial faculty meeting they released a statement pledging "to cease classroom instruction and undertake a review of our relationship to the university in the light of this intolerable and, one would have thought, unthinkable situation."

And at the Wednesday meeting, after Perkins endorsed nullification of the reprimands to the three blacks, James J. John, history professor, let the administration know that confrontation was preferable to selling out, saying, "If Mr. Jones says he is going to destroy this university, I say let him try it.... My particular field of study is the history of universities. In the nearly 800 years that they have existed, many eminent universities have come and gone and the world has survived their departure. But those that have departed because they stood for nothing have not even been missed."

The heavyweights made their positions known. Walter F. Lefeber, chairman of the history department; Alan Sindler; Walter F. Berns; George McT. Kahin; and Alan Bloom—among others—all defined the issue in terms of academic freedom. Some threatened to leave the university if this principle was not upheld.

Others, such as Nobel laureate Hans Bethke; historian Henry Guerlac; Milton Konvitz, whose Western Ethics course majestically linked the moral and intellectual traditions of Aristotle, Erasmus, and Sir Thomas Moore with Martin Luther King Jr., and the Southern freedom riders; and Andrew Hacker, an up-and-coming government professor—all went the other way. Their biggest convert was Clinton Rossiter, who seemed to have been swayed by student sentiment and an increasing empathy for the aroused black political passions. In the two critical meetings—Monday and Wednesday—Rossiter played prominent roles, on both sides of the issue.

Far more than at any similar event, at any campus, before or since, the participants at Cornell seemed to understand from the outset that an important precedent was being set, that the actions of students, faculty, administration, and alumni would have consequences beyond this event, beyond this year, beyond this university. They formulated their positions with care, articulated their thoughts, played their roles grandly.

Their insight was correct. For a generation, the faculty virtually disappeared as a force in university policy; that became a matter for the students and the administration to fight out among themselves.

After the Straight takeover confrontation was resolved, a number of COSEP students were permitted to move into "North Campus Low Rise 10." A few years later, "Dorm 10" became "Ujamaa House" and the North Campus became the area where most blacks and other minorities choose to live.

As for the faculty and administration, Perkins was eased out by alumni and trustees at the first available opportunity. True to their word, Berns, Sindler, Bloom, and others left Cornell, most to continue distinguished careers at other prestige universities or institutions.

Clinton Rossiter remained at Cornell, a hero to the administration, a pariah to many in his own department. A young university archivist named Gould Coleman started a file on the Straight takeover which he labeled, "Challenge to Governance." Coleman interviewed Rossiter at his home near Triphammer Gorge less than a year after the event and found the professor in a somber but responsive mood. The incident had taken him by surprise, he recounted, because he had been abroad on sabbatical the previous year and had been somewhat out of touch with the student mood. He had changed his mind partly because students themselves had convinced him that the blacks had more of a cause than he initially believed and partly to prevent further bloodshed.

The reaction to his performance, both among friends and colleagues, had been visceral. One friend of thirty years standing sent him a message via Western Union reading, "THE COLOR OF THIS TELEGRAM IS THE COLOR OF YOU." Rossiter did not think he was "yellow" and said, "Moral courage is doing something for which you will be accused of cowardice by some of your close friends."

In McGraw Hall, where his department had its main offices, Rossiter found an even colder reception. Not only would colleagues like Berns, Sindler, and Bloom refuse to speak with him during their final days at Cornell, some would turn their backs as he approached. He recalled one telling him, "Clinton, I'm a hard man, and when I decide no longer to have anything to do with a person, he's dead as far as I'm concerned." Rossiter said, "In all of the years I've been here, there's been nothing to resemble this. No polarization of this kind. No anger."

Weeks after his meeting with Coleman, Rossiter walked down the stairs to his basement, crawled behind an old refrigerator, and poisoned himself.

8

THE LONESOME DOVE

At the time of the Willard Straight Hall takeover at Cornell, Larry I. Palmer was completing work for his law degree at Yale University. One of ten children from a poor but well-educated black St. Louis family, Palmer had been the beneficiary of "old-fashioned affirmative action," receiving generous scholarship and other assistance from Exeter Academy, Harvard University, and Yale Law School, which all believed that a young man with academic ability and motivation ought not to be thwarted because of his race or economic situation.

Palmer began teaching at the Cornell Law School in 1975, just as the era of "program houses" was getting under way. These are special living quarters designed to provide reinforcement for communities of students seeking similar academic specialty areas—for example, music, ecology, or languages. Ujamaa promptly applied for certification as a "program house," won university approval, and set up shop, banning white students from "Dorm 10." At the same time, the university routinely honored the request of racial minorities—including incoming freshmen—

for racially homogeneous space in dormitories and other university housing. Criticized nearly from birth by the distinguished sociologist Kenneth B. Clark and others who believed that, far from discouraging self-segregation, Cornell had become a willing accomplice to the process, both Ujamaa and the unofficially segregated living arrangements managed to survive two early investigations by the New York State Department of Education, including one which declared segregated campus housing a violation of the 1964 Civil Rights Act.

Palmer gained tenure at the law school, but switched to university administration in 1979 and joined the staff of Keith Kennedy who had by then risen to provost. During his years at Cornell, Palmer had come to share the views of many of those critical of how affirmative action was working. The Committee on Special Education Projects (COSEP) program had continued to bring more minority students to campus than could reasonably be expected to work comfortably with a tough Ivy League curriculum. Even before arrival, most blacks were contacted by black upperclassmen and urged to take up residence either at Ujamaa or among other clusters of blacks on the North Campus. Once in Ithaca, they received orientation programs of their own and freshman remedial courses designed to bridge the gap between their academic credentials and those of the majority student population. These remediation courses served only to emphasize both to blacks and their white classmates that the university regarded them as academic risks, not fully capable of handling the work.

Meanwhile, black upperclassmen as well as academicians affiliated with the black studies program offered a ready-made, easy-to-wear ideology: if they had not done as well on "standardized tests" as some of their white classmates, it was because the dominant racist society had denied them the tools for equal advancement and had, in any event, transformed the tests into a means of reinforcing racist values, perspectives, and institutions. And with the ideology came brotherly and sisterly warnings not to fall into the assimilationist trap, not to judge themselves by the purportedly "objective" but demonstrably racist standards of the whites, and not to lose their own identity, their ability to help their own brothers and sisters in the never-ending war against racism.

As a result, with the probable exception of the University of Pennsylvania, Cornell had become as racially "balkanized" as any school in the Ivy League, and Palmer became convinced that the university had been complicit with each move in that direction. In fact, its entire affirmative action regime underlined the most radical black views by suggesting that the people running the institution agreed with them.

Palmer started slowly, picking his issues carefully as a member of Kennedy's staff from 1979–84. He came to believe that many of the black youths admitted to Cornell might be better off at a good but slightly less demanding university. But his principal initiative was to challenge and integrate those who had made it to Ithaca. He successfully backed revision of the freshman writing program from a post-graduate high school course for undereducated blacks to a full-credit program from which students of all races could benefit.

He also began a lengthy "conversation" about the assumptions underlying race relations at Cornell. Is there any empirical evidence to support the claim that Ujamaa or some other predominantly black environment better prepares blacks to excel academically than a more integrated environment? Do black freshmen—most of whom have attended middle-class, integrated high schools—naturally gravitate toward a segregated college environment for reasons of "comfort," or are they made uncomfortable by the blacks already there choosing some other path? Does Afrocentrism help motivate black students toward greater academic achievement, or does it provide instead an emotional "safe harbor" for underachievement?

Palmer returned to the law school in the mid-1980s. But as he prepared to leave on sabbatical in 1989, University President Frank Rhodes asked him to assume the position of vice president for Academic Programs and Campus Affairs upon his return. Palmer used his leave period to sketch out a ten-year plan, modeled on Harvard's housing system, to convert Cornell's dorms into "communities without walls," each with about one thousand students, half living in the dorms, half living off-campus with the faculty assigned to "mentor" the program. Gone would be the existing "theme houses," including Ujamaa. And those traditional institutions of social segregation, the fraternities and sororities, would be seriously undermined.

Palmer did not think the university was ready to swallow anything as radical as his ten-year plan, but he did return to Ithaca ready to proceed with a clearly focused, precisely targeted effort to integrate freshman housing and thus break the back of voluntary segregation. He quickly organized a task force, conveniently dominated by people who shared his views. In its preliminary report of February 1992, the task force found "that the current freshman housing process is not consistent with either the social or the educational goals of the university" and that rather than reflecting the diversity and heterogeneity of the entering class, "the freshman living experience at Cornell is, in contrast, characterized by ethnic, racial, and social separation." Under the task force proposal, freshmen would still be able to have various rooming choices, but racial assignments would be in the hands of the school.

The task force report ran into a buzz saw of attack from the minority community. Palmer was accused of trying to wreck the "social cohesion" of blacks on campus, of pressing for "assimilation" rather than "multiculturalism," of seeking to destroy the "support system" for individual blacks. Minorities, plus their allies of convenience, the fraternities and sororities, protested that the plan would undermine freshmen's "freedom of choice."

The task force backed and filled, adding a vigorous if not fully thought-out academic support program which it said was modeled on the "21st Century Program" developed by Professor Claude Steele at the University of Michigan. In reality, however, Palmer's efforts were turning into something of a political hodgepodge and reflected little of Steele's coherent design.

Steele, now at Stanford, has the elegantly simple theory that if you take a young student and tell him he's too dumb to do the work but that because his ancestors were badly treated you are going to give him a break and allow him to attend your university, he will quickly conclude that if you—the expert—have no respect for his intellect, neither should he. He will then attempt to save face by developing something else to care about and by which to judge himself.

Or, as Steele says, "If they detect stereotype in the domain, they will disidentify with the domain to remove the extra pressure associated with the stereotype." He calls the phenomenon "stereotype vulnerability," and argues that explains in part why blacks perform poorly in standardized tests.

Steele takes it a step further. At Michigan he found—as have others—that blacks entering the school with the same SATs as whites tend to maintain GPAs nearly a full point lower than whites. In other words, rather than unfairly underestimating the expected performance from black test takers, the SATs tend to overpredict black performance in college, often by a substantial amount.

Steele's interpretation is that, however good his scores, the black student knows he is perceived as unqualified. So, consciously or otherwise, he withdraws from the system, seeking some other standard of self-worth. At Michigan, Steele found that black students with the top third SAT scores were dropping out in greater numbers than those with lower scores.

"In the '50s," said Steele, "I knew the environment was hostile; I knew these people were racist. Now the word is, 'We like you. We support you, but we have some doubts about your ability.' So the black kid's attitude is, 'This is the man's university.' The environment validates the stereotype of inferiority."

At Michigan, the "21st Century Program" took 170 whites, 40 blacks, and 40 other minorities, all chosen at random within his or her racial group. The candidates were told they had been selected on the basis of their intellectual potential (dare one call it a "white lie"?) and were challenged with extra work in such areas as writing, physics, calculus, and chemistry. The study found that blacks inside the program did well relative to whites with the same SAT scores, while those in a control group fared as poorly as ever. Says Steele: "If I could wave a magic wand, I would get rid of every minority remediation program in the country, put them all into integrated intellectual boot camps, and work the shit out of them."

At Cornell, however, that was not to be. Regardless of revisions and new sales pitches, Palmer could never succeed in convincing Ujamaa and the frats that his freshman plan was not step one in a sequence to undermine their central role in campus life because, actually, that was its fundamental purpose. Key opposition then mounted. By the end of 1992, it was deader than a "Big Red" basketball season. And shortly thereafter, Palmer was back at his law school, beaten but unbowed. "I was trying to create an ethos on this campus where these kids could destigmatize themselves," he recalls. "We'd be much better off creating an environment where we own up to history but don't wallow in it."

In 1991, Cornell trustees approved the establishment of Akwe:kon, an American Indian theme residence. In 1994, the

Latino Living Center got going after Hispanics performed the standard ritual of occupying the Day Hall administration building. This drew another complaint from sociologist Kenneth Clark, this time joined by Michael Meyers of the New York Civil Rights Coalition on the op-ed page of the *New York Times:* "Cornell's continuing assertion that these segregated residences are not really segregated but represent residents' 'freedom of choice' eerily represents the rationalizations that guardians of the Old South offered in defense of their racist traditions."

Cornell's reply is that the residents of these three ethnic theme houses constitute only a small minority of all students living on campus and, indeed, only a small minority of Native Americans, Hispanics, and blacks. True enough, but as one of the nation's premier institutions of higher learning, Cornell's placid acceptance of the notion provides an example which many emulate. Stanford, by contrast, requires that ethnic theme houses contain no more than 50 percent of any single ethnic group, an arrangement which at least seeks to distinguish ethnic pride from ethnic cleansing.

Most on campus also feel that the Ujamaa house exerts influence among blacks at the university far beyond the mere numbers of those living at "Dorm 10" and that the administration has done precious little to distance itself from the group's racist and radical excesses. To critics, Cornell's definition of "diversity" is Ujamaa, while Ujamaa's definition of "diversity" is to invite Leonard Jefferies to campus one year and Louis Farrakhan the next.

But no one in the university administration seems to ask whether it is appropriate for the school itself to subsidize these apostles of hate, whether even one official voice should be raised after their appearances to define the university's view on anti-Semitism, race hatred, and mass schizophrenia. "Higher education is missing the point," reflects government professor Jeremy Rabkin. "We want educated blacks to feel as though they are part of the elite, as though they have a substantial stake in this society. What has been happening on university campuses shows the opposite."

Rabkin, moreover, believes this balkanization-type mentality is contagious. "There's a lot of kids here from Korea. There's a lot from Russia. It's wonderful. It's charming how quickly they become Americanized. But with each year you see more and more of an effort to mobilize them as though they were some parallel group to the blacks."

Nineteen ninety-four marked the twenty-fifth anniversary of the black takeover of Willard Straight Hall, and Ed Whitfield and Tom Jones were invited back to campus. Whitfield, still mad, still militant, knows that Jones has changed. Jones is a multimillionaire now, having gotten an MBA from Boston University and worked for John Hancock Mutual Life Insurance before becoming senior vice president and treasurer of the Teachers Insurance & Annuity Association and College Retirement Equities Fund. Today, he is president of the company, the largest pension fund in the world with assets in excess of $100 billion.

Jones has thought deeply about the events in Ithaca a generation ago and his role in them. In an eloquent and moving interview with the *Cornell Daily Star* on 19 April 1989, the day the paper published a special commemorative editorial on the twentieth anniversary of the takeover, he defended the use of guns, saying, "If the principle of academic freedom was important enough for blood to be shed then I thought it was important that it not only be black blood."

Jones described the takeover as "a tremendous event in American history. For this I am proud—that this group of what would normally be considered assimilated, upwardly mobile black students at a prestigious institution like Cornell said, 'We will be respected or we will fight to the best of our ability to have respect.'

On the other hand, Jones had come to realize the awful tragedy of the confrontation: "It was a tremendous moment of sadness, that those blacks to whom America had tried to be most accommodating in terms of undoing the wrongs of the past were involved in such an ugly confrontation. One could walk away despairing for the future of race relations in American society as we know it, an open liberal democracy."

It had not taken Jones twenty years to decide that his role would be that of a builder, not a destroyer: "Immediately after the Straight takeover, I walked away from being associated with the kind of people that create these situations, that get you into those situations without the knowledge to get you out. I'd gone through an experience where for whatever reason in that moment of history I knew how to walk onto the stage and do what had to be done. I decided to walk off the stage, that it was not how I wanted to live my life, that I had no use for it. I said, "Here is the victory. Everybody feels great. Now I've got other things to do with my life."

The militant Whitman sees Jones as an "Oreo," a "sellout," and at the 1994 reunion successfully urged a number of black students to boycott his talk.

Jones has always felt a bit guilty about costing Perkins his job, since the ex-president was a man who sought desperately to increase the representation of blacks at Cornell and make them feel at home in the small upstate town of Ithaca. So on the twenty-fifth anniversary of the Willard Straight student takeover, Jones established the James A. Perkins Prize for Interracial Understanding and Harmony, to be given annually to members of the Cornell community who have done the most to promote better relations between the races. The first recipient was awarded an honorarium of $5,000 for organizing a civil rights symposium on campus.

9

A STATE OF EXCESS

The demonstrators got so surly that the State Board of Regents had to take refuge in a secure location. Leading the protestors, Jesse Jackson rose to soaring heights of unintended self-parody, calling Jesus "an at-risk child" who required affirmative action, and declaring, "We who resist this attempt to roll back to inclusion [*sic*], to end race injustice and gender inequality, we stand in the blood of the martyrs. We stand in the blood that Medgar Evers and Martin Luther King Jr., and those who died to open these doors [*sic*]." He would later accuse California Governor Pete Wilson of becoming the "Susan Smith of national politics," because, "when Susan Smith was desperate she used an imaginary black man as diversion. When you were desperate because the economy is reeling, you did not have a budget before your legislature, you pull out the race card."

White House Chief of Staff Leon Panetta called it a "terrible mistake" and vowed to review the flow of federal funds to California's state university system. A respected Berkeley professor emeritus of physics, Charles Schwartz, told the *New York Times* that the regents' action was like introducing 1950s-style loyalty oaths since it showed that "the regents were a conduit for political intrusion into the university."

The occasion was the 20 July 1995 decision by the State Board of Regents, by a vote of 14–10, to ban the consideration of race as a factor in admissions, faculty hiring, or contracting by state institutions of higher learning. Wilson, condemning race preferences with the same vigor with which he had defended them for most of his years in public life, defined the issue this way: "Thirty-five years ago, if a fully qualified African American, a better qualified African American, had been denied a place in the medical school and his place had been given to a less qualified Caucasian, we would have called that what it is—racial discrimination. But today, if a better qualified Asian or Caucasian who applies to a medical school is denied his place and it is given instead to a less qualified member of a favored racial group, today we call that affirmative action. But it's still racial discrimination."

The action of the regents was opposed by the academic senates at all nine campuses of the University of California as well as by the chancellors and vice chancellors and the president of the university system. Opposition from traditional defenders of quotas and other forms of extreme racial preferences was, of course, expected. Among other Californians who cared about the issue, opinion was divided. Many could find no justification for racial discrimination, whatever its name. Others predicted that the order would only prove bearable if, under the rubric of color-blind consideration of economic disadvantage, at least some way could be found to admit blacks and Hispanics to the university in numbers that exceeded, at least modestly, those who would gain admission by virtue of academic credentials alone.

The state college and university system, sometimes prodded, sometimes merely encouraged by the California legislature, had brought the crisis upon itself by pursuing singlemindedly a program to achieve racial balance among student bodies that was, by any reasonable standard, extreme. It was also so far beyond the limited license afforded by Justice Powell in the *Bakke* case as to be illegal on its face. Nonetheless, the schools persisted until both their legal and political positions became untenable. Under the Board of Regents action, beginning with admissions for the year 1997, 50 percent to 75 percent of all admissions must be based on academic criteria alone. And while admissions officers are permitted to consider the special merit of applicants who have overcome economic or social disadvantage, that leeway does not technically extend to the consideration of race nor does it apply to hiring or tenure decisions.

The problem as it stands could hardly be stated more simply: the credentials of black and Hispanic graduating high school seniors are materially below those of whites and Asians. But under state law, the university, consisting of nine schools, is responsible for educating the top 12.5 percent of high school graduates while the California State University system, with twenty-one campuses, educates others in the top one-third. California also maintains more than one hundred open-enrollment low tuition community colleges appropriate for general education and from which deserving students can transfer to one of the two university systems. According to a September 1995 research paper published by Michael Lynch of the Pacific Research Institute, for the year 1990, among the state's graduating high school seniors, 32.2 percent of the Asians and 12.7 percent of the whites were eligible for the nine top universities, while for blacks and Hispanics the figures were 5.1 percent and 3.9 percent, respectively. To achieve their diversity goals, the top schools had to go beyond academic credentials to favor blacks and Hispanics.

At Berkeley, the state's flagship institution, the office of undergraduate admissions has estimated that strict reliance on academic criteria—SATs, GPAs, and achievement tests—would reduce the percentage of blacks from 6.4 percent, their number in the 1994 freshman class, to between 0.5 and 1.9 percent of the entering freshmen, and Hispanics from 15.3 percent to between 3.0 and 6.3 percent. The percentage of Asian Americans would increase from 41.7 percent to between 51.6 and 54.7 percent, while white percentages would increase from 29.8 percent to between 34.8 and 37.3 percent. With race-neutral consideration of socioeconomic status factored in, the percentages would be Asian Americans, 49.3 to 52.1 percent; whites, 31.8 to 33.3 percent; Hispanics, 5.6 to 10.0 percent; and African Americans, 1.4 to 2.3 percent.

Three months before the regents acted, Chancellor Chang-Lin Tien and Admissions Director Bob Laird, both of whom opposed the new policy, acknowledged the potential impact of the even more sweeping California Civil Rights Initiative—a 1996 ballot referendum which would ban race preferences by the state or its institutions—and dismissed suggestions that socioeconomic considerations could substitute for race. "Nothing that we could come up with that would preserve current levels of diversity would ever pass what could be called 'the straight face test' in the courts," said Laird. "We simply could not defend it without a betraying grin. Further, when you start favoring the poor, the Asians benefit, you divide the Hispanic community between Latinos, who are relatively well off, and Chicanos, who are not, and you bring in a sizeable number of whites."

Chancellor Tien also acknowledged that a race-neutral mandate would change the numbers at Berkeley, but he hoped the system would retain some flexibility. "I don't want to say we are preparing, but we are studying various scenarios.... I will obey the law. But we will find ways to provide students with the best educational environment experience.... There are many different ways to cut the pie."

Consistent with the views of most senior educators, Tien indicated that requiring race-neutral faculty hiring could affect decisions on who becomes an assistant professor—in virtually every institution of higher learning today, minorities have an advantage here—but would have little impact on promotions or tenure. Stunningly, even the most academic "deconstructionists" seem to develop an instant commitment to traditional notions of merit when jobs in their own departments are at stake. "At judgment time, there is a uniform standard," said Tien.

The conflict between California's goal of maintaining one of the world's great university systems while expanding opportunities for ethnic minorities who would not gain admission under traditional standards traces back more than three decades to the *Master Plan for Higher Education in California* adopted by the state legislature in 1964, which established the various university mandates and eligibility formulas. The plan included an Equal Opportunity Program (EOP) which allowed 2 percent of the freshman class to be selected from low income, educationally disadvantaged students who did not rank among the top one-eighth of their high school classes. It recommended that by 1980, "[e]ach segment of California public higher education shall strive to approximate the general ethnic, sexual, and economic composition of recent high school graduates," a principle restated by the legislature in 1974, again in 1983, and again, in slightly altered form, in 1988.

While the Asian population of California—almost entirely Chinese and Japanese—made up a small fraction of the total population in the 1960s, it accounted for more than 5 percent of the student population in the state university system. A review of Berkeley admissions policies published in 1989 by a special committee chaired by Jerome Karabel observed, "On a much smaller scale, Berkeley was to California's Chinese and Japanese what the City College of New York had earlier been to New York City's Jews: a pathway to upward mobility to which entry was granted not on the basis of who one was, but rather what one had achieved."

But few blacks or Hispanics were able to take advantage of the open door of educational opportunity because then, as now, only a small percentage of them met the eligibility requirements. Today, only 3.9 percent of Hispanic high school graduates are in the top 12 percent of their high school classes. For blacks, the figure is 5.1 percent; for whites, 12.5 percent; and for Asians, 32.3 percent. Thirty years ago, it was worse. The antidote fashioned by the regents was to drop the standards by doubling the EOP exemption to 4 percent in 1968. In 1979, the figure was raised to 6 percent. By the early 1970s, the admission of minorities under EOP required admissions officers to "redirect" at least a handful of eligible whites to other universities.

While the university system was nibbling at the margins of race preference, the Cal Davis medical school took the more direct 16 percent quota approach, leading to Alan Bakke's lawsuit and the historic 1978 Supreme Court decision. Because of Justice Powell's opinion, Bakke won acceptance to the Medical School of the University of California at Davis. And because the University of California relied on Justice Powell's opinion, "to employ a facially nondiscriminatory admissions policy" as a "cover for the functional equivalent of a quota system," thousands of white and Asian students were either "redirected" from Berkeley and the University of California–Los Angeles (UCLA) to lesser state universities or were shuttled to them through a "multiple admissions" procedure that treated an application for any one school in the University of California system as an application for all nine.

Their places at the top schools were taken by black and Hispanic students, some of whom had not even met the minimum academic standards supposedly required for admission to the state university system. Instead of providing state university admissions officers limited flexibility while maintaining official race neutrality in the vast majority of cases—clearly the result Justice Powell intended—his opinion, in the hands of University of California officials, became a "how-to" manual for evading the Equal Protection Clause of the Fourteenth Amendment.

Despite the tricky business, each freshman class at Berkeley remained heavily white and Asian, with blacks and Hispanics still faring poorly. In 1983, for example, 56.7 percent of the freshman class was white; 28.0 percent, Asian; and another 3.9 percent was Filipino, while only 6.1 percent was Hispanic and 5.6 percent was black. This situation was altered dramatically when Chancellor Ira Heyman decided to "change the face of the university." Heyman, who as head of the Smithsonian Institution would later preside over the Enola Gay debacle, instituted an aggressive "Three Tier" admissions process. This first reduced the number of Tier One admissions—those based strictly on academic merit— from 50 percent to 40 percent, and then (Tier Two) reviewed near misses on the basis of "supplementary criteria," which included race and ethnicity. It then moved onto a Tier Three "complemental" admissions category which tried hard to find any qualifying minority not admitted under the first two tiers. Since even this administrative gadgetry couldn't generate the desired numbers, the "special" EOP next swung into operation, reaching down to nonqualifiers, all in the name of Justice Powell's "diversity" standard and all while university officials publicly denied that anything like a quota system was at work.

Heyman's creative approach produced precisely the sort of results one would expect when a merit-oriented admissions process is corrupted to serve one man's concept of social engineering. But as black and Hispanic applicants were admitted in record numbers, Berkeley also found Asian students began to enroll at a significantly higher percentage than formerly due to their relatively low socioeconomic status and the low state tuition. Heyman then tried to "cure" the overrepresentation of Asians by recommending that greater weight be accorded verbal SAT scores—where Asians do relatively less well—rather than math, where they excel. Unsatisfied, he sought to emphasize extracurricular achievements, again to weed out Asian applicants. When the large Asian community reacted with anger to these initiatives, the school backed down, shifting the affirmative action burden back to the whites.

By 1988, only 37.0 percent of Berkeley's freshman class was white and 20.8 percent, Asian. Filipinos were at 5.4 percent, blacks at 10.8 percent, and Hispanics at 18.6 percent. It was clear that far higher standards were being demanded of whites and Asians than blacks and Hispanics. Consider the mean SAT and GPA scores of entering freshmen that year:

Mean SAT Scores (1988)

Blacks	Chicanos	Latinos	Whites	Asians	Filipinos
979	1013	1053	1267	1269	1126

Mean GPA Scores (1988)

Blacks	Chicanos	Latinos	Whites	Asians	Filipinos
3.19	3.46	3.49	3.79	3.91	3.82

Not only were highly qualified white and Asian students failing to gain admission, but with the exception of a relative handful of white athletes and others admitted under special circumstances, the lowest groups of entering freshmen were overwhelmingly minority. In 1978, for example, 69.3 percent of freshmen with SATs under 1000 were white or Asian. By 1987, they made up only 13.9 percent of that category. Moreover, more than half the entering minority freshmen were failing to graduate within six years. So while university administrators made much of the fact that despite the emphasis on diversity, each year's class had higher SATs and GPAs than the previous one, the reason was that, with tuition relatively low, exceptionally well-qualified whites and Asians continued to apply in large numbers. It was their superior performance that provided Berkeley's race preference program with the veneer of academic respectability. At the same time, as with the School of Industrial and Labor Relations at Cornell, most of the relatively few minorities with superior credentials were snapped up by Stanford or out-of-state prestige schools while those with solid but lesser credentials were going to the same institutions under affirmative action programs. "They're like thousand-yard running backs," mused Bob Laird. "Everyone wants them."

Nor was the socioeconomic justification for special treatment of "disadvantaged minorities" self-evident. Perhaps the most pervasive myth in the affirmative action educational debate is that the black freshmen receiving special treatment have earned it by overcoming childhoods of de facto segregation and decrepit elementary and secondary school systems. In truth, at Berkeley, as at Cornell, the University of Virginia, and most other prestige schools, the overwhelming majority of entering black freshmen came out of good, thoroughly integrated or predominantly white high schools and were themselves comfortably middle class. Today, the average family income of a black freshman at Berkeley is $39,000, somewhat above the national median. In 1987, when the non-quota system at the school was in high gear, two-thirds of the black freshmen had family incomes at or above the then mean of $30,000; 39 percent were between $50,000 and $75,000; and 13 percent were above $75,000.

With complaints from the Asian and white communities starting to make political waves and a number of new "reverse discrimination lawsuits" threatened, the system was partially reformed at the behest of the 1989 Karabel Committee. The percentage of freshmen admitted under purely academic criteria was restored to 50 percent. Latinos, two-thirds of whom had at least one parent with a college degree, were dropped from the preferred racial category unless they could prove individual disadvantage. Tier Two was technically eliminated, and the remaining criteria were merged into a complex "matrix" of admission standards. Under this new standard, a student received two rankings: The first, his Academic Index Score (AIS), was based on his high school GPA, the verbal and math SATs, and three required achievement tests. The other index, his Social Diversity Score (SDS), awarded points on a descending order of diversity value. In computing the score, the university employed the following chart:

> *SDS A:* (1) California residents who are American Indian, African American, or Chicano AND low socioeconomic status (SES) or disabled; (2) California residents who are low SES and disabled; (3) California residents who are reentry applicants (over twenty-four years of age).
> *SDS B:* (1) California residents who are American Indian, African American, or Chicano; (2) California residents who are Latino and SES or disabled.
> *SDS C:* (1) California residents who are Latino; (2) Non-resident American Indian, African American, or Chicano applicants.

SDS D: Very low SES.

SDS E: Rural and other high school.

SDS F: (1) Non-resident Latinos; (2) Other low SES.

SDS G: California residents.

SDS H: Domestic non-residents.

SDS I: Foreign applicants.

Again, 50 percent of the admissions went to those with the top academic scores while second and third groups of applicants in the top 12.5 percent of high school graduating class had their positions on the matrix helped or hurt by their SDS scores. But even this wasn't enough for the Berkeley Admissions office, so 189 students, most minorities, were accepted even though they did not meet the 12.5 percent standard and were thus not statutorily entitled to admission. *Thus, in every single year not only were minorities who finished in the top 12.5 percent of their high school classes vaulted over whites and Asians with better academic credentials, not only were nonresident wealthy blacks and Hispanics given preference over impoverished resident whites and Asians, but some whites and Asians finishing in the top 12.5 percent were rejected to make room for blacks and Hispanics who had failed to make the statutory cut off point.*

"One of the things *Bakke* tells you as an admissions officer is to make the process as complicated as possible," recalls a former policy advisor to the admissions dean. Neither this advisor nor any other university official interviewed thought it at all appalling that in the United States of America in the 1990s, applicants to one of the most prestigious state university systems in the world were receiving Social Diversity Score rankings based on their race and ethnicity. That anyone familiar with the history of this century could condone such a system strains credulity. That its most zealous defenders would describe themselves as "liberal" is a harsher indictment of that political tradition than any of its intellectual foes could possibly propound.

The revised procedures produced fewer black and Hispanic admissions. Enrollment of blacks among 1995 freshmen was down to 5.5 percent; Hispanics dropped to 15.1 percent. Even so the gap in SAT scores remained wide. For blacks, the combined verbal and math mean was 994; for Hispanics, 1032; for whites, 1256; and for Asians, 1293.

Berkeley has in recent years softened its image as a sort of academic Galapagos Islands where, off in pursuit of Nobel Prizes, faculty and administration disdain to intervene in the darwinesque game of student survival. These days the school arranges a number of programs to support minorities and others, advising them on everything from course selection to student life. This has improved the percentage of those graduating within six years, but by the standards of prestige institutions, the gap is still very wide: 88 percent for Asians, 84 percent for whites, 64 percent for Chicanos, and 59 percent for blacks. And while there are clearly areas of what Admissions Director Bob Laird calls "social overlap," the school, as even the most casual visitor can discern, remains highly self-segregated, an observation confirmed by Berkeley sociologist Troy Duster in a study of racial associations on campus published in the early 1990s. It would be ludicrous to expect anything else since so few blacks would be there but for race preference. For example, in the freshman Class of '94 only 33 of the 558 blacks were among the 50 percent admitted strictly on the basis of academic credentials. In the same class, 1,701 of the 2,701 whites got in on academic credentials alone, as did 1,960 of the 2,961 Asians.

None of these inconvenient facts received any mention whatsoever when in March 1996 the Department of Education's Office of Civil Rights (OCR) issued an opinion clearing Berkeley of discrimination in its admissions policies. Once again, the Powell rationale—the historic right of a university to seek diversity in its student body—was used to cloak practices that came about as close to the bald imposition of racial quotas as possible while still preserving a semblance of derivability. A careful reading of the fifteen-page document reveals no mention whatsoever of the specific difference in SAT or GPA scores between the favored and disfavored racial and ethnic groups, nor of the percentage of minorities admitted under Tiers designed to compensate for any shortfalls in academic credentials, nor of the percentage of minorities that would have been admitted under standards that made no allowance for race, nor the difference in academic performance and graduation rates among various admission categories. Rather, the agency's giddy endorsement of Berkeley admissions practices, including its Social Diversity Score procedure, simply confirms its own bias in favor of race preferences in admissions.

Berkeley was far from unique in its approach to the minority admissions issues. UCLA had its own strikingly similar Three Tier admissions procedure with strikingly similar results and was apparently guided by the dictate of its admissions dean, Rae Lee Siporin, that, "Emphasizing grades alone would produce a bland class."

That certainly did not happen. Under Ms. Siporin's guidance, UCLA in 1994 chose only 45 percent of its entering class from the best group of state high school graduates, those with a 4.16 GPA and SATs of at least 1252, putting them approximately in the 92nd national percentile. Another 27 percent of the class came from a second group with an average GPA of 3.96 and an SAT average score of 1120, putting them in the 81st percentile. A third group averaged a 3.74 GPA and SATs of 977, putting them in the 62nd percentile, while a fourth group had a GPA of 3.4 and SATs of 900, the 50th percentile. Most of the third group—12 percent of the class—and nearly all of the last group,

16 percent, were black or Hispanic. The final composition of the class was 43 percent Asian, 24 percent white, 20 percent Hispanic, and 7 percent black. But the average high school GPAs ranged from 3.58 for blacks to 4.14 for Asians, and the black–white SAT gap was well over 200 points.

These differences carried over to performance as students. In the 1990s, the white graduation rate from UCLA has been 80 percent; for Hispanics, 60 percent; and for blacks, 52 percent. GPAs have averaged 3.34 for Asians, 3.26 for whites, 3.11 for Hispanics, and 2.86 for blacks. And this at a university with a well-earned reputation for grade inflation.

If anything, these figures understate the problem. Professor Gail Heriot of the University of San Diego School of Law noted that students from the lowest of the four groups are fourteen times more likely than students from the highest group and four times more likely than those from the second highest group to have a GPA of 2.0 or less. After two years, the average GPA for the third group students is 2.62 while that for the lowest group is 2.28.

Ms. Heriot suggests that consciously or otherwise, the faculty changes both the curriculum and the depth of classroom discussion to accommodate those less able to keep up. She adds: "Students in this position often feel like losers. Of course, they aren't losers; they are above average high school graduates who might have performed well at less competitive colleges. They are not, however, of the same academic caliber as most of their peers. Not surprisingly, some attempt to justify their poor performance. 'It's all politics' and 'The teacher is racist' become common complaints. Some students seek to segregate themselves from the rest of the school—separate social groups, students organizations, and student lounges. Some even seek to segregate themselves during class hours by gravitating toward less competitive racial and ethnic studies departments. The result has been a tragic lesson in racial resentment."

In his powerful paper, *Choosing by Color: Affirmative Action at the University of California,* Michael Lynch of the Pacific Research Institute cites the 1994 record of many of the state's graduate schools:

- UC Berkeley School of Law admitted every black applicant with a GPA of 3.5 and Law School Admission Test (LSAT) of 90.0 or above, while only 42 percent of similarly qualified whites were admitted.
- UC Davis School of Law admitted all three black applicants with GPAs between 2.75 and 2.99 and LSATs in the 70.0–74.9 range, but none of the twenty-three whites or Asians with similar ranges.
- UCLA School of Law admitted 61 percent of black applicants but only 1 percent of whites and 7 percent of Asians having both a GPA between 2.5 and 3.49 and an LSAT between 60.0 and 89.9.
- UCLA School of Medicine admitted twenty-seven blacks but no whites or Asians with GPAs of 3.24 or below and Medical College Admissions Test biology and chemistry percentile scores of 93.4 and below.

In a separate review of California medical school admissions practices, Lynch noted that during the period 1991–93 minorities were admitted to the UC Davis School of Medicine at a rate equal to four times the rate of whites and Asians. Lynch writes: "If the school is to be believed that it gave no special preferences based on race and ethnicity, then the chance of this many URMs [under-represented minorities] being accepted... is less than one in a million."

Throughout the university system, the average GPA of whites and Asians rejected for admission to medical school was higher than the average GPA of blacks and Hispanics accepted for admission. The result in medical and other graduate schools was precisely and predictably what it has been at the undergraduate level: minority beneficiaries are bunched at the bottom of the class where they more often require remedial work, frequently fail to graduate with their classmates, and often find the going rocky when the time comes to pass medical board exams.

So when the winds of change blew hard in California, diversity as an entitlement had its share of defenders, but as an educational value it had precious few. That is because in content and in result, education was never its mission. Diversity was instead always a numbers game, or, as Justice Powell feared, "the functional equivalent of a quota system." From the time of Powell's *Bakke* opinion until the Board of Regents mandated reform, the admissions policies of the elite schools in the University of California system amounted to little more than a colossal lie.

10

HISTORICALLY BLACK STATE COLLEGES AND UNIVERSITIES

Consider: You are a resident of a state below the Mason-Dixon Line who has been newly appointed to its Board of Regents, responsible for determining educational policy at state-supported institutions of higher learning. Your state has both historically white institutions (HWIs), where black enrollment ranges between 8 and 23 percent, and historically black institutions (HBIs), where the white enrollment is in each case less than 5 percent. At your first meeting, you are informed of a comprehensive plan to reform the system, which includes the following points:

- The requirement that high school students wishing to attend one of these institutions complete a "core curriculum" that includes a range of math, English, and science courses will be dropped.
- Admissions requirements at the prestige state universities offering comprehensive fields of study, including doctoral programs and, at some, degrees in medicine

and law, will be lowered to where at least 65 percent of graduating black high school seniors are automatically eligible for admission (under current standards, 45 percent already are).

- A policy of "open enrollment" will prevail at all other state institutions of higher learning.
- At least 10 percent of each freshman class at all HWIs must henceforth be black.
- At least 10 percent of all new faculty hires at all HWIs must henceforth be black.
- In order to make blacks feel academically comfortable at the HWIs, the curriculum will deemphasize Western philosophical, political, and literary traditions and introduce a greater degree of Afrocentric themes, including the mental, moral, and physical superiority of the black race and the way Western society developed racist institutions to counter that superiority.
- One state medical school and one law school will be transferred from HWIs to HBIs in order to encourage white students to enroll at these schools, thereby reducing the degree of racial segregation at state institutions.
- A proposal to reduce segregation more directly by merging a HBI with a nearby HWI offering the same basic program will be scrapped because of the unique "nurturing" role HBIs play with black college students, even though this particular HBI has a six-year graduation rate for its students of just 25 percent, the lowest of any state school.

As a newcomer, you are tempted to rise and to question the need for many if not all of these "reforms," but you hold your tongue. A few minutes later, you are glad you did because you learn that several of these proposals are at issue in a court case your state has been litigating for twenty years, while others are under consideration in neighboring jurisdictions.

In much of the country, the racial zealots of academia have become cautious. Political correctness is an outrage turned farce. Shrinking budgets are converting affirmative action into a zero sum game. Quotas and exclusive minority scholarship programs are under furious counterattack.

But after centuries of racial oppression and segregation many Southern states retain the remnants of a segregated system of higher education, one which has been subject to years of quiet give-and-take with civil rights groups and officials of the Justice and Education Departments in Washington but which, prior to 1992, had never reached the Supreme Court. Indeed, many states assumed that a state-supported college has more in common with a state-supported 4-H club than a public elementary or secondary school since, like the former, the decisions whether to attend and which to attend are voluntary. And in *Bazemore v. Friday,* involving a 4-H club, the Supreme Court held that the only constitutional violations by a state were those that limited access on the basis of race. But then, in the 1992 case *U.S. v. Fordice,* initiated in 1975 when a black student named Jackie Ayers sued the governor of Mississippi hoping to end the dual system of higher education which the state had maintained for nearly a century, the Court took a different view. It held that if the challenged policies and practices were traceable to former de jure segregation, continued to have segregative effects, were without sound educational justification, and could be eliminated in a practicable way, they must be. And—as with employment discrimination, voting rights, or bias in awarding public contracts—once the violation was established the potential remedy was limited only by the imaginations of lawyers and courts.

The magnitude of the human and constitutional insult against blacks in the South can never be overstated. Before the Civil War, most of the slave states made it illegal to educate blacks. When the first Morrill Act of 1862 provided land grants for the establishment of institutions to provide liberal education to the working classes, among the Southern states, only Mississippi, Virginia, and South Carolina would later use part of the resource to educate blacks. While a network of private black colleges funded mainly by Christian groups and Northern philanthropists offered schooling in some liberal and professional disciplines to Southern blacks, the publicly funded Southern schools trained agricultural workers, mechanics, and teachers for the segregated elementary and secondary schools. Only in response to Supreme Court decisions in the 1930s and 1940s did some of the Southern states finally establish at least a handful of doctoral and professional programs for blacks.

Following the 1962 admission of James Meredith to the University of Mississippi—courtesy of federal troops—the state legislature passed a law requiring an American College Test (ACT) score of 15 for admission to the University of Mississippi, Southern Mississippi University, and Mississippi State University, while a score of 13 was needed for admission to any HBI. At the time the average scores were 18 for whites—the approximate national average—and 7 for blacks.

Jackie Ayres lost his case in the lower federal courts, and by the time it got to the Supreme Court, the Bush Justice Department had become heavily involved. Most of the remaining black litigants were more fearful of "victory," which might actually phase out state-run HBIs, than they were of defeat. The Court found four possible areas where the residual effects of past segregation were clear and continuing: (1) admissions governed by the "ACT only" criterion, which had been erected as a barrier to black enrollment after Meredith's admission; (2) overlapping missions of the various schools; (3) duplicative courses of study; and (4) the number of institutions, which suggested the possibility of consolidation. In a strange and convoluted bit of reasoning, the majority rejected the blacks' quest for more resources on the grounds of constitutional right—after all, "separate but more equal" was pretty old hat—but suggested they might be able to prevail if they claimed that more resources would help them to compete for white students, thus furthering desegregation.

But the plaintiffs' joy in contemplating remedies was overshadowed by concern that the Court's opinion could really lead to desegregation—the merger of black institutions with white ones. Concurring Justice Clarence Thomas was the first to sound the tocsin: "Although I agree that a State is not constitutionally *required* to maintain its historically black institutions as such [citation omitted], I do not understand our opinion to hold that a State is *forbidden* from doing so. It would be ironic, to say the least, if the institutions that sustained blacks during segregation were destroyed in an effort to combat its vestiges."

Sure enough, the state education commission did come up with a plan for merging one of its three HBIs—Mississippi Valley State University (MVSU) in Itta Bena—with Delta State University (DSU), the HWI in nearby Cleveland. All students at MVSU would be guaranteed places at the merged university, which was already 23 percent black, and all MVSU faculty members would be assured equivalent positions within the state university system.

But the blacks and their liberal allies would have none of it. The National Association for the Advancement of Colored People organized a march of ten thousand people in Jackson, Mississippi, where former Executive Director Benjamin Chavis thundered, "You kill our schools, you kill our communities." William H. Gray, CEO of the United Negro College Fund, commented, "I am alarmed that they are saying the black college should merge with the white college, instead of saying the white college should merge with the black one, or that the black college should be upgraded." William Blakely, a Washington lawyer long active in civil rights litigation, offered what has since become a familiar line of argument: "Nobody has ever suggested that because Catholics can go anywhere to college they should close Notre Dame. Likewise, nobody has ever suggested that because Jews can go anywhere to college, that we ought to close down Brandeis University. Our churches and colleges are the most treasured things we have. If they take our colleges away from us, we won't need the churches anymore. You have got to be able to read your Bible." In their report, "Redeeming the American Promise," the Southern Education Foundation's Panel on Educational Opportunity and Postsecondary Desegregation—a group that has never met a radical black demand it didn't like—weighed in on the issue: "The Panel emphatically rejects closing HBCUs [historically black colleges and universities] to promote desegregation. Both traditionally white and traditionally black institutions are vestiges of purposeful state-imposed segregation. No set of institutions has any more right than the other to survive. The burden of desegregation should not fall exclusively or disproportionately on the HBCUs."

Alex Johnson, the radical University of Virginia law professor, was among those most troubled by the Supreme Court's integrationist rumblings, explaining, "Ironically, a significant portion of African Americans came to view the liberal notion of integration as undesirable. African Americans who supported integrationism as a means of improving the plight of African Americans won the battle but lost the war." He continues: "Coercive assimilation is as wrong and harmful as the forced exclusion of African Americans that was mandated by the doctrine of 'separate but equal'.... African Americans are now in a position to choose whether or not to maintain their separate society and its distinct norms and institutions." And Jackie Ayres's widow, Lillie, now demonstrating against her late husband's goal, said, "We learned that being mixed with the white folks doesn't work."

The reaction is perplexing on a number of fronts. For one thing, the devotion to institutions simply because they "sustained blacks through segregation" seems misplaced. The same could have been said for all black elementary and secondary schools, not to mention "blacks only" hotels, theaters, and eating establishments. The regime was ended because society concluded, in the words of *Brown v. Board of Education,* that "separate but equal has no place. Segregated schools are inherently unequal."

Second, the comparison with Notre Dame, Brandeis, or, for that matter, Yeshiva is inapt, since these are all private institutions, as are more than forty HBIs about which there is no dispute. For a state or the federal government to maintain a Catholic or Jewish university would not only be inappropriate, it would be unconstitutional. But no one is urging the elimination of state-run historically black colleges and universities, since we are clearly not writing on a clean slate and tens of thousands of black students do rely on these institutions. No, the issue is whether society should seek to expand these institutions into new areas. In an era of budgetary scarcity, this would mean placing a bet on them to outperform others in serving black education interests. The alternative is to provide enough support to maintain most of them in their current roles while remaining alert to the occasional opportunity to merge them with a nearby historically white institution in circumstances where the quality of education can be maintained or improved for both races, and the degree of racial integration enhanced.

Third, the HWIs in Mississippi and elsewhere across the South are among the most integrated schools in the nation, and becoming more so. By 1992, blacks composed about 8 percent of the student body at Ole Miss, 13 percent at Mississippi State, 12 percent at Southern Mississippi, and 23 percent at DSU. Elsewhere in the South blacks make up more than 10 percent of enrollment at the University of Alabama, the University of Virginia, North Carolina, North Carolina State, Louisville, Florida, Louisiana State University, and Maryland, and blacks make up more than 20 percent at Georgia State and Memphis State. This list is not comprehensive. To pour new resources into the state-run HBIs, particularly to transfer or add new graduate and professional schools on the grounds that they will promote integration by enticing more whites into the student body is worse than misguided; it is a lie. Such a policy would retard integration by keeping more black students from attending the integrated HWIs.

All this would be understandable if those who soar to lyrical heights about the unique and nurturing role the public HBIs play had any evidence to support their case. Unfortunately, the thing the state HBIs appear best at is nurturing college dropouts. At MVSU, the percentage of freshmen graduating within six years is only about 25 percent, as low as any in the state. Moreover, while black plaintiffs in *Fordice* complained about the "hostile environment" at the HWIs, these schools had better retention rates for black students than did the state HBIs. The excuse is usually that the HBIs cater to poor kids who often drop out for financial reasons. But in Mississippi more than 90 percent of all black students, regardless of their college or university, receive financial assistance.

The situation is similar across the South. A 1994 paper written by Professor Michael T. Nettles of the Center for the Study of Higher and Postsecondary Education at the University of Michigan studied the six-year (1985–91) retention and graduation rates for whites, blacks, and other ethnic groups at public colleges and universities in the southern and border states. Among his conclusions:

- The more selective schools had the best retention and graduation rates for both white and black students.
- With few exceptions, "the retention, progression, and graduation rates for African Americans is far below their white counterparts and their Hispanic counterparts both statewide and within the same institutions."
- "[T]he historically black public universities appear to have retention, progression, and graduation rates for African American students that lag behind even the state regional colleges and universities in the same state."

Nor has Nettles found two-year community or "junior" colleges able to serve as a bridge from high school to four-year institutions for very many blacks, despite the huge reliance on these facilities in recent years. Consistently, his studies show that fewer than 15 percent of blacks entering these institutions graduate from four-year colleges after six years.

The reason for the abysmal matriculation rates is that the admissions standards at HBIs are so low that few candidates are screened out even if the prospects are dim that they will ever perform college-level work satisfactorily. During the years 1988–92, 60 percent of the students enrolled in Mississippi's HBIs scored below 15 on the ACT exam. Providing even a little higher education for these youngsters is a defensible undertaking, and no doubt finding the occasional "diamond in the rough" is a rewarding experience for an HBI. But at best that makes the case for keeping enough of these institutions in business during the transitional period from segregated to integrated higher education to serve as a safety net for those reluctant or unable to adjust. It does not argue for expanding the public HBI's role or for the state to maintain indefinitely a robust quasi-segregated system of higher education in order to accommodate the separatist ideologies of the black militants and their white apologists.

Although the Supreme Court accepted in *Fordice* the fact that the ACT standard had become a screen for unpreparedness rather than a tool for discrimination, it found that "this mid-passage justification for perpetuating a policy originally enacted to discriminate against black students does not make the present admission standard any less suspect."

Plaintiffs seized the issue to attack a favorite minority target, standardized tests, or other admissions criteria that have a disparate impact on blacks, urging a policy of "open enrollment" at regional state institutions while eliminating the need for students to take a core college preparatory curriculum in order to be considered for the state university system. The state responded with a plan that would automatically accept any core curriculum student who had achieved a 3.2 GPA, regardless of his or her ACT score. Those with GPAs of at least 2.5 could get in with an ACT score of 16, and those with at least a 2.0 could get in with an 18. Students not meeting any of these criteria can participate in a state-sponsored "screening program," which determines the level of remediation needed to prepare the applicant for college. Those choosing to do so then participate in a ten-week summer program employing "state-of-the-art computer-based assessment, instruction, software, and management."

Still, the minority plaintiffs found this unacceptable. Alcorn State University (ASU) Admissions Director Emanuel Barnes worried that those told they need remediation would be intimidated and that "students will apply to schools elsewhere rather than agree to a screening exam."

The plaintiffs were happier about the state's treatment of graduate school applications, by virtue of their dropping any cutoff grade on the graduate record exams (GREs). National figures show that blacks average 129 points below whites on the verbal portion of the GRE and more than 150 points lower in the quantitative and analytical exams.

On remand from the Supreme Court, the shrewd and experienced District Judge Neal Biggers, Jr., refused to be goaded into junking all admissions criteria or abandoning the requirement for core curriculum high school courses. He found no statistical evidence that community wealth or per capita school expenditures had any relationship to the ability of students to choose core courses or to their performance on the ACT exam. In fact, "[a]ccording to the testimony, students working toward goals will usually do that which is expected of them. If they believe they need not prepare themselves for college by taking the core curriculum in high school, they will not do so. Such unpreparedness may bring them to college campuses unable to execute the rigors of college work and result in low retention rates, college debt accumulations, and years expended with no degrees.... It has also been shown that institutions of higher learning that open their doors to unprepared students via open admissions not only do a disservice to many of the students admitted, but can lower the quality and, concurrently, the prestige of the institutions generally."

Fair enough, but the court went further than necessary by imposing uniform admission standards throughout the system of four-year colleges and universities, much along the lines recommended by the state. With higher ACT and GPA standards suddenly thrust upon them, the HBIs suffered an immediate drop in applications and admissions. According to a *New York Times* report of 24 April 1996, by early March of that year applications at Jackson State University (JSU) for the fall semester were down 25 percent, admissions were down 60 percent, applicants eligible for their remedial summer program were up 61 percent, and the projected freshman class size of about 500 was down 60 percent from a year earlier. It was far better for the court to have allowed admission requirements that were uniform for all races and ethnic groups, but which were permitted to vary from school to school.

To his credit, however, Judge Biggers rejected all of the exotic "hostile environment" remedies, although a federal circuit court reviewing an Alabama case did instruct the lower court to explore whether a more Afrocentric curriculum might attract more blacks to HWIs. The state did offer to fund an expanded agriculture and an MBA program at ASU, while rejecting the medical school raid and other power moves proposed on behalf of JSU.

As to the most emotional question—whether the state could, for purposes of integration, merge MVSU and DSU—the court substantially ducked the issue, telling Mississippi to study the matter further. With no substantial voice from either race demanding merger, and with most blacks actively opposed, it appears a merger is unlikely to happen anytime soon.

Biggers ordered the state to look further into the feasibility of adding law, pharmacy, allied health, business, social work, and urban planning professional school programs to the school. When that examination takes place, those who would urge a major new expansion of graduate programs at HBIs are likely to encounter some inconvenient facts about the prospects for such programs. In 1995, the National Research Council (NRC), a branch of the National Academy of Science, published an assessment of graduate school programs in the areas of arts and humanities, biological sciences, engineering, physical sciences and mathematics, and social sciences. The study embraced forty-one separate disciplines. A total of 3,634 doctoral programs at 274 public and private universities which had awarded 90 percent of the 143,000 doctorates earned between 1986 and 1992 were rated, based on the opinions of nearly 8,000 graduate faculty members, as well as the amount of federal grant support, the number of papers published, publication citations for scholarly works, and honors and awards.

The survey included sixteen doctoral programs at Howard University and three at Clark College in Atlanta, the only two HBIs included. Howard's sociology graduate program ranked 76 out of 95 rated, and its psychology program ranked 119 out of 185. All others ranked in the bottom quarter of their respective disciplines. In both biochemistry and molecular biology, Clark College was rated 180 out of 193. In political science, it nosed out Idaho State to finish 97 out of 98.

Still, the report noted that of the 5,800 minority scholars earning doctoral degrees during the period, 40 percent attended programs ranked in the top 25 percent and nearly two-thirds were in programs ranked in the top one-half. Reviewing the report, the *Journal of Blacks in Higher Education* (*JBHE*) noted, "It appears that many academically gifted black students who choose the nurturing environment of a black college or university for undergraduate studies are opting for graduate programs in which academic strength and reputation are the prime considerations."

JBHE found the data persuasive that financially strapped HBIs will never be able to compete with the major research universities in the quality of graduate programs. So why pour scarce resources into the creation of a new wave of second- or third-rate programs? The editors found no persuasive reason: "At black universities, meager financial resources may be more wisely allocated to undergraduate teaching programs that will adequately prepare black students for graduate programs at the leading research universities. At the very least, the NRC statistics should dissuade black universities from establishing additional financially draining doctoral programs."

11

VOTING RIGHTS:
AS YE SOW...

The 1980s were a period of mixed Republican fortunes. With the election of Ronald Reagan in November 1980, the GOP would control the White House for the entire decade plus two years. Reagan swept a Republican Senate into office with him. But it would revert to the Democrats after the elections of 1986. As for the House, it had not been Republican since 1955 and seemed much less likely to change hands. In the House, incumbent reelection rates were at 98 percent and holding, high even by historical U.S. standards. No fewer than 387 of the 435 congressional districts were controlled by the same party throughout the 1980s. Such were the advantages of incumbency that in only 174 of the 1,305 elections during the decade did the winner get less than 55 percent of the vote. Nearly half of the congressional winners in 1988 received more than 70 percent of the vote.

In partisan speeches at the time, Republican National Committee Counsel Benjamin Ginsberg, now a partner in the muscular Washington, D.C., lawyer–lobbyist firm of Patton and Boggs, and other GOP officials argued that one way House Democrats had managed to preserve their advantage was through old-fashioned gerrymandering, like the late Democrat Phillip Burton's cosmic 1981 "fix" of California. "Our communities," Ginsberg claimed, "have been packed, cracked, fractured, and manipulated." Then, with the beguiling innocence of a choir boy, he would implore, "Redistricting should be a process that ensures competitive elections that allow the voters, and not computer-toting gerrycrats, to determine who wins elections."

One Republican response to Democratic gerrymandering was to field an army of "computer-toting gerrycrats" of their own. With vastly improved hardware and access to the Census Bureau's "Tiger System," which provides computerized population maps in statistical detail, the pros of both parties plus other interested constituencies were able to get into the reapportionment game big time. The Republicans developed software packages worth as much as $360,000 apiece capable of designing districts favorable to the GOP or analyzing Democratic designs with the contrary effects. As Justice John Paul Stevens noted, "Computers now make it possible to generate a large number of alternative plans, consistent with equal protection guidelines and various other criteria, in a relatively short period of time, and to analyze the political characteristics of each one in considerable detail."

A continuing problem for state Republican organizations, however, was that in many of the key states Republicans were not even "at the table"; they controlled neither the state house, senate, or the governorship, and thus were unable to participate directly in redistricting. In 1981, following the last census, they had been represented in states containing only 188 of the 435 congressional districts. And although by 1991 that number had increased to 242, the void remained considerable, particularly in the Southern states where steady Republican gains in presidential and congressional elections were unmatched in state legislative and gubernatorial contests. In a state like Alabama, a Republican governor could fight Democratic redistricting to a standoff, throwing it into the lap of the courts, but that was seldom the case.

Fortunately for Ginsberg and his Republican allies, a remarkable alliance of convenience was coming into focus. The nation's minorities, particularly African Americans, also felt they were seriously underrepresented in Congress. Nationally, minorities composed 20 percent of the population but only 10 percent of the House of Representatives. In the 11 states of the Old Confederacy, blacks made up 17.4 percent of the voting age population, but only 5 black representatives held seats among the 116 elected members.

There were reasons to think this was about to change. The Voting Rights Act of 1965 had been amended in 1982 in a way that seemed to ensure that, during the redistricting following the 1990 census, a large number of new black majority districts would be created. To assemble these new "majority–minority" districts, black voters from surrounding areas would be siphoned into them. This could help Republican candidates in the surrounding districts by depriving Democratic candidates of groups of voters more than 90 percent of whom tended to vote Democratic. The new majority black districts would almost certainly produce a Democratic congressman... a black Democratic congressman at that. But if, in order to create one decisively black district, narrowly Democratic surrounding districts lost black Democratic voters, the end result could be a net Republican gain. As for the surrounding Republican districts, the transfer of Democratic voters would ensure that they remained in GOP hands.

This could be a boon to Republican chances across the South, and perhaps elsewhere. And while they may have had no seat at the negotiating table, there was nothing to prevent their providing political and technical support to blacks to increase the number of majority–minority districts, or even to intervene in legal proceedings where racial redistricting was the critical issue.

The community of interest was there, at least on the surface. "Cracking" black voters—dividing a concentration of minorities among the most districts possible—helped elect Democrats but not blacks. But "packing" them—drawing boundaries to include minorities from geographically diverse areas into a smaller number of districts—could mean more blacks and more Republicans in the 103rd Congress.

So the GOP went to work. In Georgia and Texas, its state organizations formed alliances with black groups challenging Democratic redistricting plans. Republicans in Illinois already had a lawsuit going; in North Carolina, they not only filed a suit of their own but also joined in litigation initiated by black organizations. Other minorities also received GOP help. In California, where the Reagan Justice Department had for years been in league with Mexican American voting rights groups, the pro-GOP Rose Institute shared several of its computer-generated redistricting schemes with the Mexican Americans.

So the two became strange bedfellows. The Republican party and black political organizations sought to bolster their strength in the U.S. Congress and state legislatures. But while the principal consequence of their activity, a loss of Democratic numerical strength, was the Republican raison d'être, it could also undercut the base of black political power and the substantive policy interests of the larger black community.

■　■　■

It is not always easy to understand why a technical, highly complicated issue like redistricting generates the political passions and the intellectual energies that it does. One simple answer is that voting is, by definition, at the heart of our system of representative government. Another is that though nearly everyone has an inherent sense that the political process should fairly reflect "popular will," that is not always easily defined or gauged. Further, the outcome of a political process can be manipulated fairly easily by tinkering with the mechanics of the vote. When it comes to the issue of fairly representing African Americans, and to a far lesser extent, other ethnic minorities, emotions are already close to the surface. Not only were blacks historic victims of the most virulent forms of racism, but for a full century following passage of the Thirteenth, Fourteenth, and Fifteenth Amendments, the manipulation of voting rights and procedures was one of the principal tools used by the white South to maintain Jim Crowism masked as the expression of "popular will" at the ballot box.

To illustrate with a simplified example, let us take our imaginary political jurisdiction with one hundred residents entitled to elect a total of ten representatives. Let us further assume the jurisdiction is divided between seventy-six "As" and twenty-four "Bs" as follows:

A	A	A	A	A	A	A	A	A	A
A	A	A	A	A	A	A	A	A	A
A	A	A	A	A	A	A	A	A	A
A	A	B	B	B	B	A	A	A	A
A	A	A	A	A	A	B	A	A	A
A	A	B	A	B	A	B	A	A	A
A	A	A	B	B	B	B	A	A	A
A	A	B	A	B	A	A	B	A	A
B	B	A	A	B	A	B	B	B	A
B	B	A	A	B	A	A	A	A	A

We can see that if all representatives run "at large" with all residents entitled to vote once for each of ten different candidates, the "As" at least in theory have the power to elect all ten of the candidates they prefer. On the other hand, if the jurisdiction is divided into ten voting districts with each electing one represen- tative—so called single-member districts—the "Bs" will be able to elect anywhere from zero to four of the ten representatives depending on how the voting districts are drawn.

Of course, those are not the only options. The jurisdiction can be divided in half with each side electing five representatives— multimember districts. Or, voters can be given ten votes and allowed to cast as many as they want for any candidate or candi- dates—so-called cumulative voting—which would ensure their ability to elect at least some of their preferred candidates, even in an at-large vote.

Now if instead of "As" and "Bs", the jurisdiction is divided between blacks and whites, several issues arise:

Should the government take account of race in drawing voting district lines?

Do people of the same race vote for candidates of their own race all or most of the time?

How much influence does one race have in a district where it has, say, four of the ten votes?

If the districts are in fact drawn with the intent of maximizing the number of representatives blacks can elect, does this really maximize their political clout since the whites retain 60 percent of the elected positions, and the blacks have no presence at all in districts where they are not the majority?

■　■　■

It is doubtful that very many of those who voted overwhelmingly to adopt the Voting Rights Act of 1965 were personally familiar with the term "affirmative action." The act, after all, was designed to eliminate an assortment of ugly, undemocratic, and occasionally brutal practices whereby a large number of blacks across the South were denied the right to vote. Fewer still likely thought that what they were doing had any relationship to the obscure labor law term which had been borrowed a few years previously by the Kennedy administration to describe a voluntary plan for government contractors seeking to end racial discrimination in employment. More likely, their thoughts were on Colonel Al Lingo's Alabama State Troopers who had ferociously beaten voting rights marchers on the Edmund Pettus Bridge in Selma as they dramatized the state's unwillingness to register black voters. Some may well have been recalling the words of Martin Luther King Jr., "Give us the ballot and we will no longer have to worry the federal government about our basic rights.... Give us the ballot and we will quietly, lawfully, and nonviolently, without rancor or bitterness, implement the May 17, 1954, decision of the Supreme Court.... Give us the ballot and we will transform the salient misdeeds of bloodthirsty mobs into the calculated good deeds of ordinary citizens."

The tiny scattering of blacks in Congress at the time may well have had enough of a sense of history to recall the 1901 farewell of Representative George H. White, the twentieth black to serve in Congress during the post–Civil War era and the last until Oscar DePriest was elected from the black wards of Chicago twenty-seven years later. White said goodbye on behalf of an "outraged, heartbroken, bruised, and bleeding people," but a people who one day, "phoenix-like," would "rise up and come again."

To do that, however, they would have to overcome a vast assortment of weapons in the Southern Jim Crow arsenal: poll taxes, shifting property ownership requirements, racially exclusive primaries, gerrymandering, "good character" certification requirements, bogus literacy tests, economic pressure, or, when all else failed, physical intimidation and violence.

Three civil rights acts, passed during the late 1950s and early 1960s with only token opposition from Southern congressional moderates, had not done the job. Though the percentage of blacks registered to vote in the Old Confederacy had risen from 3 percent on the eve of World War II to just over 40 percent at the end of the second Eisenhower term, the figure was much lower in states with the highest black populations. In Mississippi, for example, only 6 percent of the state's black voting age population was registered. As Congress prepared to vote, a convention of elected black Southern officeholders could have been held in a one-room schoolhouse.

As passed in 1965, the Voting Rights Act was not an affirmative action law. It was a pure civil rights statute providing that no "qualification or prerequisite to voting, or standard, practice or procedure" could be imposed by any state to restrict the right to vote on the basis of race or color. Two additional provisions gave the act real teeth. One permitted federal registrars to assume responsibility for registering voters where necessary. The other required jurisdictions which had used literacy tests and had voter turnout of under 50 percent to obtain "preclearance" either from the Justice Department or the U.S. District Court of the District of Columbia before making any change in their voting procedures. Preclearance would eventually apply to all or parts of twenty-eight states, including many jurisdictions as disparate as New York City and Alaska, which had never prevented minorities from voting, but where the use of literacy tests and occasional low voter turnout brought in the feds.

At the time it was passed, most assumed the act applied only to the right to register, vote, and have the vote counted, rather than to such questions as at-large versus single-member district electoral arrangements. But it was not enacted in a vacuum. Since 1960, the Court had begun applying the Equal Protection Clause to questions about the configuration of voting districts and the populations they represented. The combination of statutory protection for the physical process of voting, together with evolving judicial application of the Equal Protection Clause to the drawing of political boundaries, held high promise for black voters across the South.

For example, in 1960, the state of Alabama, perhaps anticipating strong voting rights legislation, redrew the boundaries of the city of Tuskeegee to what the Supreme Court would call an "uncouth 28-sided figure" for the obvious purpose of excluding most black residential areas from the municipality. Striking down the law in *Gomillion v. Lightfoot,* Justice Felix Frankfurter, overcoming his distaste for the "political thicket" of redistricting questions, wrote that the Fifteenth Amendment "nullifies sophisticated as well as simple-minded modes of discrimination," and outlaws "onerous procedural requirements which effectively handicap the exercise of the franchise by the colored race although the abstract right to vote may remain unrestricted as to race."

Two years later, in its historic *Baker v. Carr* decision, the Court held that a state violates the Equal Protection Clause when it organizes legislative districts with wide population disparities. And by 1964, in *Reynolds v. Sims,* it was ready to articulate the principle of one man, one vote, declaring, in other words, that each voting district must have equal population. Protected now both by the Court and Congress, black influence at the polls grew dramatically. There were districts in Alabama and Mississippi where the number of black voters climbed from a few hundred to nearly 10,000 in the space of a single election. In Alabama, the percentage of registered blacks reached 52 percent by 1967, doubling in just two years.

Not surprisingly, blacks began running and winning in local elections and finding a more receptive audience among the region's white elected officials. Still, Southern districts proved resourceful in attempting to skirt the intent of the act. Their most effective vehicle was simply to convert single-member districts where they existed to larger entities where all candidates would run at-large, a device which, as seen in our hypothetical district, can effectively dilute minority voting power. But in 1969, the Supreme Court dealt a heavy blow to such chicanery, holding in *Allen v. Board of Elections* that the preclearance provisions of the Voting Rights Act applied to efforts to dilute the votes of blacks as well as to efforts to disenfranchise black voters directly.

Throughout the 1970s, the courts generally sanctioned an expansive interpretation of the act. Whether the issue was redistricting, annexation, or any other change, the emerging standard employed by the Civil Rights Division at Justice and sanctioned by the federal courts was "nonretrogression": If the minority suffered no damage to its political strength as a result of the change, neither Justice nor the courts would intervene. But neither would permit any "retrogression" in minority political power, even where the primary motivation for the move was nonracial. Across the South, this kind of political protection translated slowly but relentlessly into paved roads, improved municipal services, jobs, and patronage for blacks.

Then, in 1980 the Supreme Court seemed to change direction. The Court refused to throw out Mobile's "at-large" election system, even though it appeared to dilute minority voting strength, unless it could be shown that the city employed the at-large system with the *intent* of discriminating against blacks. This would be difficult to prove. Not only had at-large voting been widely accepted for years, it had grown originally not from racism but from the "good government" reforms of the turn of the century. The same was true of other "good government" measures that might incidentally or even inadvertently reduce black political power, such as office-holder qualifications, run-off elections, and borough or county government arrangements. All these can work to the incidental detriment of minority voters determined to elect one of their own. For that reason, since the early 1970s, Justice and the courts had routinely declined to approve the imposition of changes that had such an effect. But now, the Supreme Court appeared to be moving to an *intent* standard, and the civil rights lobby saw more than a decade of political gains suddenly at risk.

The Leadership Conference for Civil Rights, a lobbying coalition of nearly 150 minority and labor organizations, under the able and spirited guidance of Ralph Neas, immediately mounted a hugely successful legislative effort to amend the Act while extending it for an additional twenty-five years. By the time Congress's work was complete, it had enshrined the notion of group rights into the law and imposed an "outcomes" or "results-oriented" test on election processes alien to the spirit of the 1965 Act and to U.S. political tradition. In effect, the new act would bring affirmative action to elections—not affirmative action to bring blacks to voting booths, but affirmative action to elect black candidates to office.

Under the new act, it would be a violation of the law when, "based on the totality of circumstances," it was shown that the political processes were not equally open to members of a protected class or that "its members have less opportunity than other members of the electorate to participate in the political process and to elect representatives of their choice." The act listed a number of circumstances that might count as evidence of racial exclusion, including the extent to which voting in state and local elections was racially polarized and whether campaigns had been characterized by appeals to race. But all were dwarfed by the seventh criterion: "[t]he extent to which members of the minority group have been elected to public office in the jurisdiction." In other words, where few black officials were *elected*, black voters could conclusively be presumed to have been discriminated against.

Senator Robert Dole, the once and future majority leader, managed to add a "clarifying clause," disclaiming that anything in the legislation "establishes a right to have members of a protected class elected in numbers equal to their proportion in the population." Nevertheless the amended act eliminated the requirement that a plaintiff must show that the state or local jurisdiction intended to discriminate or even that its action would cause retrogression of black political power. Instead, it issued an engraved invitation to minorities to claim victimhood based on a package of social and political data interpreted by that most corruptible breed of social scientist, the expert witness. As has been and would be the case in such related affirmative action issues as employment testing and "disparity studies" used to prove discrimination against minority contractors, voting rights litigation often came to turn on whether the expert witness swearing that voting statistics proved discrimination was more or less believable to the court than the expert witness swearing that the statistics proved just the opposite.

For blacks and other minorities, the priority now was to organize into ethnocentric voting blocs regardless of individual political sentiments, rather than forming coalitions based on common ideas and interests and aimed at electing politically compatible candidates. Instead, black leaders would insist on maximizing the number of blacks; they would read racism into what may have been and often was nothing more than philosophical disagreement, invite massive and continuing federal intervention in the most mundane local electoral affairs, and claim elective office as a virtual entitlement, not unlike an outright quota. A right of all blacks to vote would be transformed into the right of a few blacks, drawn predominantly from that same leadership, to be elected.

What made Congress's action doubly reprehensible was its explanation for dispensing with the requirement of intent. In a dynamic era when racial attitudes and practices have undergone momentous salutary change, the amended act tended to freeze political institutions on the basis of past sins, keeping those sins always before us while effectively eliminating incentives to repent and reform. Ironically or hypocritically, having made the most wrenching form of social analysis a prerequisite to successful litigation and having eliminated innocence as a defense, the Senate committee report on the bill explained that its brand of no-fault racism was preferable to the search for an evil purpose because "[s]uch inquiries can only be divisive, threatening to destroy any racial progress in a community." In the end, 183 Southern congressmen and senators joined the vote to amend and extend the act—perhaps the clearest evidence that no such amendment was needed— strengthening it in ways that would have been unthinkable even to most legislators who had voted for its initial passage, let alone to Southerners who had opposed it seventeen years earlier.

It remained for the Supreme Court to determine the full reach of the new provisions. Four years later, in 1984, in *Thornburg v. Gingles,* the Court considered a black challenge to seven multi-member state house districts established years before by the North Carolina legislature. Backed by the Reagan Justice Department, the state argued that the arrangement represented no dilution of black voting power. In most of the districts, blacks routinely received 25–50 percent of the white vote. Since 1974, blacks had won elections in five of the seven districts. In the most recent (1982) campaign, blacks had been elected in those districts in numbers roughly proportional to their percentage of the voting population.

Nonetheless, the Court ruled that the arrangement violated the new act. Writing for a Court plurality, Justice Brennan held that, "[f]or purposes of [the act] the concept of racially polarized voting incorporates neither causation nor intent. It simply means that the race of voters correlates with the selection of a certain candidate or candidates." So long as the minority population tended to vote as a bloc, and so long as its candidates usually lost to candidates backed by the racial majority, Justice Brennan said the act had been violated. The obvious remedy was to draw districts where racial minority voters would constitute the majority of voters and then to hold elections organized on a single-member district basis rather than a multimember district or at-large basis.

Moreover, since the dispersal of minority residents across most states makes it extremely difficult to draw any district scheme that ensures the election of minority candidates in proportion to their total population, states and localities could be certain of avoiding challenge only if their plans maximized the number of minority candidates that could be elected. If, for example, the voting population could be organized to provide minorities with one, two, or three safe seats, the three-seat solution was the only one certain to gain preclearance by the Justice Department or federal courts or to sustain a challenge by minority voters. By implication at least, considerations of race took precedence over all other factors that traditionally influenced redistricting: geographic compactness, the preservation of historic neighborhoods, respect for municipal and county boundaries, even protection of incumbents. Thus, the 1982 amendments, together with *Gingles,* imposed what was essentially a "disparate impact" test on electoral processes and converted ethnic entitlements into a game which any number could play.

■   ■   ■

During the first thirty years of administering the Voting Rights Act, the Civil Rights Division of the Justice Department found 3,004 instances where state or local voting procedures failed to meet its standard of fair treatment in dealing with minorities and were thus denied preclearance. Though this is but a small percentage of the more than 250,000 proposed modifications to electoral procedures that had been submitted to Justice during the same period, the vast majority of submissions have been minor, technical, and of negligible impact. The division preferred to intervene in highly visible or novel situations that it could use to set an example or establish a precedent. Favorite Justice targets have included:

- Annexation plans and other devices to alter political boundaries, usually of cities, counties, or townships. Particularly in the early years, some of these were thinly veiled efforts to dilute minority influence. More recently, nearly all have been undertaken as part of good faith efforts to broaden the tax base or provide a more coherent system of governance. (Metro-area governance is a passion with political scientists and other good-government types.) Undeniably, some have had the tangential effect of lowering the percentage of minority voters in the jurisdiction.
- Procedures designed either to register voters or to "purge" from the rolls the names of those who have failed to exercise the franchise over a sustained period.
- Majority vote or run-off provisions which theoretically make it more difficult for a minority candidate to win a race against two or more white candidates in districts where the majority of voters are white, although actual experience has produced little support for the theory.
- Candidate qualification rules, such as a requirement limiting school board eligibility to high school or college graduates.

- Provisions requiring that one or more candidates for judgeships or other offices be elected at-large.
- The location of polling places.

One of the more prolific areas of litigation today involves judgeships. Invariably, these suits develop evidence showing that blacks are "underrepresented" in the number of elected judges. As is the case with so many affirmative action issues, viewing the facts through lenses that can discern nothing but racial bigotry is quite blinding. The key reason, of course, for the shortage of black judges is the smaller pool of black lawyers from which to pick. Black attorneys who are backed by professional bar organizations or state party machinery often win overwhelming support from white voters. And the reelection rate for black judges is about the same as it is for white judges. In most cases litigated in the South, black judicial candidates have been shown to run as well or better than national Democrats in the state.

Sometimes federal efforts fail to account for the evolution in political power which already has occurred. In New York City, for example, Deval Patrick, head of the Civil Rights Division at Justice for the Clinton administration, objected to a process whereby party organizations in Brooklyn, Manhattan, and the Bronx nominated the names of judges to appear on the November ballot. Patrick argued that this minimized the influence of black and Puerto Rican voters. The minority citizens were less than effusive in their gratitude, since at the time the borough presidents of Brooklyn and Manhattan were black and the Bronx borough president was Puerto Rican.

■ ■ ■

Nationwide, no group watched the development of the new act more closely than the Congressional Black Caucus (CBC). The

Caucus had grown from an informal group of three of four Northern black congressmen called the "Democratic Select Committee" and centered about Charles C. Diggs of Michigan, into what in 1989 was a bloc of twenty-four Democrats, most of them comfortably settled on the political left, many of them senior, a few chairing powerful committees or subcommittees, and a couple in positions of party leadership. White members of the House, regardless of their constituencies or political views, were excluded from membership and allowed to participate in some caucus functions only as "associate members."

For many years, the CBC's influence on policy and most legislation was marginal. The organization's best known project, an annual alternative budget, regularly commanded only about seventy votes. But the redistricting that would follow the 1990 census had to be conducted under the standards of the new act. And that would add materially to the numbers and clout of the Caucus on Capitol Hill.

In its early days, the few members of the Caucus were big city blacks whose large, compact districts gave them the sort of political bases and tenure enjoyed mostly by their hated white colleagues from the one-party Democratic South. Both in the South and nationwide elected black officials were so few that the political community still took its lead from the big, soon to be vestigial, civil rights organizations like the NAACP, the Southern Christian Leadership Conference, and the Student Nonviolent Coordinating Committee. That changed as more and more blacks were elected to office. Viewing the problems of the NAACP in the mid-nineties, a senior member of the CBC was asked what the venerable civil rights organization could do to restore its position of influence. "Nothing," he said. "We now have more than 8,000 elected black officials. That's where black folks look for answers to their problems, and that's where they should look." Black leadership was becoming more and more synonymous with black elected officials.

With redistricting occurring only once per decade, black representation from the South had grown slowly. Barbara Jordan of Texas and Andrew Young of Georgia had been elected in 1972. Young, from what was then a majority white district, won a far higher percentage of the white vote than he would in later contests for mayor of Atlanta and governor of Georgia, testimony either to the fact that white voters had grown more bigoted or that UN ambassadors who praise the Ayatollah Khomeini as "a saint" and get fired for unauthorized meetings with terrorist organizations tend to lose support among moderate and conservative voters.

By 1983, the number of black Southern representatives had grown to five, but the decennial redistricting in the wake of the 1980 census had been substantially completed before the 1982 Act was passed. In the wake of the 1990 census, and with a strategically sympathetic Bush Justice Department enforcing the act, major black gains could be expected in the South. Indeed, with the exception of Arkansas, at least one new black representative was anticipated from every state of the Old Confederacy in 1992. The CBC stood to become a far greater power in the Democratic party and the House.

The political power of the CBC, however, was totally dependent on the Democratic party retaining control of the House of Representatives. And the creation of majority–minority districts would require draining blacks from adjoining districts, thereby depriving neighboring white Democratic candidates of assured voters. This was far more true in the South where, even in urban areas where most blacks live, whites in adjoining districts are likely to be Republicans. In the North, by contrast, whites in ethnic inner-city neighborhoods tend to be Democrats, so transferring black voters from one district to the next has less partisan impact. Unless the process was accomplished with exceptional craftsmanship in the South, one black Democratic seat could cost one or more Democratic seats in neighboring districts. Repeated often enough the process could threaten the Democrats' control of the House.

The great firewall against this potential disaster was to be the Democratic control over the redistricting process throughout the South. In the critical year of 1991 when the districts would be drawn, not a single state house or state senate, and only one governorship in the eleven states of the Old Confederacy, was in Republican hands. And so Democrats set to work to save as many Democratic seats as possible while accommodating the presumed legal obligation to maximize the number of majority–minority districts. Where possible, black voters for the minority districts were carved from neighboring Republican districts. In 1992, 73 percent of black voters transferred into new majority black districts in the South had previously been represented by Republican members of Congress. Where that proved impossible, state Democratic leaders tried to replace blacks lost from a white Democratic district with blacks from one controlled by the GOP. Where even that would not suffice, Democratic district designers revved up their computers and tried to shave white Democratic districts as gently as possible, hoping to preserve the Democratic majority, although with less margin for error than they might wish.

The elections of 1992 seemed to vindicate the strategy. Thirteen new black seats had been delivered, twelve of them in the South. White Republicans had gained a total of seventeen seats across the region, but the bleeding was less than feared, Democrats told themselves, and the black gains were important.

In truth, the 1992 results were ominous, especially in a year when Democrats had gained the White House. A good many marginal Republican districts were strengthened. Principal among them was Newt Gingrich's Sixth Congressional District in Georgia.

Gingrich had received a threadbare 50 percent majority in the 1990 vote. In 1992, he emerged with one of the safest Republican seats in the nation, due to the transfer of black voters out of his district and white voters into it. Across the South, safe Democratic seats became hard-fought. In a Democratic year, hard-working incumbents mostly prevailed. But should those seats become "open" in a year when a Republican tide was running, much could be washed away.

At the time, however, most politicians focused on the facts that the Republican's net House pick-up was six and that the institution, along with the Senate, remained in Democratic hands. The Clinton presidency was the product of a 44 percent plurality constructed on a solid national base of black support. For the CBC, a period of unprecedented political influence lay immediately ahead. The Republican National Committee, which had sacrificed its philosophical abhorrence of race-conscious districting in supporting the black power grab, seemed to feel it was all for nothing.

In the 103rd Congress members of the CBC chaired powerful committees and subcommittees, including Armed Services and Government Operations. They held senior positions on Appropriations, Ways and Means, and Rules. Their presence was felt not only on policymaking committees but also on those that deliver projects to the districts back home. David T. Canon of the University of Wisconsin–Madison has documented that the CBC reached unprecedented power—in the leadership on committees, on pivotal votes, and over the policy direction of Congress. "The CBC has become an institutional player rather than an outside critic," he concluded. "The CBC played a central role in shaping and then passing [in the House] legislation on the budget, the space station, crime and campaign finance reform. The CBC played hardball with the budget, threatening to kill it unless more funding was provided for the inner cities, the earned-income tax credit, food stamps, and mandatory immunization for poor children." Its members were also instrumental in blocking the line-item veto.

Yet this apparent triumph carried the seeds of future disaster. The South's largest single constituency consisted of white conservatives whose ties to the Democratic party had been eroding since 1964. Already they tended to go for the GOP in presidential contests, often feeling alienated from the liberals who prevailed more often than not in the nominating process. Now, with newly elected blacks pushing Southern congressional delegations further to the left and with defecting to the GOP seeming less like an exercise in futility as redistricting created winnable Republican districts, white conservative ties to the Democratic party began to erode more rapidly. The ultimate Democratic nightmare was emerging: a region divided between a Republican majority and a Democratic minority, the latter substantially black, the former overwhelmingly white. In Democratic circles, the racial politics of CBC began to be seen as having provoked the "white flight"— not from the neighborhood, but from the party.

The creation of majority black districts was also having its impact on Southern legislatures, where future redistricting fights would be fought. In 1992, black representation in Southern state senates increased from 43 to 67 and, in state houses, from 159 to 213. And Republicans captured control of the North Carolina state house and the Florida state senate for the first time in this century. They also narrowed substantial legislative gaps in Virginia, Texas, and Tennessee. Two years later, the South Carolina state house would go Republican. Even more revealing, in the period following that election, seven white South Carolina state house Democrats switched to the Republican party, leaving Democrats with a mere 50 of the 124 seats in a chamber they had controlled since Reconstruction.

Benjamin Ginsberg had known what the game was, and so had the late Lee Atwater, Boyden Gray, and other GOP political strategists. In an extremely prescient 1993 book, *Black Faces, Black Interests,* Carol M. Swain of Princeton University observed, "Republicans give African Americans the opportunity to increase their descriptive representation, but, quite possibly, at the expense of their substantive representation." Swain noted that with white majorities in 90 percent of the nation's 435 congressional districts, blacks by 1993 had just about achieved the upper limits of what color-conscious redistricting had to offer. Should the continuing Republican political trend transfer the House into GOP hands, "most African American legislators would automatically become minority members of the minority party. Gone would be the committee chairmanships, the leadership posts, and other key assignments."

In public statements and private argument, black leaders and their liberal apologists have tried to minimize the importance of replacing white Southern Democrats with white Southern Republicans by claiming that the so-called "Southern Democrat" had long been aligned with the forces of racism and had offered little legitimate representation of black interests. But this argument had lost much of its validity during the 1970s and by the end of the 1980s had become pure nonsense. David Bositis, a scholar at the Joint Center for Political and Economic Studies—an organization formed and funded by the CBC and its allies—has published a paper in which he traces the "nationalization" of white Southern Democrats in Congress during the 1980s, where he notes that by the end of the decade, the Southern Democrats voted very similarly to Midwestern Democrats. Bositis writes:

> [The party shift] is significant to the representation
> of black political interests in the South because the

change from a Southern white Democrat to a Southern white Republican represents a major shift in support for the CBC in two ways: First, any Southern white Republican will vote with the CBC, and by extension black political interests, much less frequently than any Southern white Democrat. Second, the loss of white Democrats in the South and elsewhere undermines the influence of the CBC (and again by extension black political interests) because the CBC's power is leveraged on the Democrats being in the majority.

To the Republicans, victory was in prospect if not in sight, and the coalition had worked, though slowly and with some pain. Blacks won the battle but might well be on the verge of losing the war. For in their single-minded struggle for power, defined solely as black numerical representation, the issues they cared about and shared with mainstream Democrats were soon under siege. What they forgot, as Carol Swain had written, were that those issues were "real and color blind." Her wisdom would become apparent after the 1994 election.

12

SO SHALL YE REAP

On 29 November 1995 members of the Congressional Black Caucus (CBC) obtained a special order in the House of Representatives permitting them to devote floor time to discussing voting rights issues, particularly the creation of majority–minority legislative districts. One of the speakers pointed to the recent political arrangement sanctioned by popular vote in South Africa wherein representatives of the white minority were assured positions in the elected parliament and the government itself:

> Do you think that the United States of America would have been satisfied if the black majority in South Africa had come forward with a proposed democracy that said we are going to be color-blind; we are not going to take race into account at all; we are not going to assure the white minority in South Africa representation in this new Democratic government?

After answering the question in the negative, the speaker continued: "If the white minority in South Africa was going to have any chance of having a fair shot at representation and having its views reflected in that democracy, the only way it was going to happen was to set up a system that allowed them to have representation."

The argument has been repeated hundreds of times with only minor variation by black lawyers, legislators, and political activists even though the two situations are totally different. South Africa is a society that went from total apartheid and black exclusion from all political power to majority black rule virtually overnight. Some political concessions were necessary to achieve white agreement to so massive and fundamental a transfer of political power. Blacks, moreover, had a vested interest in running the country without scaring into exile a white population which had a near monopoly on legal, medical, scientific, engineering, agricultural, administrative, financial, commercial, and military expertise. By contrast, the United States today has thousands of elected black officeholders, a long history in the North of black participation in the political process, and a tradition of inclusive two-party politics where the interests of ethnic and other groups find expression and representation.

There have been numerous other attempts to justify writing a de facto requirement of result-oriented racial districting into the law—or electoral schemes like proportional representation which achieve the same result—from the sophisticated computerized analysis of voting behavior by Chandler Davidson and Bernard Grofman in *Quiet Revolution in the South* to the intellectual advocacy of Lani Guinier in a number of law review articles, symposia, and a book. Reduced to basics, they stand or fall on twin assertions: first, that white racism at the polls continues to deny to black or other minority candidates a meaningful opportunity to win in predominantly white districts and second, that the political interests of blacks are somehow so special that they cannot be represented adequately by whites regardless of their political persuasion. In this view, fairness requires that black officials be elected in rough proportion to the percentage of blacks in the general population.

True, racial prejudice remains a quantifiable factor in the attitudes of some white Americans. When he testified before the House Subcommittee on the Constitution in October 1995 on behalf of a community of scholars that had developed nuanced and sophisticated techniques of gauging racial prejudice, Professor James H. Kuhlinski of the University of Illinois at Urbana-Champaign indicated the group's studies had found evidence of rather acute antiblack attitudes in 42 percent of white Southerners and 12 percent of white non-Southerners, with milder prejudicial attitudes in perhaps an additional 10 percent of each population.

The force of Kuhlinski's study was that its methodology was designed to avoid the "social desirability" problem of poll taking, which is a phenomenon where people change their answers to match what they think is the "right" or "moral" answer. But the extent to which the reported prejudicial attitudes translate into voting behavior was beyond the scope of his study. Consistent with the work of Stanford's Paul M. Sniderman and other distinguished scholars, Kuhlinski did find that many nonracist whites resent race preferences. Manifestly, however, sufficient numbers of unprejudiced whites exist in every Northern state, and, most likely, in every Southern one as well—particularly when combined with black voters—to elect a black to any given office. And even antiblack prejudice afflicting 42 percent of whites in the South has not prevented blacks from winning any number of statewide contests in that region.

Of course, it is intuitively obvious that a liberal black Democrat campaigning for a Southern state legislative or congressional seat will also face political obstacles in a predominantly white district that have little or nothing to do with race beyond the extent to which race is itself a factor in determining one's political outlook. Most black candidates are Democratic and politically liberal. And increasingly, white Southern voters tend to be not only political conservatives, but also Republicans as well. But even whites with a threshold prejudice against blacks may rise above such prejudice if the "right" kind of black candidate comes along. Representative Cleo James, a liberal Democrat, lost his 1995 race for the governorship of Louisiana in a contest where whites and blacks voted along racial lines nearly 90 percent of the time. But would a conservative black Republican like Representative Gary Franks or J. C. Watt have suffered the same fate? Unlikely. And according to early public opinion surveys on the 1996 presidential campaign, had General Colin Powell chosen to run, those who feel most strongly that blacks cannot compete without race-conscious districting could well have wound up making their case to the nation's first black president.

As to the ability of minorities to win elections in predominantly white districts, the trend is overwhelmingly favorable. Political scientists have worn out their hard drives trying to calculate black chances in white districts and whether racial redistricting was necessary. Susan Welch of the University of Nebraska found that at-large systems in cities with large black populations do not provide quite as much representation as the single-member district method, but "the differences among systems no longer achieve statistical significance." Interestingly, Welch's study also found that local election structures did not seem to make any difference for Hispanic candidates.

A recent study by Charles S. Bullock III and A. Brock Smith of local runoff elections noted that since 1977, black primary front-runners have fared about as well as whites when facing a white in the runoff election. The two found that black primary leaders were nominated in 71.4 percent of the contests after 1977, compared with a 20 percent success rate over the previous seven years. Their conclusions explicitly rebuked both the complaints of Jesse Jackson, who found racism in the runoff system, and the Civil Rights Division at Justice, which routinely refuses to preclear every runoff arrangement it can get its hands on. According to Bullock and Smith, "[i]t already appears that runoffs constitute little more of a barrier for black than for white primary leaders. Black candidates for whom runoffs are most troublesome are those who face another black and those who placed second to a white in the primary."

Likewise, according to statistics compiled by the Joint Center for Political and Economic Studies, there were 1,469 black elected officials in 1970, the first year a survey was taken, and 8,015 in 1993, the last year for which figures are available. While these particular figures are not broken down into the kind of district involved, the available evidence is that the increase includes progress across the range of electoral districts—single-member, multimember, and at-large.

As of January 1994, a total of eighteen blacks held statewide office in fifteen states including Alabama, Florida, Georgia, North Carolina, and Texas. The previous year, L. Douglas Wilder had completed his term as governor of Virginia and, the year before that Carol Moseley-Braun was elected to the United States Senate from Illinois, becoming the first African American to sit in the Senate since Edward Brooke of Massachusetts lost his 1978 bid for a third term. In November 1994, J. C. Watt was elected to the U.S. House of Representatives from the Fourth District of Oklahoma, becoming the seventh black since the 1970s to represent a congressional district where a majority of the voters were white.

That same month H. Carl McCall, an African American, was the sole statewide Democrat to survive the Democratic debacle in New York State, winning reelection as state comptroller on a ticket headed by former Governor Mario Cuomo.

Blacks have tended to fare well in municipal elections. As of June 1995, they served as mayors in thirty-four cities with populations of 50,000 or more. Thirteen of those cities had majority white populations, including Dallas; Seattle; Cleveland; Denver; Kansas City, Missouri; St. Louis; and Minneapolis. Within the past decade, blacks have served as mayors of the nation's three largest cities—New York, Chicago, and Los Angeles—all of which are predominantly white.

The second half of the argument, that so-called "black" interests cannot be represented without bean-counting racial proportionality, is both manifestly false and contrary to political experience. The election of Franklin Delano Roosevelt in 1932 ushered in an era embracing two-thirds of a century in which political forces increasingly sympathetic to the black social, political, and economic agenda, and often backed by black voting power, controlled the White House, the House of Representatives, the Senate, or all three, not to mention federal and state judiciaries. It has been an era in which industrial unions, traditionally more open to blacks than craft unions, gained primacy in much of American industry; a social safety net was put into place; the heinous regime of "separate but equal" was dismantled; Medicare and Medicaid were enacted; special and remedial educational needs were addressed in unprecedented fashion; voting rights were fully secured; and trillions of dollars were poured into low income housing, urban mass transit, legal aid, welfare, public school assistance, and other programs intended to benefit minority citizens. Regardless of the wisdom of any of these measures, political coalitions embracing and reflecting minority interests have had a monumental impact upon public policy for the better part of seven decades. The inescapable conclusion is that substantive black interests have received a sympathetic hearing in the councils of government for many years running.

The notion that racial groups have an inherent right to hold elective office in rough approximation to their percentage in the population likewise fails on more obvious grounds. Not only were the Fourteenth and Fifteenth Amendments written to preclude racial factoring in the allocation of political rights, but this nation, in devising its electoral system, made a conscious decision to shun the tool of proportional representation in allocating legislative seats. The national tradition instead is "winner-take-all" within legislative districts, the theory being that too much democracy—the representation of every political faction able to achieve a threshold total of the vote—can be as troublesome as too little. The system assumes that over time there will be a "balancing of inequities," that the party underrepresented today will be overrepresented tomorrow, and that, in any event, the system will benefit from the kind of coalition building that occurs among factions aware they will never get to the table if they insist on going it alone.

Italy, New Zealand, and other Western democracies have chosen to go the proportional route. Israel rewards every political party achieving at least 2 percent of the vote with at least one seat in its Knesset (Israel's parliament). As a result fanatical religious parties are often able to topple a government. In the mid-1980s, the same system meant that the parliamentary answer to the highly emotional question, "Who is a Jew?" and therefore entitled to immigrate to Israel, turned on the votes of Palestinian communists elected to the Knesset from Arab communities inside the state's pre-1967 boundaries. It may be that the Congress of the United States could benefit from a handful of "Perotistas," some black Islamic representatives spouting the numerological insights of

Louis Farrakhan, a fanatic or two in the mold of David Duke, and a handful of other fringe characters unable to win pluralities in traditionally drawn districts. But it is not self-evident that in deciding otherwise, the architects of American Democracy burdened future generations with a wrong begging for correction.

Advocates of race-conscious districting have two further policy hurdles to overcome even on the assumption that they face some electoral disadvantage arising from white prejudice. The first, to borrow from the economic realm, is simply one of marginal value versus marginal cost. How many black congressional or state legislative districts would disappear if the special effort to create such districts were abandoned, assuming of course that all the other non-affirmative action–style protections of black voting rights were left in place? At the congressional level, estimates vary, but a district-by-district review suggests that no more than a dozen would be seriously vulnerable to legal challenge, nearly all in the South. As to state legislatures, Democratic and Republican state chairmen and executive directors throughout the South say that although they tried to increase black state house and senate representation following the 1990 census, most of the districts so created could pass muster under traditional districting standards.

Juxtaposed with the modest additional number of blacks who owe their seats directly to racial gerrymandering are the costs of the intramural battles between black and white Democrats; the numerical Republican gains—remember, the creation of a single majority black district can create GOP opportunities in two or three surrounding districts; "white flight" to the Republican party; the segregationist mentality fostered; and the perception that blacks are somehow "different" from the rest of society, unable to participate equally in traditional endeavors without special help from a paternal government.

The separation of voting blocs by race tends to polarize the political behavior of each. A black and a white running for a school board seat in an at-large or multimember district, or a racially heterogeneous one, may campaign for the equalization of per-school expenditures, a new bond issue, or the need for greater efforts to hire well-qualified, experienced teachers in schools throughout the district. That same black, campaigning in a specially constructed majority–minority district, may push for an Afrocentric curriculum and a faculty bulging with black role models, while the white running in an overwhelmingly majority district may wind up campaigning for a voucher program to support parents electing to send children to private schools together with a freeze on property tax increases. Such polarization is already evident in state legislative and congressional districts apportioned by race.

The fact that a minority may have only 25 percent or 30 percent of the voters in a particular district does not mean that its influence there is negligible. On the contrary, the combination of a number of diverse groups in a single district often produces the compromise, mutual concessions, and even mutual understanding that create not only democratic law, but *a democratic society*. As Supreme Court Justice Souter has written, in words that would have been familiar stuff to every ethnic ward healer of halcyon days, "minority voters are not immune from the obligation to pull, haul, and trade to find common political ground, the virtue of which is not to be slighted in applying a statute meant to hasten the waning of racism in American politics."

Thirty years earlier in a voting district case, Justice Douglas wrote, "When racial or religious lines are drawn by the state, the multiracial, multireligious communities that our Constitution seeks to weld together as one become separatist; antagonism that relates to race or religion rather than to political issues are generated; communities seek not the best representative but the best racial or religious partisan. Since that system is at war with the democratic ideal, it should find no footing here." Likewise, many years earlier, protesting the bifurcation of a Hasidic community in New York City in order to establish a majority black district, Chief Justice Burger wrote that such practice "tends to sustain the existence of ghettos by promoting the notion that political clout is to be gained or maintained by marshaling particular racial, ethnic, or religious groups in enclaves."

Minorities have the right to institutions that are neutral and officials who perform fairly. They have the right to full protection in the exercise of their franchise and to protection against deliberate acts designed to dilute their voting strength. But attempts to cure bias by introducing more bias into the law disserves all concerned. Such an approach rankles white constituencies, even those not given to lengthy reflection on the shape of their voting districts. It is increasingly questioned by thoughtful blacks and is being challenged and, in some leading cases, overturned by the courts. And, as was demonstrated in 1994, it undermines the very political interests of those it was enacted to protect. Perversely, it appears to be creating its own reality as whites, particularly in the South, flock to a Republican party whose legislative agenda could not be farther from that of black America.

Yet racial redistricting continues to enjoy the fervent endorsement of most black leaders. As with their support for the welfare institutions of the 1960s, this leadership seems in many cases to have moved beyond politics, even beyond ideology, to a self-destructive cultist form of advocacy. Here ritual, cant, and mindless political orthodoxy are exalted. Results are all but ignored.

■   ■   ■

Of all the black members of Congress now in their first or second terms, Melvin L. Watt seems to inspire as many heartfelt expressions of respect as any. A tall, slender, highly articulate graduate of the University of North Carolina and Yale Law School, Watt worked his way up from a "tin-roofed house with no electricity or running water," to a high visibility civil rights law practice in Charlotte. He also served as an advisor to Mayor Harvey Gantt and had helped run Gantt's losing campaign for a second term as mayor of Charlotte and his later narrow loss for the U.S. Senate seat held by the venomous Jesse Helms.

Watt would come to consider Gantt's defeat in Charlotte a betrayal by a white business community which had invited international attention to his election as proof that Charlotte was, like Atlanta, "too busy to hate." And he would never forget Helms's last minute appeal to white concerns about affirmative action with ads that showed white hands being passed over for blacks' in the quest for jobs. Reminded that Gantt ran about as strongly against Helms as had the popular white Democratic governor, Jim Hunt, Watt replied, "Yes, but the profile was different. We didn't get anywhere near as many white votes."

In his own newly defined district, North Carolina's Twelfth, Watt didn't need many white votes. In fact, while he got tens of thousands of them, he could have been elected by black votes alone. His district is the product of an apportionment scheme forced on the state by the Bush Justice Department. The odd shape of the district ultimately drawn has been widely remarked upon, rarely in kindness. Mickey Micheaux, who trailed Watt in the 1992 primary, said, "I love the district because I can drive down I-85 with both car doors open and hit every person in the district."

When white residents of the district sued to dismantle it on the ground that it unlawfully segregated North Carolinians by race, the state found itself in the rather anomalous position of defending a scheme it had done everything it could not to enact. But without approval from Justice, North Carolina couldn't conduct an election.

By the time the case reached the Supreme Court, the Clinton Justice Department had replaced the Bush Justice Department and the style of the case now read, *Shaw v. Reno*.

Writing for a 5–4 Court majority in *Shaw*, Justice O'Connor noted that of the ten counties through which it passed, "five are cut into three different districts; even towns are divided," and likened it to the "uncouth 28-sided figure" which had been struck as an illegal exclusion of black enfranchisement in the seminal *Gomillion* case nearly thirty years earlier. The Court held that the odd manner in which the district was drawn established a presumption of racial preferencing, which is subject to "strict scrutiny," and must be justified by a "compelling state interest."

O'Connor also seemed to imply that had those who had drawn the boundary been less blatant while achieving the same end, the district may have passed constitutional muster. The most eloquent and quoted passage of her opinion reinforces the view that, for Justice O'Connor at least, image is everything:

> We believe that reapportionment is one area in which appearances do matter. A reapportionment plan that includes in one district individuals who belong to the same race, but who are otherwise widely separated by geographical and political boundaries, and who may have little in common with one another but the color of their skin, bears an uncomfortable resemblance to political apartheid. It reinforces the perception that members of the same racial group—regardless of their age, education, economic status, or the community in which they live—think alike, share the same political interests, and will prefer the same candidates at the polls. We have rejected such perceptions elsewhere as impermissible racial stereotypes.

Liberal commentators were stunned and irate, and more than a bit puzzled by *Shaw*. The opinion did seem to raise more questions than it answered:

■ If the state is required by the act and *Thornburg v. Gingles* to establish majority–minority districts, doesn't that in turn establish the sort of "compelling state need" necessary to justify the race-conscious remedy?

■ Why is it "apartheid" to establish a district which is 55 percent black and 45 percent white while some districts in the United States are 95 percent to 99 percent white?

■ If "a reapportionment scheme so irrational on its face that it can be understood only as an effort to segregate voters into separate voting districts because of their race" is subject to strict judicial review, at what level of ugly draftsmanship is the Court's taste for geographic symmetry offended?

■ If a district were less bizarre but no less race conscious in origin or purpose, would that be okay?

The Court would eventually address these very questions in the 1995 case *Miller v. Johnson*. That case, which would not be decided until seven months after the 1994 elections, arose from the results of the 1990 census. Following that census, Georgia gained an eleventh House seat. The legislature prepared a redistricting plan that created a second majority black district for the state, the most that could be conveniently drawn for the state's 27 percent black population.

Black leaders, however, assisted by the NAACP and the American Civil Liberties Union (ACLU) came up with a "max-black" plan of their own, providing for a third black district. The Bush

Justice Department supported the "max-black" plan and told the legislature it would accept nothing less than the three black seats. The ultimate result was a third minority district stretching for 260 miles, embracing four distinct and different urban centers, and uniting some of Atlanta's upscale black community with the poor rural communities of coastal Chatham County.

The results were devastatingly clear, not only in Republican gains, but racial polarization and white flight from the Democratic party. As *The Almanac of American Politics* put it, "[t]he plan had two unintended consequences: huge Republican gains and a lawsuit that threatened the third black-majority seat. Republicans won four of the eight white-majority seats in 1992, two because black voters in adjacent areas were cordoned off into black-majority districts; they won three more of the white-majority seats in 1994, two of the seats made more Republican by the black-majority district lines...."

After the election, Representative Nathan Deal was Georgia's sole remaining white Democrat in the House of Representatives. A conservative, he was the author of the Democratic alternative to Newt Gingrich's welfare reform plan. In March 1995, he told a reporter, "I am the last Democrat who will ever represent the Ninth. The day of the white conservative Democrat in Georgia is over." Two weeks later, Deal declared himself a Republican. The Georgia congressional delegation now consisted of three black Democrats and eight white Republicans. "The racial-partisan polarization of Georgia's delegation represents the realization of the majority–minority districts' critics' worst fears regarding the long-term implications of current voting-rights policy," acknowledged David Bositis of the Joint Center. Months later, on 9 October 1995, Sam Nunn, the last surviving white Democratic member of Georgia's congressional delegation and a true institution in the United States Senate, added an exclamation point to

Bositis's analysis, announcing he would retire from the Senate after twenty-four years of service.

With Republican control of the Congress came the Contract with America program of recision packages, welfare cuts, Medicaid revisions, projected budget balances, and substantial tax cuts. By outmaneuvering the GOP politically during the closing days of the first session, President Clinton was able to prevent most of the conservative agenda from immediately becoming law. But he had done so at the cost of allowing Republicans to define national priorities, and the series of continuing resolutions he was forced to accept did little to invigorate Democratic hopes for better times ahead. Perhaps Clinton himself wrote the definitive epitaph for the black political agenda in his 1996 State of the Union message when he declared, "The era of big government is over."

To House Democrats, the power and amenities that went with majority status had become a way of life and few enjoyed the loss of staff, the absence of any real control over the legislative agenda, or the lack of attention from the media and the lobbyists.

But to CBC members the days were particularly painful. The Great Society edifice of Lyndon B. Johnson, shaky for years, seemed in danger of crashing down on the backs of its longtime beneficiaries, their constituents. Affirmative action was under attack. Each day brought another assault on a favored program and more frustration and anger for CBC members who had felt so triumphant two years before.

Following one legislative setback, Major Owens of New York described his Republican protagonists as "high tech barbarians." When the House passed legislation revoking tax benefits for those selling broadcast licenses and related assets to minorities, Charles Rangel of New York compared the "scapegoating" of blacks with Hitler's assault on the Jews. Georgia's John Lewis, long ago viciously beaten on the voting rights march to Selma and later an official in Bobby Kennedy's presidential campaign, also likened Republican social policy to the Nazi roundup of Jews and other disfavored citizens: "They're coming for the poor. They're coming for the sick, the elderly, and the disabled. This is the Contract with America." And in early 1996, as if to underline the diminished Black Caucus role in the new Congress, Kweise Mfume, the former CBC chairman and among the most brilliant and articulate men in the Congress, left to become executive director of the NAACP, an organization many believed had been eclipsed by the power of elected black officials.

Black representatives and interest groups reject suggestions that their fetish with majority–minority districts was even partly to blame for their plight. Yet, the evidence suggests that racial redistricting had directly cost Democrats about thirteen House seats, had strengthened GOP control of others, and had placed still others within Republican reach. David L. Lublin of the University of South Carolina, among the foremost academic students of redistricting, estimates that the Democrats lost as many as two seats in Alabama, two in Florida, three in Georgia, one in Illinois, one in New Jersey, and three in North Carolina, while strengthening one in Maryland and two in South Carolina.

Less visible but of equal importance to the public is the transformation of Southern politics at the state legislative level. In South Carolina, for instance, a coalition of blacks and Republicans, aided by pressure from the Justice Department, worked together to create at least seven additional minority districts. The result: in the 1994 election, the South Carolina state house went Republican for the first time since Reconstruction. The house was made up of sixteen Republicans, all white, and six Democrats, all black.

"There is no doubt that the application of the Voting Rights Act is generating white flight from the Democratic party," says Trey Walker, executive director of the state GOP. "To be honest, some conservative Republicans like myself would rather not be doing this because, in principle, we're against racial districting. But golly, this thing has just been thrown in our laps."

Now the same black–Republican coalition has created a new redistricting plan for the state senate. Walker predicts that in 1996, that chamber will go Republican as well. Similar trends were evident throughout the South, though in a few states such as Louisiana and Texas skillful Democratic gerrymandering controlled the damage. Still, in every one of the eleven states of the Old Confederacy, redistricting after 1990 increased black Democratic seats, but cost the Democrats seats overall.

On 29 June 1995, the Court in *Miller v. Johnson* threw out the Georgia "max-black" plan. Writing for a 5–4 majority on a bitterly divided court, Justice Kennedy minced few words. The Fourteenth Amendment guarantees equal protection of the law: "[i]ts central mandate is racial neutrality in governmental decision making." Further, he held, defenders of the apportionment scheme had misconstrued the Court's holding in *Shaw v. Reno*. There, the bizarre configuration of the district was not the evil. Rather, it was merely evidence "that the state has used race as a basis for separating voters into districts. Just as the state may not, absent extraordinary justification, segregate citizens on the basis of race in its public parks, buses, golf courses, beaches, and schools, so did we recognize in *Shaw* that it may not separate its citizens into different voting districts on the basis of race."

And since the authority for the "max-black" plan was the amendments added to the Voting Rights Act in 1982, many students of constitutional law believe that those amendments, utterly central to the act today, are just a whisker—or, more to the point, a plucked eyelash—from being declared unconstitutional by five Justices.

In her *Miller* dissent, Justice Ginsburg issued a strong

reminder of the role ethnic and racial politics has played in political life and wondered why what was so right in Boston, New York City, and Chicago should be so wrong in Georgia. "To accommodate the reality of ethnic bonds, legislatures have long drawn voting districts along ethnic lines," she wrote. "Our nation's cities are full of districts identified by their ethnic character—Chinese, Irish, Italian, Jewish, Polish, Russian, for example." She cited a horseshoe district in Jersey City which lumped together most of the city's Irish Catholics and a San Francisco legislator who wanted a district drawn following Catholic parish lines so as to keep all parishes where he attended baptisms, weddings, and funerals in his district. "The creation of ethnic districts reflecting felt identity is not ordinarily viewed as offensive or demeaning to those included in the delineation."

No, it isn't, and without the heavy hand of federal intervention once it was no longer needed to ensure the right to vote, one could easily imagine things developing precisely that way in the South. State Democratic leaders would have approached black leaders trying to spread out the blacks in a sufficient number of congressional districts to elect the maximum number of Democrats. In return, black leaders would have demanded patronage, services, important projects, and programs, moving from there to the inclusion of black candidates on the ticket for a variety of offices, perhaps then demanding a newly created district which, while respecting traditional political boundaries, would have ensured the election of a black to Congress or the state legislature.

These are all voluntary and natural political acts, part of the "pushing and hauling" Justice Souter had referred to.

But it is *unnatural* for state political leaders to carve out minority districts that result in *fewer* elected representatives for their own party. It is *unnatural* to risk the resegregation of political parties in the South in a way that is inimical to the interests of the party controlling the process. It is *unnatural* to give the opposition party a chance of winning and keeping control of the U.S. House of Representatives and of unprecedented gains in the state legislatures. And when these *unnatural* acts are forced upon state parties by the Department of Justice, asserting that it is enforcing federal law in so doing, we are no longer playing ethnic politics as it always has been played. Rather than legislatively ratifying political deals made at the grassroots level, we are imposing abnormal racial prescriptions on normal political processes. And that the Constitution forbids.

Reaction to *Miller* was strong, with most black leaders criticizing Kennedy's position. Cynthia A. McKinney, the two-term representative from Georgia's Eleventh District, called the Georgia redistricting decision "the ultimate bleaching of the U.S. Congress," and Wade Henderson, director of the Washington, D.C., office of the NAACP, called it "the first step in the resegregation of American Democracy."

Both black and white Georgia Democrats were left with bitter feelings. The blacks felt that with a few discreet changes of boundary, three majority–minority districts would have survived. Whites, led by the retiring state house speaker, Tom Murphy, could not comprehend how liberal black Democrats could align themselves with Republicans in moves that would cost their party one or more congressional seats. And Benjamin Ginsberg, an architect of the strange black–Republican coalition back in the 1980s, expressed contemptuous wonder that so many conservative Republicans had, on ideological grounds, turned against racial redistricting. "Until the mid-1990s," he said, "the blacks were underrepresented and the Republicans were underrepresented. Now we are both enjoying a semblance of justice and my good friends want to throw it away."

Within days of the decision, the state's black and GOP leadership were again conferring on plans to salvage as much of the arrangement as possible. By late August, when a special legislative session convened in Atlanta, the black–Republican entente was the single most significant feature of the gathering, elegantly reflected by the makeup of the state's congressional delegation—which by then featured three black Democrats and eight white Republicans. But the session ended in stalemate, returning the matter to the lower federal courts which in late autumn mandated an arrangement providing for only a single majority black district.

Some weeks after the Georgia decision, Melvin Watt, whose North Carolina District was the subject of *Shaw v. Reno* which would soon be coming back to the Supreme Court, mused over whether maximizing the number of blacks in Congress was worth Republican control. "I can answer that question informationally or as a black politician," he said. "Informationally, we are not the ones who lost the House to the Republicans and no study says we did."

Granted, came the reply, but you played a role. And the notion of the South dividing into black Democrats versus white Republicans might have been a subtle factor in a number of other districts.

"Or I can answer it as a black representative," he continued, ignoring the observation. "Black folks are different from white folks. They think differently. Look at the O. J. trial and the differences in perceptions between whites and blacks. And black folks need people representing them who understand them."

Well, don't answer it informationally. And don't answer it as an elected black official. How about answering it as a man who sits on the Judiciary Committee and waits to be recognized by Republican Chairman Henry Hyde. Answer it as a representative with no legislative agenda except trying to stop as much of the Contract with America as you can. Answer it from the standpoint of what kind of power the Congressional Black Caucus wielded when you came to Washington four years ago and what power it wields today.

"That's tough," smiled Watt. "That's tough."

13

EDUCATION VERSUS IDEOLOGY

The *New York Times* of 4 June 1995 reported a controversy at the high school in Ithaca, New York, over whether to discontinue the honors program for academically gifted students. The program offers advanced placement college level courses in English, math, and the sciences for students who excel in these subjects and who, for the most part, are heading for the nation's premier institutions of higher learning. The percentage of honors students at Ithaca High is substantial. More than a quarter of the student body have parents on the faculties of Cornell University or Ithaca College. A reverence for learning in the home is about as good a predictor as there is of high-achieving children.

A substantially less difficult series of academic courses is offered for students planning to attend less selective colleges, while those unlikely to pursue higher education usually enroll in "local" level courses. The school's superintendent, Dr. James E. Lothridge, described by the *New York Times* as "a black educator who grew up in the segregated South and has a strong interest in promoting diversity," sought to end the honors program as a first step in what he hoped would be the total elimination of all forms of "tracking."

In Dr. Lothridge's view, putting high school seniors capable of understanding college-level science in the same class as those who would have a hard time explaining why Newton's apple didn't fall up, has its charm. As the *Times* explained, "students would be exposed to a richer spectrum of humanity and those with, say, good mechanical intuition could help those more adept at abstract theory and vice versa." In other words, Joey—talented in the sciences—may now come home from physics class knowing less about the theory of relativity than had the class been composed of uniformly good science students, but when Daddy's car rattles, the "good mechanical intuition" Joey developed by associating with Herb—a future Exxon station proprietor—may lead him to suggest a visit to the Midas shop. The long-run beneficiary of all this, of course, is neither Joey nor Herb, but Japan.

Many parents in Ithaca seemed to fear their children would be swept out to sea in the undertow of this educational egalitarianism. Without exception, the nation's premier universities like to see challenging courses on a high school resume. The preparation itself has future value. "They won't be prepared to take chemistry at Cornell," warned one Ithaca parent, himself a chemistry professor. "It's a shameful way to treat bright students." Shortly after initiating the controversy at Ithaca High School, Dr. Lothridge moved to Long Island and another superintendent's job. Ithaca retained its tracking system.

With the notable exception of Southern and border state school districts still under federal court supervision as they complete the transition away from segregation, most state and local districts control the character and financing of elementary and secondary schools.

Nevertheless, such issues as school financing, ability grouping, and alternatives to the exclusive state reliance on public schools are being contested in dozens of states and hundreds of individual districts nationwide. And when one explores the situation in the trenches, the old face of affirmative action can be spotted wearing yet another mask. Educational arrangements rooted in sound theory and practice find themselves under attack because of their "disparate impact" upon blacks and other minorities. Hard numerical funding formulas (more money = better schools) are pushed as though their logic were self-evident, when in fact the data suggest otherwise. Quack racial theories drive policy in many a minority-controlled district. A worthy striving for fairness degenerates into crass egalitarianism. In such an environment, the rights of the gifted are sacrificed, as is the ability of more ordinary but conscientious students to receive an education unburdened by the unruly, the borderline truants, and those whose physical or emotional disability distracts teacher and student alike. At the same time, communities committed to spending what it takes to provide the best education are effectively enjoined by legislative fiat from making their schools too good, lest their advantage over less affluent districts be magnified.

Not all students are alike and not all efforts to organize them in ways that enhance their individual educational talent are alike. In any given grade, 5 percent to 10 percent of the students may have exceptional math and science skills and a similar percentage—often with considerable overlap—may have reading and writing skills far beyond their grade level. At the other end of the spectrum a similar percentage—also with substantial overlap—may be slow learners in math and English. At the present, districts with high concentrations of black and Hispanic students tend to have relatively fewer "gifted and talented" students and relatively more slow learners and behavior problems. In districts with mixed populations, the black and Hispanic students, on average, perform less well academically than whites and Asians. The gap has been closing slowly for a number of years and, on any given day, the media may report programs which have actually raised the level of minority student achievement, particularly in the lower grades. Still, the bias toward equal outcomes runs so deep within the community of the politically correct that any program recognizing the fact of different aptitudes and seeking to provide reasonable opportunity for the gifted as well as the disadvantaged is bound to come under intense fire.

Let us take a hypothetical fifth grade with one hundred children having the range of abilities described above and enough space and faculty to accommodate five classes. School administrators could theoretically avail themselves of any of the following options:

- Randomly assign the students to the five classes, and cover the material suggested for fifth graders by the state board of regents.
- Employ what is known as the "XYZ Ability Grouping," placing the highest twenty achievers as measured by math and verbal aptitude scores plus IQ in one class, the next highest in a second class, and so on. But under the XYZ method, teachers cover identical material in all classes.
- Randomly assign each class, but ask the teacher to work informally with different students who require a faster or slower pace. If time permits, introduce the best students to more advanced material.
- Randomly assign each class, but during reading, math, and perhaps social studies periods, arrange the students into various ability groups. Try to enrich the program of the better learners by including special material and,

if possible, accelerate their work so they begin covering sixth grade material before the year is over.

- Randomly assign each class, but during reading, math, and perhaps social studies periods, mix the students from one class with those from another, or even another grade so that substantial groups of students are working with others of similar ability. Enrich the programs of the better learners with outside reading and special projects, and accelerate their learning, permitting them to cover some sixth grade work by year's end. "Top 5 percenters" in math or English may well end up working not only at seventh or eighth grade levels, but actually with students from those grades. Less challenging material is covered in the "slower" classes.

- Same as the above, only try to enrich the curriculum for the more modest achievers as well, devising ways of stimulating their minds along with their personal commitments to learning. Further, permit "group jumping" so that any student developing his or her skills can move up to a higher level.

- Simply describe the enriched curriculum and accelerated learning opportunities available, and permit a student or parent to determine whether the student should enroll. Then go at a "sink or swim" pace for each class, encouraging reassessments as the year progresses.

(Keep in mind that although the term "tracking" is sometimes used by casual commentators to describe what we have defined as "ability grouping," educators usually employ "tracking" to mean a process that occurs early in high school whereby, usually through self-selection, students are given a curriculum of "academic," "general," or "vocational" courses in math, English, and other subjects. Certainly, the group to which a student is assigned in the lower grades will be somewhat predictive of the "track" he or she winds up in later on; this is not, however, because the student was favored or disfavored, but because the initial selection process tends to identify students by their academic potentials with considerable accuracy.)

Contemplating the need to explain things to, let us say, a PTA meeting, it is clear that any one of the above options except the first will involve some "ability grouping"—defined by Professor James J. Gallagher of the University of North Carolina as "the separation of same-grade schoolchildren into groups or classes according to school aptitude or past school performance."

It is also clear that in all situations but the first, relatively more of the black and Hispanic children in our fifth grade will wind up either in a class or a group of slower learners. Clearly, both tracking and ability grouping can be abused to herd children into programs along racial or ethnic lines no matter their individual capabilities, as shown in a handful of documented instances. But the record is also clear that tracking and ability grouping can be of considerable benefit to all students if the program is run in a way that takes account of individual differences and seeks to improve the performance of all. There is nothing progressive about treating all students alike. Rather that sort of mindless egalitarianism all but ensures that neither the gifted nor the slow learner will reach his or her full potential.

Ability grouping has been with us for more than a century, at least since 1891 when the "Cambridge Double Track Plan" put the high-achieving children into classes that covered six years in four. By 1900, New York City had established "special progress" classes in which grades seven to nine were covered in two years. The practice has been a tempting target over the years for John Dewey progressivists, social reformers, civil rights activists, and others, and is under continuous assault in hundreds of districts nationwide. By carefully selecting data from hundreds of studies over the years, and ignoring the rest, they have tried to make the case that ability grouping produces negligible positive results while imposing the stigma of academic mediocrity upon blacks and others. Once the performance of ability grouping is sufficiently discredited, critics of the practice find that school boards, PTAs, or city councils tend to be more sympathetic to social equity concerns.

But the record is otherwise. Both Johns Hopkins University and the University of Michigan have conducted massive "mega-analysis" studies of ability grouping, and both have concluded that where properly employed the practice can be of material benefit to gifted students.

Professor Robert E. Slavin of Johns Hopkins opposes most ability grouping on social equity grounds. But he is an impeccably honest scholar who does not dodge the evidence. In the Summer 1993 *College Board Review,* Slavin conceded that algebra enrichment programs for talented seventh graders produced good results. He further noted: "There is also evidence to support use of the Joplin Plan, in which students are placed in mixed-ability classes for most of the day, but are regrouped according to reading performance across grade lines. Acceleration programs for extremely able students have been supported by research, and advanced placement and other advanced course work for high school students can be beneficial."

The Michigan study showed that ability grouping accompanied by curriculum adjustments benefited students of all groups. According to Dr. James A. Kulik of Michigan, "[t]he typical pupil in a mixed ability class might gain 1.0 years on a grade-equivalent scale in a year, whereas the typical pupil in a cross-grade or within-class program would gain 1.2 to 1.3 years. Effects were similar for high-, middle-, and low-aptitude students."

Further, the study showed that when ability grouped classes were discontinued, the performance of gifted students regressed. Albert Shanker, who has spent much of his quarter-century tenure as president of the American Federation of Teachers battling an attack on academic standards that has sometimes masqueraded as ethnic pride and sometimes as egalitarianism, says, "If tracking and ability grouping are bad for elementary and high school students, why are they so good at Harvard and Stanford? If an honors program isn't a glorified form of ability grouping, what is it?"

In fact, contrary to the cries of those who discern some massive psychic insult to those of modest academic talent, even where the academic benefits of grouping are negligible, as with XYZ grouping, the effect upon the self-esteem of those in the lower group is positive. The reason: with the high achievers out of the way, they can "come out of their shells" and express themselves in class with greater self-confidence.

Dr. Joseph S. Renzulli of the University of Connecticut's National Research Center on the Gifted and Talented says that those who want to get rid of school honors programs and other enriched programs are aiming at the wrong target. "Programs for the gifted and talented are working well," he says. "Further, since the mid-'60s, we've spent close to a trillion dollars on compensatory education for the disadvantaged. But we're doing a bad job getting their scores up."

Renzuli adds, "We have failed because we're using special education departments as 'drill and kill' centers. We find out what the kid can't do, won't do, doesn't want to do, and never will do, and then we spend most of the year drilling it into him."

According to Renzuli, the answer is to improve programs for the disadvantaged, not to "dumb down" the better programs. "At a time when our own students are falling farther and farther behind the international competition, I fail to see why we should take the calculated step of eliminating programs that provide opportunities for our best students to reach their full potentials."

Professor Gallagher has argued that "the modest educational strategy of ability grouping has become hostage to major social forces in the society struggling for power and influence." He does not agree with "the champions of political correctness" that the relatively poor performance of blacks and Hispanics is attributable to Western-oriented subjects or a long-range vista that is short on economic opportunity and promise. Instead, he sees something far more basic at work. "Students from black and Hispanic cultures do not, as a group, appear to spend as much time on their academic lessons as do other groups in the society that are outperforming them. It is also the reason for the perceived superiority of Asian students—who do seem to work harder and longer hours than the students with whom they are competing. The rules of practice are immutable on this point."

The rule of law is also immutable on the subject of ability grouping. It is lawful even if its application tends to concentrate the races in specific classes. In the leading 1975 case, *McNeal v. Tate County School District*, the Fifth Circuit Court of Appeals held: "School districts ought to be, and are, free to use such grouping whenever it does not have a racially discriminatory effect. If it does cause segregation, whether in classrooms or schools, ability grouping may nevertheless be permitted in an otherwise unitary system if the school district can demonstrate that its assignment method is not based on the present results of past segregation or will remedy such results through better educational opportunities."

In furtherance of President Clinton's "Goals 2000: Educate America Act," an increasing number of states have begun requiring high school graduating seniors to pass minimum competency exams in such areas as reading comprehension and math in order to earn their diplomas. The theory, of course, is that colleges, future employers, the military, and others have the right to interpret that diploma as reflecting at least the ability to read, write, understand simple mathematical concepts, and appreciate elementary concepts of citizenship, because these skills are considered the basic foundation upon which future learning can be built.

In Ohio, a not atypical state, the exams are pegged to the level of ninth grade proficiency. Yet from the outset, inner-city school districts with high concentrations of black students were experiencing pass rates in the area of 25 percent. In 1994, the Cleveland branch of the NAACP filed a lawsuit to block the tests and fired off a letter to the U.S. Department of Education's Office of Civil Rights (OCR) urging "your immediate suspension of the requirement for Cleveland students to pass a proficiency test to receive a high school diploma," arguing that "the requirement disparately impacts and violates the rights of the district's minority student population under Title VI (of the Civil Rights Act of 1964)."

Ohio refused to roll over and accept either the implicit racism in the complaint of those purporting to defend the interests of black schoolchildren—that it is unfair to expect black high school seniors to master basic ninth grade level concepts or that the schools they attended were so inadequate as to ill prepare them for the test. The state presented evidence that educational funding levels were generally adequate, with the state itself paying 51 percent of all school district expenditures. Moreover, while the state required every school to teach prescribed courses, the school districts in question were under strict local control with black school boards dominating the educational regime and presiding over teacher hiring.

"We were able to establish that the great variable in test results was school attendance, not race," explained Dr. Robert Moore, assistant superintendent of public instruction for the Ohio Department of Education. "Of those students who came to school on at least 90 percent of the total school days, 92.4 percent passed the proficiency exam. In poor white rural areas, where attendance was no better than in the predominantly black inner cities, the pass rates were as bad as or worse than the inner-city schools. By identifying low attendance patterns and intervening with tutorial assistance, the schools were able to elevate pass rates statewide to over 95 percent." The suit was dismissed, and OCR decided that no action on its part was necessary.

A victory for common sense and educational sanity? Perhaps. But consider that the subject of this controversy was a ninth grade proficiency exam required for a high school diploma. What happens when Ohio, Florida, or any other state seeks to implement standards that truly measure a student's mastery of the work he or she has been pursuing, an exam that is relevant for the student who wishes to become a skilled and productive member of the workforce following high school graduation and for that student's prospective employer? Imagine the fuss that will be raised by the community of advocates whose stock in trade is victimization. And then ask whether those who shape and conduct public policy have the courage to defend their actions. Albert Shanker thinks the inception of the program is not auspicious. "Right now we have the tests and the scores, but they can't be used for any purpose for five years because that would discriminate against those who don't do as well on the tests. And I thought that the purpose of testing was to distinguish levels of performance."

■ ■ ■

When is enough, enough?

Having initially ordered states to put an end to segregation in the schools "with all deliberate speed," the Supreme Court watched for more than a decade and a half as school districts throughout the South defied the decision, circumvented it, or took their "deliberate" time in implementing as little as they could get away with. Finally, in the 1971 case that effectively wrote the end to de jure school segregation, *Swann v. Charlotte-Mecklenburg Board of Education,* the Court not only ordered the immediate eradication of segregation "root and branch," but where segregation had been proven to have resulted from government action, it decreed that the remedy involve not only student attendance patterns, but also faculty hiring and assignments, the placement of auxiliary staff, transportation, extracurricular activities, and facilities.

Thus began a seemingly endless parade of lawsuits in all sections of the country in which individual minority plaintiffs and organizations purporting to represent their interests challenged elementary and secondary school arrangements as racially discriminatory. In those places where district court judges agreed, the litigation often ended with a decree requiring busing to achieve a degree of racial mixing in each school roughly equivalent to that throughout the court's jurisdiction, the targeted hiring and assignment of teachers and other staff, the construction of new facilities so as to equalize opportunity throughout the jurisdiction, the introduction of special education programs to compensate victims of past discrimination, and even the levying of new taxes to pay for all the steps ordered by the court. And where the school district or districts subject to the order had an insufficient tax base to meet the newly required expenditures, the courts might transfer that responsibility to the state, whether or not it had played any role in the initial discrimination.

So long as the federal courts maintained their control over the districts in question the arrangement proved a nifty way for many school systems to acquire the most modern facilities and the finest faculty and staff money could buy while circumventing the often messy business of getting local taxpayers to approve the expenditures. And since for years no court had ever bothered to define what degree of progress was sufficient to bring the period of federal oversight to an end, many local federal judges in effect became one-man boards of education, city councils, and state legislatures, an arrangement for which a fair number acquired a taste.

Finally, in the 1991 case of *Dowell v. Board of Education of Oklahoma City,* the Supreme Court held that in determining whether a school system had, in fact, become unitary, the district courts should review its performance in the light of the old *Swann* criteria, and if procedures involving student assignments, faculty, staff, transportation, extracurricular activities, and facilities could all pass muster, the system should be returned to local control notwithstanding that local officials intended to discontinue mandatory busing and assign children to their own neighborhood schools.

In the wake of *Dowell,* dozens of actions to end federal oversight have been initiated. Many have provided a disturbing glimpse into the results of up to two decades of desegregation efforts. Cleveland, for example, had been under a massive busing regime since 1978. There was no question about the system's "original sin," which involved the deliberate gerrymandering of attendance zones to promote segregation along with "intact" busing whereby children bused from black neighborhoods to predominantly white schools were assigned to classes as a group, thereby reestablishing segregation at the end of the bus ride.

The massive busing ordered by the court was designed to remedy the impact of these earlier practices. But the results have been contrary to the intent of the original black plaintiffs and the court, and contrary to the interests of all of Cleveland's schoolchildren. During the period of court supervised busing, both overall school enrollment and the percentage of white students in the system dropped appreciably, SAT scores in both reading comprehension and math dropped sharply, and the percentage of students graduating from high school dropped from well over 40 percent to below 35 percent. Over the years, the school system computed that desegregation efforts have cost more than $791 million, more than $276 million of which has been spent on busing to achieve racial balance. This during a period when the district was so cramped for funds that elementary school pupils were asked to share textbooks.

An embittered population has approved only one tax increase to support public education in the past twenty-five years. During the spring of 1995, the federal courts ordered the state of Ohio to take over the Cleveland public school system because the district was no longer able to administer or pay for it. In February 1995, George Forbes, president of the NAACP's Cleveland chapter, told the *Cleveland Plain Dealer*, "We have to be honest with people, whether they be black, white, whatever. And being honest means saying that busing no longer serves any useful purpose toward the education and welfare of children in Cleveland today. It must end."

The schools in and around Wilmington, Delaware, which came under federal jurisdiction in 1974 due to the state's history of de jure segregation, provide an even more striking example of judicial futility. By designing a plan whereby students from the inner city were bused to surrounding districts for a total of nine years while those from outside the city were bused to inner-city schools for three consecutive years, the district court was able to achieve perhaps the most integrated school system in the country, in which the white:minority ratio remained at or near 70:30 and in which there were only minor deviations from this ratio among the overwhelming majority of the system's elementary and secondary schools.

But the arrangement was expensive, the costs were borne by the state, and eventually the Republican-controlled state legislature brought suit to end the period of federal oversight. The evidence was overwhelming that all six *Swann* criteria had been met. But although nearly every student in the entire school system had from kindergarten on attended school in conditions of near-perfect equality, black student performance was depressingly far behind that of white children. Among sixth graders in 1992, for example, with a national norm of 50.0, the average reading score for whites was 55.6 and for blacks, 39.0. In math, it was 52.0 for whites and 36.0 for blacks. Whites were represented in far higher numbers in classes where the curriculum was enriched for high achievers and in high school classes associated with the college-bound tracks, even though participation in all such programs was voluntary. Many of the schools' extracurricular activities were similarly self-segregated. Blacks were also subject to disciplinary proceedings at rates far higher than whites.

In opposing the effort to have the Wilmington system declared unitary, an ad hoc civil rights group calling itself "The Coalition to Save Our Children" asked the court to maintain control until black students performed as well as whites on standardized tests and other measures of academic achievement, that is, ensure that blacks elect courses of study that ensured racial balance in each class; participate in extracurricular activities in numbers sufficient to ensure racial balance; not exceed white rates of disciplinary action; have drop-out rates no higher than whites; require special education services at rates no higher than whites; and enroll in and graduate from college at the same rates.

Recalling that even the oldest of these students had not been subjected to so much as a day of racially segregated schooling and that all had participated in one of the most thoroughly integrated school systems in the country, the argument amounted to little more than a naked plea for the courts to use the educational system to attempt to remedy more fundamental problems in society at large, something that would defy the Supreme Court's warning in the *Swann* case that "One vehicle can carry only a limited amount of baggage."

Just how much baggage was evident in statistics recited by the district court from the 1990 U.S. Census and the 1992 Vital Statistics Report of Delaware? The court noted that black households are 2.54 times as likely as white households to have a reporting householder who lacks a high school degree. They are 6.47 times as likely to have children classified as being in poverty, and those that have children are 3.55 times as likely to earn less than $25,000 per year. Blacks are 2.06 times as likely as whites to be unemployed. Their households with children are 3.21 times as likely to be headed by a single parent. The black teenage fertility rate is four times that of white teenagers. Single black women are five times as likely as single whites to give birth to a child. Black children are 5.25 times as likely as white children to be born after inadequate prenatal care and their rate of infant mortality is 2.42 times that for whites.

A leading expert witness in the case testified that these horrific societal disparities are sufficient to explain all but a small fraction of the difference in academic performance between whites and blacks. In other words, white children coming out of the same home and community environment as blacks would fare only marginally better on most standard tests. But the court, finding that the Wilmington school system for years followed remedial court orders in good faith and had in fact established a unitary school system, declined to consider the work still left to be done to close a racial performance gap that was clearly not the product of the way schools were being conducted. Federal jurisdiction was held to be at an end. The case was taken to the Third Circuit Court of Appeals.

By far the most egregious rape of the public treasury in the name of remedial treatment of past victims of discrimination occurred in Missouri where, at the time of the 1954 *Brown v. Board of Education* case, the state was among those segregating schoolchildren on the basis of race. But, unlike its sister states to the south, Missouri engaged in no "massive resistance," but instead pledged compliance with the decision, a pledge which was, in the main, executed in good faith.

During the 1954–55 school year, 18.9 percent of the students in the Kansas City, Missouri, School District (KCMSD) were black. During the next two decades Kansas City's experience was similar to that of other large urban centers. Many whites migrated to the suburbs. Others began sending their children to private schools. As the percentage of blacks in the school population increased, "white flight" gained momentum. By 1961–62, 30 percent of the KCMSD students were black, by 1965–66, the figure reached 40 percent, and by 1975–76, it was 60 percent. At the same time, the academic performance of district students relative to their national peers declined, with most students performing below their grade levels.

In 1977, the KCMSD and several individual residents of the city filed what can most charitably be described as a collusive lawsuit against the state and several federal agencies before District Court Judge Russell G. Clark, who maintains jurisdiction over the case to the present day. The suit alleged that defendants had caused and maintained a pattern of racially segregated schooling throughout the Kansas City metropolitan area. Over the course of a seven-month trial, the case was first dismissed against federal defendants, who clearly had not done anything to contribute to segregation. The court next found that the impact of the alleged segregatory behavior was limited to the KCMSD itself. Therefore, any cure must be limited to that district, thereby ruling out, for example, a merger of city and suburban attendance zones.

The court then converted KCMSD from a very real plaintiff (it had helped initiate the lawsuit in the hope of obtaining state or federal aid) into a nominal defendant and "adversary" of the individual plaintiffs. Judge Clark concluded that both the state and KCMSD had failed to remove the vestiges of segregation from within the district. He found evidence of this in the fact that student achievement scores had been forced down by segregation's aftereffects and, further, that twenty-five schools within the KCMSD could be identified which had at least 90 percent black enrollment.

Coming up with a remedy was tricky. With no interdistrict violation, the court lacked power to order, say, cross-district busing or any other relief directly affecting nonresidents of KCMSD, and, as for the school population within the district, it is very difficult to order additional desegregation with a white population that is under 40 percent and shrinking. Finally, Judge Clark simply "allowed District planners to dream" while the court "provided a mechanism for those dreams to be realized." The dream took the form of a concept the court termed "desegregative attractiveness": building a school system so modern, advanced, and individualized that whites would come flocking back from their private schools and suburbs and, together with resident blacks, would achieve Nirvana—and perhaps raise their performance on standardized tests—in their educational Eden community.

Under the plan, every high school and middle school and most elementary schools in KCMSD were designated "magnet schools." Enforced by district court decrees over the next sixteen years, the facilities included, as the state would note in a Supreme Court brief, "a performing arts middle and high school, a technical school offering vast and varied programs, a school with a large farm and wildlife area, and a $32 million dual-theme high school for computer and Classical Greek-style education, including an indoor running track, gymnastics room, and an Olympic-sized swimming pool and natatorium." In a 1993 Supreme Court decision involving some technical financing issues in the case, Justice Kennedy listed some of the other amenities: High schools in which every classroom will have air conditioning, an alarm system, and fifteen microcomputers; a 2,000-square-foot planetarium; greenhouses and vivariums; a twenty-five-acre farm with an air-conditioned meeting room for 104 people; a model United Nations wired for language translation; broadcast-capable radio and television studios with an editing and animation lab; a temperature controlled art gallery; movie editing and screening rooms; a 3,500-square-foot dust-free diesel mechanics room; 1,875-square-foot elementary school animal rooms for use in a zoo project; swimming pools; and numerous other facilities.

Plaintiffs, together with the American Federation of Teachers, also petitioned the court to order increases in pay for both teachers and other noninstructional employees. Again, Judge Clark proved pliant, to the delight of KCMSD's cooks, custodians, carpenters, laborers, electricians, parking lot attendants, security guards, secretaries, clerical workers, business administrators, and data-processing personnel.

As of early 1995, the costs of the magnet school program, including extra transportation, had amounted to $448 million. Capital expenditures ordered by the court had amounted to over $540 million. Per pupil annual expenditures in KCMSD—excluding capital costs—came to $9,412 compared to figures ranging from $2,854 to $5,956 in the surrounding school districts. With capital costs included, the per pupil KCMSD expenditure came to $13,500 annually, $3,000 more than the next highest district in the state of Missouri.

But none of this seems to have had the desired effect. Since 1986, when the first of Judge Clark's decrees went into effect, there has been some improvement in the performance of KCMSD students, but several grades remain at or below national standards. Overall enrollment in the district's public schools is down 30 percent since 1986; white enrollment is down 40 percent beyond its already low base. Today, the school system is more segregated than ever with black students accounting for 68.3 percent of the school population.

Judge Clark had imposed a remedial regime on the delighted defendant, KCMSD, which was far beyond its ability to finance and which thus drew the state into the picture at a potential cost far exceeding $1 billion. The state appealed on what appeared to be fairly narrow grounds. It challenged the establishment by the district court of student performance on standardized tests as a test of compliance with desegregation, as well as the necessity of salary increases for noninstructional employees.

Astoundingly, the lower court order was affirmed by a divided Eighth Circuit Court of Appeals. But the dissent was vigorous. On the issue of student performance, the dissenters wrote: "To require achievement test scores at or above the national norm is to require the school system to be responsible for circumstances beyond its control. Segregated housing patterns, poverty, street violence, drug usage, criminal activities, and lack of parental involvement, if they exist in the KCMSD, are not the responsibility of the public school system."

And on the question of salaries, the dissenters noted acidly that "logic does not directly relate the pay of parking lot attendants, trash haulers, and food handlers, for instance, to any facet or phase of the desegregation plan or to the constitutional violations."

In the Supreme Court's June 1995 *Missouri v. Jenkins* decision, somewhat overshadowed by public interest in the voting rights and minority set-aside issues also coming down from the Court, a narrow 5–4 majority reversed the Eighth Circuit decision not only on the two grounds actively contested by the state, but also on the issue of the scope of the relief embraced in the "deseg-regative attractiveness" approach. Chief Justice Rehnquist sent the case back to the district court with instructions to weed out any further requirements whose principal purpose was to attract white students from outside the KCMSD since "this *inter*district goal is beyond the scope of the intradistrict violation identified by the District Court." In effect, wrote Rehnquist, "the District Court has devised a remedy to accomplish indirectly what it admittedly lacks the remedial authority to mandate directly: the interdistrict transfer of students." Unless Judge Clark proves even more resourceful than his critics suspect, the Rehnquist decision will begin at least to contain the financial damage from what must surely rank as one of the great constitutional scams in the history of American jurisprudence.

In a noteworthy concurring opinion, Justice Thomas complained that "[i]t never ceases to amaze me that the courts are so willing to assume that anything that is predominantly black must be inferior." Going all the way back to the sociological studies that underpinned *Brown v. Board,* he said, the courts had assumed that black students "suffer an unspecified psychological harm from seg-regation that retards their mental and educational development." Thomas suggested that the approach "relies upon questionable social science research rather than constitutional principle," and that it also "rests on an assumption of black inferiority."

The point of *Brown,* of course, was not that separation itself produced feelings of psychological inequality in blacks, but that such feelings were a product of a regime imposed by a politically dominant white society which relegated blacks to a position of inferiority in both the great and petty pursuits of daily life:

education, employment, access to public and private facilities, voting, housing, even worship. Such a regime would be no less damaging today than it was then, no more constitutionally permissible. Nor would it be acceptable for a society-wide network of private arrangements to impose a degree of de facto segregation which could become as rigid and pernicious as the old de jure system, though in a different way.

The problem is not a black neighborhood any more than it is a Jewish or Italian neighborhood, but rather a series of arrangements that erects a wall of separation between communities. Whether such a system would feed white notions of superiority or black notions of inferiority is speculative. What we do know is that a society in which the most important credential is one's racial or ethnic badge is a society divided against itself, vulnerable to organized group violence, even to dissolution. There is little evidence to show whether the Moslems of Bosnian Herzegovina, the Druse of Lebanon, or the Hutus of Rwanda "suffer an unspecified psychological harm from segregation," but evidence aplenty that a society where tribal associations are exalted above all others is a society in very deep trouble.

The KCMSD situation also suggests the pitfalls of creating institutions less for their well-established traditional educational values than for their usefulness as indirect desegregation tools. Specialty schools, for example, have a long and useful tradition of offering programs of enormous interest to students with exceptional ability or talent. The Bronx High School of Science, Manhattan's High School of Music and Art, Boston Latin School, and Thomas Jefferson High School in Northern Virginia have all provided qualified young people the kind of educational opportunity at the secondary school level which is comparable to or better than the best offered at private schools.

Like most of the specialty schools, the magnet schools offer a distinctive curriculum organized around a particular theme or method of instruction. And like the specialty schools, they draw students from several attendance zones; indeed, nearly 2,500 federally subsidized magnet schools operate in the hope of attracting white students from other zones specifically for the purpose of furthering desegregation efforts. That mandate defines the major difference between magnet and specialty schools: students compete for admission to specialty schools by virtue of aptitude tests or auditions whereas they elect to attend magnate schools because of their interest in its program or facilities and usually need no special credentials to get in.

Because the magnet program is often the product of a court desegregation decree or a deliberate policy decision to enhance integration, it is often inserted into a school in a minority neighborhood. Very often, instead of a "full-site" magnet program which involves the entire school, the authorities adopt a "partial-site" magnet program, where, according to a 1994 article by Kimberly C. West in the *Yale Law Journal,* the program becomes "an enclave in a larger regular school." This can often produce the anomalous result of an integrated school building, but one with classes which are substantially segregated by race, with the white students enrolled in all the magnet courses and the neighborhood black children taking the regular curriculum, a situation compounded by the frequent need to adjust classes to transportation schedules. According to Ms. West's article, "[t]his segregation has led to a horrible irony: desegregation-oriented magnet schools have placed an explicit label of inferiority on the minority children they were designed to serve."

The attempt to achieve diversity through artificial means has led to results which have justifiably made school authorities look like social engineers, idiots, or both. In Montgomery County, Maryland, two Korean girls were prevented from enrolling in a nearby French specialty program because officials did not want to upset the racial balance of their existing school. In nearby Prince George's County, Maryland, a magnet program for gifted and talented students was underenrolled because an insufficient number of white students had applied for it. According to the *Washington Post*, some fifty qualified black children languished on the waiting list for the classes, their slots reserved for whites who were needed to promote integration.

Notions about how to offer the best possible education to the district's schoolchildren seem to have taken a back seat to the question of arbitrary racial balance. Even the venerable Boston Latin School is presently maintaining a 35 percent set-aside for black and Hispanic students, and race-norming its entrance exams. This led the ubiquitous Abigail Thernstrom, best known for her brilliant criticism of the 1982 amendments to the Voting Rights Act, to complain in a *Boston Globe* column, "Give all our kids a high-class education. And treat them not as members of racial and ethnic groups, but as individuals whose skin color is not relevant on a science quiz."

14

WHITES NEED NOT APPLY

om Stewart's stepfather, Frank Gurney, liked to think that he and his boys could work so hard that their little subcontracting company would compete successfully with firms three and four times its size. Frank Gurney, Inc., was founded in Spokane, Washington, in 1959. Its specialty was and is constructing road signs and highway guardrails.

Two of Frank Gurney, Inc.'s, toughest competitors have been Junlo Corporation and Peterson Corporation. Both are larger than Gurney, well run, and skillful. The former, owned by Asian Americans, and the latter, by a woman, always got a good chunk of the available market, but Gurney would fight them for every contract.

On 7 April 1981 Gurney received a letter from the chief estimator for the Associate Sand and Gravel Company, prime contractor on a state road deal on which Gurney had submitted a subcontractor bid. The letter acknowledged that while Gurney had submitted the lowest bid, "we were obligated to use the higher quotation to satisfy the 6 percent Minority Business Enterprise goal as set forth in the specifications for the subject project." Peterson got the award.

On 23 March 1983 Gurney got a similar letter from the NPC Corporation; on 1 February 1985, from two others; on 15 February 1985, from one more; and so on.

Frank Gurney died in 1989, taking what Stewart would later call "a great deal of frustration with him to his grave." That frustration would, like the company, be passed to his heirs, as year after year, the letters kept coming, depriving Tom Stewart's company of millions of dollars worth of business they had earned. Frequently, the contracts went to the better heeled firms of Junlo or Peterson, because of their "minority" ownership.

"In theory, I could sue the government myself," Stewart, a tall, white-haired, dignified man, later told a congressional committee. "But that's not realistic. A small firm like mine cannot begin to finance a lawsuit against the federal government. The U.S. Department of Justice is the largest law firm in the world. For all practical purposes, its resources are unlimited. By the time my firm won a lawsuit, it would be in bankruptcy."

"We realize that affirmative action is deeply rooted in American society," Stewart continued. "I am told and I believe that the vast majority of Americans continue to support affirmative action. They want it to continue. So do I. But I urge you in the strongest possible terms to put affirmative action back on its original course. It was never intended to give special preferences to a favored few. It was never intended to require a general contractor to reject a lower bid from a subcontractor simply because that subcontractor is someone like me."

Months later Stewart reported, "I still get the letters every week and still lose business. Believe me, it's a tough, unfair situation."

■   ■   ■

In 1977, a black Democratic machine politician from Baltimore, Representative Paren Mitchell, added an amendment to that year's

$4 billion "Public Works Employment Act" providing that, absent a waiver, states and localities must use at least 10 percent of their grants to procure services from "minority business enterprises," a term defined as U.S. citizens "who are Negroes, Spanish-speaking, Orientals, Indians, Eskimos, and Aleuts."

A similar amendment was added on the Senate side by Republican Edward Brooke of Massachusetts and, after conference, with no hearings and little floor debate, the measure became law. The law was challenged by white government contractors as contrary to the Equal Protection Clause of the Fourteenth Amendment and the due process clause of the Fifth Amendment. The Supreme Court, however, sustained the act in the 1979 decision, *Fullilove v. Klutznick.*

The era of minority set-asides had begun. *Fullilove* was, in effect, a friendly alarm bell waking both Washington and state and local governments to a way of funneling money into minority communities which might otherwise have been overlooked. Within a decade at least 250 minority set-aside programs were in existence throughout the country. And by 1995 when Senate Majority Leader Bob Dole requested a survey of federal race preference programs, the Congressional Research Service was able to identify scores of statutes and administrative edicts that fit the description.

In 1993, "Small Disadvantaged Businesses," or SDBs, the term applied to those owned and controlled by protected minorities or, in some cases, women, received $13 billion out of $180 billion federal contract dollars, a sixth of that through subcontracting. Most of the beneficiaries were participants in the Small Business Administration's (SBA's) "8(a) program," which establishes the SBA as the certification agency or government clearinghouse for firms seeking to qualify as Disadvantaged Business Enterprises (DBEs). As recently as 1994, before the Republicans took over both the

Senate and House of Representatives, a bill establishing a 5 percent minority target in federal contracting passed both houses without a dissenting vote in either.

There is no great mystery as to why minority set-asides have proved so appealing to lawmakers at every level of government. They address one of the most critical problems in our society, the creation of a class of minority businessmen, and they do it on the cheap by funneling money already in the pipeline to minority contractors and subcontractors. Few additional dollars must be appropriated that are publicly identified with race preferences, and only a minimal additional bureaucratic structure is required to preside over the programs. The additional dollars spent may be substantial, but they are buried in the costs of the programs themselves. Studies on such extra costs, which almost certainly would include the government's acceptance of higher bids or bonuses and the increased risks of default by those less than fully qualified to perform the work, are close to nonexistent.

To some extent the approach works. Any civil rights lobbyist worth his expense account can cite from memory the old set-aside beneficiary which is today an official supplier of athletic clothes to the 1996 Olympics; the metal fabricator in Washington, D.C., who refuses to move his facility from the inner city despite far greater growth potential in the suburbs; or the female Hispanic former Illinois cop who started a firm designing security systems with four employees in 1986, got certified for the 8(a) program in 1990, and today employs 375 people at five locations, coast to coast.

While the stock of black-owned businesses remains disturbingly small, that number did increase by 37.6 percent between 1982 and 1987, from 308,260 to 424,165. That means that the minority business formation rate is now at least as high as that of whites, although in terms of dollar volume their share of the economy has remained relatively stagnant for the past decade. According to *Black Enterprise Magazine,* in 1994, the largest one hundred black-owned businesses had sales of $11.7 billion compared with $473 million in 1973. A 1994 SBA study showed that thirty-two of the one hundred largest black-owned firms in the country and seventeen of the top one hundred Hispanic-owned firms got their start in the 8(a) program. In fiscal 1994, federal set-aside contracts purportedly injected an estimated $14.4 billion into the minority business community.

Further, while set-asides are targeted at minority capital formation, not jobs, the link between the two is strong. Black male self-employment rates are today about 4.1 percent compared with more than 11 percent for whites. (In 1940, the figure for blacks was 6.0 percent. The decline over the past half century has much with do with the decimation of the black family structure, denying would-be black entrepreneurs the sort of family support system needed to get started.) But black-owned firms are far more likely to hire black employees. According to the 1980 census, blacks constituted half or more of the employees in 93.5 percent of firms owned by blacks but in only 23.2 percent of the firms owned by whites, and 57.8 percent of the white-owned firms had no black employees at all. Even in predominantly minority neighborhoods, blacks constituted a majority of employees in 96.2 percent of the black-owned businesses but in only 37.6 percent of the white-owned businesses, and 32.9 percent of the white-owned firms had zero black employees. So the public interest in stimulating black business ownership extends meaningfully to the employment area.

To the contracting community at large, however, the notion of rigid racial set-asides is anathema. As with objective civil service standards in government hiring, the procedure of awarding public procurement and construction contracts to the lowest qualified bidder was not an inevitable development. Rather, where it has been won, it has been hard won, offering the small honest contractor protection against the political influence of such giants as Brown and Root, Bechtel and Hyman, or, at the local level, the corruption and cronyism that have long plagued the business of public contracting. "The awarding of government contracts on the basis of minority set-asides fails at two very basic levels," says Mike Kennedy, general counsel for the national organization, Associated General Contractors. "It fails the Equal Protection test because it favors one race over another. And it fails the test of elemental fairness because it forsakes the principle of awarding business to the lowest qualified bidder."

Not that access to the political process is, or should be, irrelevant. To the contrary, the ability of large numbers of blacks to win elections as aldermen, councilmen, mayors, county executives, state legislators, and congressmen is one of the happy developments of our time. It opens doors to patronage, swells the number of those in positions of power and responsibility, ensures that the black business community receives timely notice of government-generated business, and fortifies legal strictures against discrimination. This is better than formally designated set-asides or other forms of "affirmative action" because it is "earned" through the political "pushing and hauling" endorsed by Justice Souter in the voting rights context. And it is civically integrating rather than isolating.

The notion of "merit" has many disguises. "Equality" sometimes means having a political action committee (PAC) no smaller than one's opponent. The Establishment may be powerful and forbidding, but in the context of the American political system, its genius is that it has always been open to newcomers willing to play by the rules. In thousands of daily transactions favoritism abounds. But the process is dynamic, and the beneficiaries change. So long as public institutions themselves remain fair and neutral our constitutional and political traditions are not jeopardized.

The fundamental failing of the Congress that passed Representative Mitchell's minority set-aside amendment, and other Congresses and other legislative bodies that passed hundreds of similar laws, was their implicit assumption of a static, pre–civil rights era, political power structure rather than a dynamic, evolving nation where blacks, armed with the right to participate fully in the political process, were learning rapidly how to acquire and use their political muscle. By the mid-1990s, they would hold more than eight thousand elective offices. Such major cities as New York, Chicago, Los Angeles, Houston, Seattle, New Orleans, and Birmingham had been or were being run by black mayors. City councils, county and borough governments, and key state legislative and congressional committee chairmanships were in the hands of blacks and other "disadvantageds." In California, Ward Connerly, the conservative black member of the Board of Regents, which oversees the state educational system, observed, "Over a period spanning the last fourteen years, a black man, Willie Brown, has had the power of life or death over every piece of legislation and every dollar approved in our state budget. Both of our U.S. senators are women. Our state treasurer is an American of Asian descent. Two of our constitutional officers are women."

Clearly, blacks, a race once subject to the indignity of the term "boy," were in the process of becoming "Old Boys." They were in positions to get "inside" information, take advantage of connections, and get their "fair share" of the pie the way most other ethnic and immigrant groups have done.

In such circumstances, the adoption of racial set-aside quotas should not have been necessary. But that did not stop the process. The Richmond City Council that, in the mid-1980s, adopted the Minority Business Utilization Plan requiring prime contractors to subcontract at least 30 percent of construction contracts awarded by the city to a Minority Business Enterprise (MBE), was itself controlled by a black majority. During debate on the evening of the vote, proponents noted that the city's population was 50 percent black and that black prime contractors received less than 1 percent of city construction business. They claimed that black contractors had difficulty amassing working capital, meeting bonding requirements, and keeping abreast of bidding procedures.

But there were no claims of deliberate exclusion. Representatives of several contractor groups told the council they had repeatedly and unsuccessfully solicited minority members. And there were indications that, due to extensive subcontracting and separate tabulations for projects financed largely or entirely by the federal government, the real involvement of minority contractors in city construction projects was far higher than the council's estimate. The 30 percent quota requirement seems to have been pulled out of the air.

The Richmond ordinance was challenged in the federal courts by a white contractor who had submitted the low bid on a contract for plumbing fixtures in the city jail only to see the job awarded to a minority whose bid had been higher. When the case, *City of Richmond v. Croson,* reached the Supreme Court in 1989, Justice O'Connor, in one of the more important decisions of the decade, declared that "an amorphous claim that there has been past discrimination in a particular industry cannot justify the use of an unyielding racial quota." Rather, she held, all such racial classifications would be subject to strict judicial scrutiny, meaning they would be upheld only where needed to redress proven past discrimination and where the remedy had been "narrowly tailored" to right the proven wrongs.

But rather than closing the door on racial set-asides, Justice O'Connor, perhaps unintentionally, left a loophole large enough to accommodate a four-lane superhighway by suggesting in a footnote: "Where there is a *significant statistical disparity* between the number of qualified minority contractors willing and able to perform a particular service and the number of such contractors actually engaged by the locality or the locality's prime contractors, an inference of discriminatory exclusion could arise..." (emphasis added).

Alas, from *Croson* was born the "disparity study" industry and the instant army of lawyers, consultants, and expert witnesses that flourished around it. From Baltimore to San Francisco, from Atlanta to Dallas, from Dade County, Florida, back to Richmond itself, scores of communities undertook to discover the evils of racism in contracting in order to justify "remedial" programs long on the books. Professor George LaNoue of the University of Maryland, Baltimore, perhaps the nation's leading expert on disparity studies, has estimated that through 1994, more than one hundred disparity studies had been completed at a total cost exceeding $45 million, including thirteen subsidized to the tune of $14 million by the federal government's urban mass transit authority. LaNoue says the amount "may be the largest sum ever spent on social science related research in our nation's history," and all in order to justify continuing or expanding MBE programs. Some used scholars, some accountants, some consultants. A few jurisdictions conducted their own studies, and a handful used minority activist groups.

Unremarkably, this outcome-driven research has found in nearly every case pervasive evidence of race discrimination requiring precisely the sort of relief already on the books or contemplated, the sole exception, according to LaNoue, being a Louisiana study which was promptly discarded and a new consultant brought in who, to no one's surprise, found the desired evidence of discrimination.

A good indication of the quality of analysis provided by these studies in their effort to satisfy Justice O'Connor's *dictum* involves consultant Andrew F. Brimmer, once a Carter appointee to the Federal Reserve Board.

Brimmer was called to Philadelphia more than a decade after the fact to provide *post hoc* justification for a 15 percent minority set-aside program enacted by the city in 1982. Following *Croson*, various contractors associations filed suit to stop the program under the Fourteenth Amendment. Twice they prevailed in the District Court. After the second District Court decision, the Circuit Court of Appeals, noting Brimmer's statistical study, concluded that he had made out a prima facie case for discrimination and asked the court below to review the matter more thoroughly.

Brimmer's methodology vindicated the axiom, "There are lies, damn lies, and statistics." He began with a 1982 national federal census of construction contractors operating in the Philadelphia area and then found another 1982 list compiled by the city and purportedly containing the names of 195 minority contractors "qualified, willing, and able" to undertake city work. Then, from old Philadelphia records, he calculated the dollar volume of prime contracts awarded by the city to minorities in fiscal years 1979, 1980, and 1981. Using these three sets of numbers he compared the percentage of minority contractors (for 1982) with the percentage of business awarded to minorities (in three earlier years). The result was what Brimmer termed a "disparity index," which equaled the amount of minority participation as a percentage of what could have been expected on the basis of their percentage of available contractors.

Brimmer testified, "We have found a substantial statistical disparity in the participation of M[B]E's in the city of Philadelphia Public Works contracts for fiscal years 1979 to 1981, when compared with their availability in that market, from which we conclude that the disparity is attributable to racial discrimination." Brimmer also testified that in his view blacks had been subjected to "discriminatory exclusion and token participation" in contractor organizations and that they "have had few, if any, opportunities to participate with white-owned contractors through subcontracting and joint ventures."

In its January 1995 decision in the case, the U.S. District Court rejected Brimmer's work as "methodologically flawed." The court found that contrary to Brimmer's list, in 1982 only fifty-nine minority contractors had been certified by the city's own Office of Minority Opportunity as qualified to perform on municipal public works projects. It found further that during the years in question, only seven had applied for prequalification, an essential first step for consideration on city contracts.

One apparent reason for the lack of minority interest was that "many of these black contractors were heavily participating in federally assisted public works projects, such as the construction of the Market East Train Station, the Center City Commuter Rail Connection, and the Airport High Speed Line." The court further found no substantiation for the claim that minorities had been unable to obtain subcontracts or to participate in joint ventures. As to contractor associations, testimony at trial indicated that no black contractor who applied had *ever* been turned down by the largest of the organizations. One reason relatively few applied was that members traditionally were the larger contractors with substantial numbers of employees and investment in heavy equipment. By contrast, the court cited federal census data indicating that in 1982, 459 out of 528 black-owned construction companies in the Philadelphia area—87 percent—had no permanent employees and thus would be unable to complete public works projects.

Once again the court struck down Philadelphia's minority set-aside program. But the case returned—for the third time—to the Court of Appeals, and no one involved is sanguine about the litigation ending during the current millennium. In short, jurisdictions boasting set-aside programs face no risk and no sanction for keeping the litigation alive, apart from trivial court costs since their legal departments, in effect, provide free services. They are therefore proving as resourceful in maintaining set-aside programs as Southern jurisdictions were in perpetuating segregation during the "all deliberate speed" years following *Brown v. Board of Education*.

Four years after *Croson*, the Joint Center for Political and Economic Studies conducted a survey of the fifty-six largest U.S. cities to determine the status of minority set-aside or goal-oriented programs in the wake of *Croson*. Fourteen cities did not reply in sufficient detail to be included in the final report, and four said they had no such program and were thus not affected by the case. Of the remainder more than twenty, including New York, Chicago, Boston, Philadelphia, Atlanta, Baltimore, Kansas City, Jacksonville, Seattle, Charlotte, Philadelphia (later challenged), and Dade County, Florida, had kept or only slightly modified their programs after post-*Croson* disparity studies. Others like Detroit, with a 40 percent minority target, felt no change was necessary. Washington, D.C., and Cincinnati had stopped their programs as a result of adverse litigation but promptly adjusted and revived them. Memphis, which had no set-aside program at the time of *Croson*, adopted one in 1993 which is so aggressive that it authorizes breaking large contracts down into smaller chunks in order to encourage minority participation. In other words, *Croson* had relatively little effect on set-aside programs other than to give work to the spanking new disparity industry.

Richmond, the loser in the *Croson* case, had been forced to suspend its set-aside program in 1987 as the result of an adverse court of appeals decision. Immediately, minority participation in contracts and subcontracts with the city dropped precipitously, from an average of 38 percent of contract dollars spent during the 1984–87 period to 2.2 percent during the balance of 1987. On the basis of a few large projects, it jumped to 26 percent in 1988, finally leveling off at about 9.5 percent in 1990. Minority advocates claim the drop was due to discrimination. Representatives of white contractors insist that the same majority black jurisdiction which had implemented the set-asides was unlikely to discriminate against black bidders simply because the set-aside program was declared unlawful; they maintain instead that the five black firms which had received the lion's share of set-aside awards in the earlier period had simply become too dependent on automatic awards to compete as successfully in the post-*Croson* environment.

In either case, Richmond soon ordered the mandatory disparity study and, to no one's surprise, found just enough discrimination to permit a goal of 16 percent minority subcontract participation for the indefinite future. The number appeared to be the city's best guess as to what the white contractor community could accept without renewed legal challenge in the courts, or, on a worst case basis, what might at least arguably be defended should litigation ensue. Dispensed with were any contracts effectively closed to white contractors or subcontractors or any technical advantage in the actual bidding procedures to minorities or primes agreeing to subcontract to a fixed percentage of minorities. Instead the targets are built into an elaborate prequalification procedure where prime contractors receive points for accepting the 16 percent target on minority subcontractors. Contractors unable to meet the target may apply for a waiver, which, according to sources in both the government and contracting community, are granted when justified by the facts. All primes with the requisite number of points are then permitted to bid on the contract in question, which is then awarded to the lowest bidder.

"It's just remarkable how year in and year out we've been able to hit our 16 percent goal," says Deborah Barnes, administrator of the city's Minority Business Enterprise program. "We're even starting to get into areas like new office construction and office building renovation where minority participation rates are in the 25 percent area." Ms. Barnes, who is old enough to remember the state's "massive resistance" days of the 1950s, thinks of Richmond as "a racially troubled city," but one where there has been "more of a change in racial attitudes among white people than I ever thought I would live to see." She says she would now "like to live long enough to see my job go away because there was no longer any need for it."

Attorney Walter "Rusty" Ryland, who successfully argued the *Croson* case, says the present program is likely to go unchallenged by white contractors "so long as no contracts are denied because of race." He adds, "If the city is skillful in the way it administers the law, as Ms. Barnes is, it can go for a long time without a suit. People who do business with the government are used to the imposition of tough conditions. The minority targets are one among many. Hell, if they said that starting tomorrow, in order to bid successfully on a contract you had to wear one white sock and one green sock, there would be a run on green socks at every clothing store in the city by 4 P.M."

At the state and local levels, even many of the nation's more conservative leaders have been slow to abandon minority set-aside programs. When, during much of 1995, sentiment in Washington seemed to be moving toward restricting set-asides, Republican Governor George Voinovich of Ohio chose to endorse the concept publicly and to privately ask Newt Gingrich to go slowly. At the same time, Houston's conservative mayor Bob Lanier increased minority set-aside targets by 35 percent. Massachusetts Governor William F. Weld defended his state's set-aside programs while acknowledging to the *Washington Post*, "I'm swimming against the tide." Wisconsin Governor Tommy G. Thompson and New Jersey Governor Christine Todd Whitman were among others to urge their party to soft-pedal the issue. Both sought no change in their own state programs.

The inescapable conclusion is that *Croson* has been a nuisance but not a showstopper, because officials seem to find it the most efficient way to get hundreds of millions of dollars into the minority community with few costs beyond those normal for the job in question. The collective local response to the Supreme Court is, in effect, that while Justice O'Connor may have a fine mind for constitutional nuance, she does not have to run the subways, collect the garbage, help support the welfare and Medicaid rolls, police the drug problem, or fret over the possible return of urban rioting. The people who do worry about those things get a warm, fuzzy feeling when they see black guys bidding for construction contracts. And well they should.

Croson, of course, had no impact on the burgeoning federal set-aside programs that continued to find their way into law with little opposition. If anything, they grew more rigid with time. The Federal Procurement Streamlining Act, passed in 1994, provided that when a contracting officer reasonably believes that two or more qualified SDBs bid for a contract, he must shelter the contract from nonminority competition. A similar "Rule of Two" was invoked by the Pentagon in its own rigid set-aside program.

Through its "1207 Program," the Pentagon has for years been excluding white contractors from a small but significant chunk of its available market. Because many Department of Defense procurement and outsourcing contracts tend to be large or technical, its 5 percent set-aside goals are heavily concentrated in construction, service, and maintenance. The White House Affirmative Action Review conceded that concentrations of contracts which are off limits to white male businesses have reached 40 percent in some locations.

In fiscal year 1995 Barksdale Air Force Base in Shreveport, Louisiana, was even more restrictive. That year 100 percent of the base's construction contracts and 75 percent of its overall contracts were restricted to SDBs. In a letter responding to Representative Jim McCrery's inquiry, Barksdale's legislative liaison wrote that Headquarters Air Combat Command had reviewed the practices and "concurs that they are proper and that the base's set-aside rate is not disproportionate." One might ask, if a 100 percent set-aside rate is "not disproportionate," what is?

"Every time you have a set-aside, that in effect is a 100 percent quota on that contract," complains Arnold O'Donnell, a gutsy Washington, D.C., construction contractor who took the District to court and won, after its 50 percent set-aside had lost him enough business to reduce his full-time employees from twenty-two to three. "More than half my guys were minorities," he recalls.

O'Donnell is also bothered by the proliferation of protected classes, a point on which legislatures across the country have squandered what little moral capital racial preferences command.

That point was inadvertently emphasized by Major Owens, the black Democrat from New York City, who proposed facetiously during House hearings early in 1995 that perhaps advocates of "race neutral" programs would be satisfied if benefits were allocated "to descendants of former slaves, regardless of race."

Not a great idea, but perhaps an improvement over current practice. It would, for example, clarify the entitlement status of immigrant Nigerians, Angolans, Somalis, Ethiopians, and other Africans who came to this country for an education, got one, and now are reluctant to return home, in most instances because of savage clan or tribal conflicts, or corrupt, brutal governments. They are a decent and worthy lot for the most part who ought to have every right to participate in the economic life of their adopted society. But preferences?

And if Hispanics are entitled to preferences because of past discrimination, they must be a race of masochists because of the numbers in which they continue to immigrate. Discussing set-asides, Drew Days, Mr. Clinton's solicitor general, observed in a *Yale Law Review* article some years back, "Such programs leave one with the sense that the racial and ethnic groups favored by the set-aside were added without attention to whether their inclusion was justified by evidence of past discrimination."

Harvard's Nathan Glazer makes a similar point. "Whatever the weight of the logic that led to the inclusion of Hispanic Americans in affirmative action at its beginnings, it no longer applies. Both groups now consist in the majority of immigrants and their children. American society and institutions have no special obligation beyond nondiscrimination for these groups."

"If the blacks came to this country in chains, how did the Argentineans get here?" O'Donnell asks. "Or the Portuguese? Or the Indians? I'm not talking about Comanches. I'm talking about the guys from Bombay who are running computers in Rosslyn, Virginia, and winning Pentagon contracts because they are a protected class."

O'Donnell faces daily competition from well-heeled Portuguese and South American construction companies that have set up business in the Washington, D.C., area to take advantage of set-aside opportunities. Between 1986 and 1990, $64 million in Washington, D.C., construction contracts were awarded to minority-owned firms. The lion's share, $39 million, or 60 percent, were won by three firms, two owned by Jose Rodriguez, the other, by his brother Francisco. The Rodriguez brothers are Portuguese, white Europeans.

In a study entitled *Affirmative Action for Immigrants,* James S. Robb notes that the combination of liberalized immigration laws of the 1960s and affirmative action set-asides of the 1970s and 1980s has radically changed the character of set-aside programs. He notes that in 1993, for example, 74.9 percent of the new immigrants came from places that qualify them as beneficiaries of affirmative action or set-aside programs.

Robb also explains that whoever gets to be a favored minority can be a game of luck, lobbying, or political largesse. Ohio's Governor Voinovich, in 1991, expanded the definition of "Orientals," to include Asian Indians, immediately qualifying sixty-four firms for sheltered state contracts who proceeded to win a total of $5.6 million the next two years. Asian Indians had contributed $278,000 to Voinovich's 1990 campaign.

In Los Angeles County, blacks are discovering that race preference is a game any number can play. Although they constitute only 12.6 percent of the county population, they had, through an aggressive affirmative action program, managed to get 30.5 percent of the county jobs. Enter the Hispanics, mostly immigrants. By 1988, they had 27.6 percent of the population but only 18.3 percent of the county jobs, a situation which evoked a stern warning from the L.A. County Office of Affirmative Action Compliance, and later, a lawsuit initiated by Hispanic organizations.

Seeing their favored position in jeopardy, a black labor leader complained, "They're trying to syphon off all our gains." She added, "What ever happened to merit? I'm not in favor of affirmative action. It shuts blacks out." Mamie Grant knows whereof she speaks. In 1970, blacks made up 66 percent of the four categories of protected groups in the United States—blacks, Hispanics, Native Americans, and Asians. Today, that figure is 49 percent.

In *Croson,* Justice O'Connor ridiculed the Richmond law's availability to Aleuts who have probably experienced as much discrimination there as have the Eskimos of Silicon Valley.

And while many Native Americans have had it tough, one must wonder about the fellow who won a set-aside contract in California, having qualified because he was 1/64th Cherokee.

With the addition of women to many state and federal set-aside programs, the protected "minorities" total roughly 75 percent of the population, giving the much abused "angry white male" something about which to be really angry.

The preferences have, of course, generated a fair amount of fraud, beginning with what might be called the "Malone factor." A recent *Vanderbilt Law Review* recalls the case of Phillip and Paul Malone, twin brothers from Boston who flunked the city's firefighters entrance exam in 1975, then changed their racial designation from "white" to "black," reapplied in 1978, and were hired. Ten years later, when they sought promotions to lieutenant, their ruse was discovered and they were fired for "racial fraud."

The federal set-aside world was for years riddled with similar fraud as a generation of black "front" companies sought and, in many cases, won contracts on behalf of their true white owners. Tighter supervision of the SBA's 8(a) program has cut back on this kind of fraud, but the Pentagon, which relies on "self-certification," continues to have its problems, as do many of the city programs. A Baltimore grand jury was kept busy for months ferreting out illegal "fronts." Indianapolis conducted a surprise review and wound up decertifying more than one-third of its DBEs. The standards vary enormously from jurisdiction to jurisdiction. In many places, decertification is the only penalty; elsewhere, criminal sanctions apply. One of the most knowledgeable individuals in the entire field confides (anonymously) that minority front companies and others headed only nominally by women are still widespread. "There is more laundering in this area than in anything since the Cali Cartel got going," the source maintains.

From their outset, the 8(a) program and its federal cousins have fallen far short of their goal: bringing large numbers of minority enterprises into the system, helping them learn to compete, and, once able, releasing them into the general marketplace. Instead, the programs have provided a bonanza for a relative handful of MBEs, many of whom never even bother to venture beyond the sheltered life of the set-aside programs.

In 1993, the SBA reported that of the 1.2 million minority-owned businesses in the country, 80 percent had no employees and only about 1 percent were in the 8(a) program at any point in time. By January 1995, there were 5,155 firms in the program, but less than half had contracts from the government and the top fifty in the program received 25 percent of the $4.37 billion awarded during that fiscal year.

The reason for the concentration is that big firms perform better, rarely default, and, if there is competition, are more often in a position to win. But once they find a satisfactory performer, the SBA and its sister agencies appear to go out of their way to preempt competition. Regulations under 8(a) provide that manufacturing contracts in excess of $5 million and others over $3 million require competition among the DBEs. But in 1994 the agency's inspector general reported that administrators frequently stretch out or break apart projects in order to squeeze in under the ceilings, preserving their ability to deal with a comfortable sole source.

The 8(a) minority program also involves a nine-year "graduation period," after which firms are no longer eligible, the purpose being to make them a permanent part of the business community rather than perpetually dependent on sheltered government contracts. Throughout the period, participating firms must show an increasing percentage of "other" business so they will land running on graduation day. Further, there are net worth limits on participating individuals: $250,000 (excluding business assets and personal residence) upon joining the program, $500,000 at midpoint, and $750,000 prior to graduation. Individuals amassing those kinds of personal fortunes are supposed to graduate early.

In practice, barely more than a third of the firms fulfill the "other business" requirements during their final years in the program and nearly 40 percent go belly-up upon "graduation." Of the firms graduating in 1989, fewer than 50 percent were in business five years later. Moreover, the personal assets requirement is often honored in the breach, particularly with the Pentagon's program which starts at $750,000 and, like its other requirements, is subject to "self-certification." Arguably, the programs are flawed because the entire concept of a "disadvantaged business" is something of an oxymoron. A firm with inadequate capital, assets, liquidity, and bondability may well be simply unqualified rather than disadvantaged. A firm without those problems should be able to compete on an even basis, perhaps after a brief orientation period.

Many further question the economic value of the entire concept, claiming it pushes the formation of minority business into areas where government procurement is heavy rather than into areas of evolving economic opportunity. Construction, for example, is widely regarded as a "mature" industry, heavy with existing firms competing for a share of a pie that is diminishing as government spending declines.

Increasingly, the federal set-aside program has come to be viewed with hostility by the community of small white contractors who see it as an economic "milk farm" for black millionaires. It was only a matter of time before the right set of facts came along to support a legal challenge. And when those facts did fall into place, Randy Pech of Adarand Constructors, Inc., pounced.

The facts were extremely simple, as was the Supreme Court's opinion. Adarand bid to become the guardrail subcontractor of a Colorado highway financed with Department of Transportation money under a program that provided the prime contractor with a 10 percent bonus for selecting a DBE, in this case, one owned by a Hispanic. Adarand came in with a bid less than 10 percent lower than the minority firm and thus lost the subcontract.

The only question of significance before the court was whether the strict standard for racial categories applied to the states in *Croson* should be applied to the federal government as well. In *Fullilove,* Chief Justice Burger, whose virtuous intuition was rarely burdened by the weight of profound legal scholarship, had suggested it did not. Burger repeatedly emphasized the unique "deference" to which acts of Congress are entitled, noting, "[i]t is fundamental that in no organ of government, state or federal, does there repose a more comprehensive remedial power than in the Congress, expressly charged by the Constitution with competence and authority to enforce equal protection guarantees."

In the last dissent of his career, the ailing Justice Potter Stewart reminded his brethren of the words of Justice Harlan in *Plessy v. Ferguson* eighty-four years earlier, that the Constitution is "colorblind," and that "[t]he law regards man as man, and takes no account of his surroundings or of his color."

The more recent *Metro Broadcasting* case had been even more emphatic in holding the federal government to a lesser, intermediate standard based on its historic role in interpreting the Fourteenth Amendment.

But in *Adarand,* Justice O'Connor swept *Metro Broadcasting* aside and dealt directly with *Fullilove:* "Federal racial classifications, like those of a state, must serve a compelling governmental interest, and must be narrowly tailored to further that interest." The case was sent back to the lower courts for specific factual determinations.

The *Adarand* decision came as the Clinton administration was in the midst of its affirmative action review, but the decision required special attention. Assistant Attorney General Walter Dellinger circulated a thirty-seven-page analysis of the decision for the benefit of agency counsel in which he noted many of the questions left unanswered by the Court. Did the federal government, he asked, have special standing to determine whether discrimination existed on a scale great enough to justify race-conscious legislative remedies, whether such findings could be made "post hoc," well after the legislation was actually passed, and whether goals such as "diversity" in the contracting community might constitute an alternative "compelling need" even in the absence of manifest past discrimination? Urging each agency to review its own affirmative action programs in the light of *Adarand,* Dellinger declared, "No affirmative action program should be suspended prior to such an evaluation."

The White House Affirmative Action Review seemed to suggest that all the questions raised by *Adarand* had been satisfactorily answered, that what was needed was simply to tie everything together in a package that would likely encounter judicial approval, and that except for a few relatively minor midcourse corrections, the programs could speed merrily along. Specifically, it cited vast numbers of studies claiming discrimination against minority contractors which could be used to justify the vast assortment of racial set-asides. The remedies had been tailored narrowly and precisely because "[a]s a practical matter, some degree of explicit targeting is the only effective way to ensure that entrepreneurial opportunities are increasingly open to minorities and women."

The president's team denied that the percentage set-asides

were "quotas" because "the statutes and regulations establish flexible goals rather than a numerical straitjacket." The team then concluded the set-asides were "balanced and equitable" because they cause "only a minor diminution of opportunity for nonminority firms." Moreover, race-neutral remedies that focused on small disadvantaged businesses as opposed to small *minority* businesses would not do the trick since that "would seriously undermine efforts to create entrepreneurship opportunities for minorities and women." This apparent suggestion, later specifically endorsed by administration lawyers, inferred that set-aside programs unable to pass muster as remedies for past discrimination might be justified as constitutionally protected quests for diversity, just as collegiate race preferences were granted at least limited license on that ground by Justice Powell in the landmark 1978 *Bakke* case.

Consistency being the hobgoblin of small minds, the president's men, in arguing for continued race preferences, chose to ignore the fact that Department of Justice lawyers in *Adarand* had tried, with straight faces, to convince the Supreme Court that the challenged program was *not* racial in nature since it was open to all "disadvantaged" contractors, not simply minorities. Of course, in the world of federal contracting, "disadvantaged" had long since become little more than a euphemism for minority.

To serious students of the subject, the Dellinger memo was glib, superficial, and legally deficient, in effect offering the president a political cover for actions he intended to take anyway, in the guise of legal analysis. For one thing, the argument appeared to rely on national data relative to some mythical national market permitting the government to proclaim discrimination, an utterly nonsensical approach. The very notion that a law placing white contractors in, say, California at a disadvantage because of discrimination which might have occurred against blacks in Kalamazoo could pass judicial muster strains credulity. Such a law would fail both prongs of the *Adarand* test since it does not identify with precision the discrimination to be remedied, nor does it satisfy the demand that the remedy be narrowly tailored to redress the wrong.

"We are going to see a number of cases which will turn on the ability of the government to establish discrimination in a particular market," predicts Mike Kennedy, the smart, tenacious general counsel for Associated General Contractors (AGC), a man who has for years been in the thick of minority set-aside litigation. "The government will find it hard to defend programs on that basis because the evidence is lacking. So they will move to an economic standard, purporting to grant preferences on the basis of disadvantage. But this ruse too will not work. At some point, it will finally dawn on people that, in practicing racial discrimination against the majority, we are in fact dealing with the same legal standard [that] was rejected by the courts when minorities were the victims. At that point, I think change will be rapid."

Given its commitment to minority set-aside programs, restated by the president in his post-*Adarand* affirmative action address at the National Archives, the administration followed a predictable path in the period after the decision. Associate Attorney General John R. Schmidt was placed in charge of mobilizing the resources needed to construct a new line of defense. This included collecting every local disparity study undertaken in the years since *Croson* in order to support the vital interest needed to justify a race-based preference and to gather every relevant study on minority contracting problems to which members of Congress may have been privy at the time they voted to establish one set-aside program or another, or which could be used to justify the program after the fact. The end result would be a federal pattern of regionally based disparity standards concluding that but for discrimination minorities would be capturing x percent of the federal contracts while they are actually winning some lesser percent which, therefore, justifies a series of federally imposed preferences designed to get them up to their rightful share of x percent.

In congressional testimony in September 1995, Schmidt noted that while the Court had required governments to identify existing discrimination before mandating race-conscious relief, "every court of appeals to consider the question has permitted reliance on evidence that the government did not have before it at the time it adopted a racial classification, so long as the government had some evidence before it when it enacted the challenged provision." Further, Schmidt suggested the government could well argue that race preferences were justifiable on the basis of "nonremedial objectives," such as diversity in contracting or the perception in minority communities that they are as fairly represented in contracting as they are in police or fire departments.

Mr. Schmidt's legal theories are, at best, spurious. The handful of federal courts to rule on set-aside programs in the wake of *Adarand* have, without exception, thrown them out. The programs remain, in the words of Mike Carvin, a former civil rights lawyer in the Bush Justice Department, "slapdash, casual social engineering without any of the hallmarks of carefully considered remedial countermeasures that are necessary to ensure genuine equal opportunity for minorities." The initial Clinton approach seemed to be that it will be business as usual until, on a case-by-case basis, it is forced to change.

A good example of this occurred at the White Sands Missile Range in New Mexico, where the army had in recent years let out bids for what were in effect three-year road construction contracts, with the first year guaranteed at about $10 million and the army able to renew the contract on essentially the same terms for an additional year or two. For the past six years, the winning low bid had been submitted by the McCrossan company, a Minnesota-based outfit. In 1995, following *Adarand,* the government informed McCrossan that the contract was now closed to white bidders under the Pentagon's 1207 Program. The same was true for a smaller contract at the nearby Holloman Air Force Base.

Only after McCrossan filed suit for injunctive relief did the Justice Department back down, issuing bids for a far smaller contract—which McCrossan won with the low bid—and telling the court it would invite bids for more substantial road-building contracts following completion of its post-*Adarand* review. But the retreat was only tactical. Instead of following the "Rule of Two," Justice said the administration would govern the bid procedures under its 8(a) program, a distinction without a difference but one which, in April 1996, somehow managed to survive a motion for a preliminary injunction sought by McCrossan.

In October 1995, the adminstration pronounced the end of all "Rule of Two" procedures, flagrantly unconstitutional under *Adarand.* And in March 1996, word was leaked to the *New York Times* that the White House had decided to declare a three-year "moratorium" on all federal programs requiring fixed set-asides for minorities or women; it would still permit other kinds of race and sex preferences, such as providing bonuses to contractors achieving a fixed percentage of minority employees or permitting the award of contracts to minorities who were not the lowest qualified bidders in a given situation. Early indications were that the Small Business Administration's 8(a) program would not be affected. All agencies were instructed to conduct disparity studies to determine whether fixed goals were warranted to remedy discrimination against minority contractors. At the same time, the 5 percent target for minority federal contracting established by legislation in 1994 was to be maintained. President Clinton, who had brilliantly managed to play both sides of the spending and balanced budget issues, was now doing the same with quotas, opposing those already in deep legal trouble but hastening to find ways to perpetuate them in practice.

The moves seemed more an attempt to adjust to the prevailing political winds than to satisfy the requirements of evolving law. For one thing, as the *Adarand* decision—which involved a bonus to road contractors hiring minority subcontractors and was not a strict set-aside—made plain, what the law finds repugnant is racial preference whatever its particular form. The administration's action came at a moment when a House committee had voted favorably on legislation introduced by Senator Dole and Representative John Canady to bar racial preferences in federal employment and contracting, and when a referendum known as the California Civil Rights Initiative, also banning race and sex discrimination or preferences by the state, was reported to have won enough signatures to find its way onto the state's November ballot. Thus, Mr. Clinton appeared to be seeking the politically defensible middle ground position regardless of its lack of philosophical underpinnings or long-term legal prospects.

The administration may also have been banking on the appointment of new Supreme Court Justices during a second Clinton term. While the current Court seems unlikely to undercut its own *Adarand* principles when confronted by disparity studies inspired by a quota-happy administration, its working majority is fragile. While the composition of the Court shifted right from the periods when *Fullilove* and *Metro Broadcasting* were decided, it started to swing back toward a more tolerant view of racial preferences with the appointments by President Clinton of Justices Ginsburg and Breyer, both of whom dissented in both the set-aside and racial redistricting decisions. One more Clinton Justice and the majority, in all likelihood, will again be 5–4 in favor of racial quotas or preferences.

But even should opponents of color-coding civil rights prevail in the long run, the goal of advancing minority capital formation in ways that do not corrupt the majority, the minority, or the law remains important. This is, after all, a nation where the racial divides are wide, where horrible disparities exist not of rights but of practical opportunities, and where both whites and middle-class blacks must encourage the black underclass to shed cultural traits that were born during centuries of enforced servitude and segregation. It is not collective guilt that must drive us, but commitment to humanity. Together, we must search for answers.

One kind of answer, a good one, is being provided in New York and New Jersey. Called the Regional Alliance for Small Contractors, it is funded by an assortment of state agencies and private firms, mainly from the construction industry, and is open to aspiring businessmen of all races. About 80 percent of the participants, however, are minorities. Its flagship program is called "Managing Growth" and involves two semesters of training in such subjects as basic construction business techniques, financial strategies for the growing contractor, hands-on computer training, managing projects between $10,000 and $1 million, construction contract law, estimating, and understanding safety. The aspiring businessmen pay $75 per semester. Corporate and state executives conduct the seminars.

Economist Tim Bates followed the program for the Joint Center for Political and Economic Studies and reported that its graduates performed far better than a control group in their first jobs. They also obtained more public contracts and more subcontracts, having taken their first steps toward corporate "networking." Sensibly, Bates urges the development of programs that reinforce minority individuals and others who have shown initiative and ability. The goal is to develop a business elite, not another welfare program. The problem with many government approaches is that they "frequently target loan assistance to low income persons who lack the education and skills that are prerequisites for success in most lines of self-employment.... In fact, available evidence indicates that small loans, targeted to low income individuals lacking the requisite skills for operating a business, very frequently become delinquent loans."

And as firms develop, Bates advises government and industry to provide even more backing. Look for opportunities for minorities and others to get into winning situations, franchises, or profitable businesses that may be for sale. Why back those who are already starting to do well? "The response is straightforward: it is the viable firms that generate economic development and create jobs."

"We were created to enable small minority contractors to learn how to compete in the post-*Croson* world without set-asides, and I think we're showing it can be done," says Mark Quinn, executive director of the Regional Alliance. But his assistant, Sioan Bethel, offers a caveat: "Most of our companies start off bidding with government agencies that have abandoned illegal set-asides but that continue to maintain 'participation goals' for minority contractors. In terms of ability, I think graduates of our program can compete. But without 'participation goals,' would our program do the job? That's the tough question we ask ourselves every day. I like to think the answer is, yes. But I just don't know."

The Regional Alliance for Small Contractors combines the sort of outreach, workshop, mentoring approach that can be of great assistance to the would-be minority entrepreneur. When such new businessmen are questioned about their problems, nearly all place access to business loans and difficulty in obtaining bonding surety arrangements needed for most state and local contracts high on the list. Reducing or waiving entirely those bonding requirements for the sorts of contracts for which minorities are likely to compete is one remedy which has been tried with some success. Standing behind the borrowing of contractors meeting certain qualifications is another. Paying a decent chunk of the contract price up-front could also help many a new businessman to get over tough early hurdles.

■   ■   ■

The Port of Portland, Oregon, had for twenty-five years prior to *Croson* hatched one scheme after another to ensure representative minority participation in construction contracts relating to the one international and three satellite airports, the import/export pier facility, and the ship repair yard that fall under its jurisdiction, but nothing worked well. The set-aside arrangement in effect in 1989 involved about 8 percent minority participation, but the awards were concentrated in a few hands, dozens of start-up minority businesses failed to get any slice of the pie, and the white contractors resented the entire arrangement as a glorified welfare program for those who needed it least. *Croson* put an end to the set-aside program since the contracting responsibilities at the Port were handled by an executive director named Ron Stemple who harbored the quaint notion that the law should be obeyed. But Stemple, the black contractors, and, to a surprising extent, the white contractor community were all dismayed when black-owned businesses won less than 2 percent of the awards.

"You'd be surprised at how quickly a consensus developed in the community that we ought to try to change things," Stemple recalls in an interview shortly before his death in May 1996. "We had three goals: increase the percentage participation of minority contractors; bring a larger number of minorities into the game; and accomplish it all in a competitive environment. In other words, at the end of the day, the lowest qualified bidder gets the contract. We just hoped to see more minority businesses winning the awards."

With the backing of the entire community, Stemple set about methodically to find out from minority contractors where the problems were. He found five principal ones:

- First, there was an ineffective working relationship between black and white Port contractors. They barely knew each other, rarely communicated, and, in the case of blacks, were often out of touch with what was happening at the Port.
- Second, communications were so poor that most black contractors rarely learned of an opportunity in time to submit a competitive bid.
- Third, the jobs were usually too big for the resources of the minority enterprises.
- Fourth, financing was a continuing problem.
- Fifth, bonding requirements were often difficult to meet.

Stemple then enlisted cooperation from the white contractors in setting up a mentoring program that was within the capabilities of the two communities. Applicants were accepted only if they were ready to step in and benefit from the program. "We limited ourselves to contractors who wanted to win awards, not people who wanted to become contractors," said Stemple. Two majority contractors were assigned to work with each successful applicant, but only after they passed a crash course on how to mentor. The "protégés" had their books gone over with a fine-tooth comb. They were taught to provide for their accounting, marketing, engineering, and legal needs; the Port provided material assistance for each protégé. "We expect a knowledge transfer to take place," said Stemple. "We demand bottom-line results. The protégés are expected to improve their profitability, their equity positions, their capacity to do the work." Special small "demonstration" projects are let for projects totaling only $50,000 to $100,000, for which only protégés are eligible and in which bonding requirements may be relaxed. Other contracts may be downsized or split to make them more accessible to protégé or other minority firms. The ones that show no inclination to improve are dropped from the program, free to compete on their own.

"We're back up to over 5 percent minority participation rates," said Stemple. "But I don't want to fool you. There's no quick fix. We've had a fair number of minority firms unable to make it, but we're encouraged by the number who have made it. We're looking at things all the time. Evaluation is key. If we ever conclude that this thing isn't working and can't work, we'll kill it. But I hate to think of that. As far as I or anyone else can remember, no other affirmative action program in this area has ever worked."

Mentor programs are promising, largely because the majority contractors enter them with enthusiasm. "It's like bringing your son into the business," said one white Midwestern construction contractor during a break at a recent AGC convention in Nashville. "Only these days, not too many young ones want to go into construction." And there are many variations. The government can play "matchmaker," putting the prime contractor in touch with a deserving subcontractor. Joint ventures are another vehicle for helping those just getting started.

And, as LaNoue and his fellow academician John Sullivan suggest, putting in place an ombudsman or even an accelerated grievance procedure to handle with fairness and efficiency situations in which minorities or others claim they are not getting a fair break in securing government contracts or subcontacts is a good alternative to letting perceived unfairness simmer.

Given the choice between integrity of government and the rule of law on the one hand and the cultivation of minority enterprise on the other, many would opt for the former. But that kind of choice may not be inevitable. A growing number of people from within the contractor community believe this nation can have both.

15

THE MORTGAGE DISCRIMINATION HOAX

On 22 August 1994 Deval Patrick's Civil Rights Division at Justice entered into a consent decree with the Chevy Chase Federal Savings Bank and its subsidiary, B. F. Saul Mortgage Company, requiring the largest home mortgage establishment in the Washington, D.C., area to undertake a number of "remedial" steps to make its product more accessible to blacks. The goal of the decree was "to obtain a market share of mortgage loans in African American neighborhoods, that is comparable to the Bank and Mortgage Company's share in white residential areas."

Among other things, Chevy Chase agreed to locate additional branch offices in black neighborhoods, offer loans at lower interest rates to black customers, hire more black agents, increase agent commissions on smaller loans, advertise heavily in the black media, and establish a special committee to take a second look at rejected minority loan applications.

This massively intrusive regime was imposed on a bank widely regarded as among the area's most progressive, one which was approving black mortgage applications at a rate of 88 percent, against a national average of 69 percent. The decree was imposed despite a fourteen-month investigation in which Justice failed to produce so much as a single individual claim of racial discrimination. Rather, Justice's complaint was that Chevy Chase had not been sufficiently active in competing for mortgages in predominantly black areas since few of its branches and relatively little of its business were located in such areas.

Patrick described the proceeding as a "classic redlining case and a novel marketing discrimination case." Redlining involves the illegal discriminatory refusal of banks to offer services in neighborhoods with high minority concentrations within the areas they serve or to do so on terms calculated to discourage business. Few familiar with Justice's evidence feel it had much of a redlining case against Chevy Chase. Both that notion and Patrick's "novel marketing discrimination" theory are really semantic covers for something far more disturbing: an effort, led by President Clinton himself, to push the regulatory envelope so as to apply the theory of "disparate impact"—a term borrowed from the thoroughly inapposite field of employment discrimination—to home mortgage lending and insurance. Thus, though no civil right has been violated, the government proposes to use the whip of civil rights law for purposes of economic redistribution and social engineering. Patrick and those who approach the law as he does clearly are frustrated by the desperate condition of many of the nation's inner cities. They want money for housing and neighborhood improvement pumped into these areas. They have targeted banks for their redistributive efforts because, as Willie Sutton discovered long ago, that is where the money is.

But their tactics, used against innocent companies, amount to little more than economic extortion. Unable to get Al Capone for murder or bootlegging, the government used tax evasion, the only available stick to beat him with. Unable to appropriate funds from banks outright, the government proposes to use the best stick available to beat them. But when the law is reduced to a convenient instrument of extortion, not only is democracy violated but the particular law, in this case antidiscrimination law, is also thrown into disrepute. Financial and insurance institutions may require vigilant regulatory oversight. Converting that oversight into a stealth affirmative action program is corruption of purpose and of process.

The government's theory of marketing discrimination is linked to the volume of loan transactions involving minority customers, to acceptance and rejection rates of loan applicants of different races and ethnic backgrounds, and to the criteria employed by lending institutions in determining which loan applications to accept or reject. Under this approach, an institution that makes relatively few loans to minority customers is immediately suspect although it may be fully meeting demand in the market in which it operates. A relatively high minority rejection rate casts a further cloud over the practices of the mortgage company involved although without knowing the qualifications of individual applicants any inference of prejudice is premature and may in fact taint an institution that goes out of its way to generate minority applications. Nor under the administration's view does an institution find protection by scrupulously and evenhandedly applying ordinary lending criteria to white and minority applicants alike if these have a "disparate impact" upon minority applicants.

Again, we are not talking about instances where minority customers are treated differently from whites or other preferred ethnic groups. That is clearly against the law. Banking law also includes a number of reporting provisions making such *disparate treatment* relatively easy to detect. Mortgage lending institutions are forbidden by the Fair Housing Act of 1968 (amended in

1988) from discriminating on the basis of race, color, religion, sex, handicap, family status, or national origin, and by the Equal Credit Opportunity Act of 1974 from discriminating because all or part of a person's income is derived from public assistance. The law is clear as to what lending institutions may not do, but neither by statute nor by regulation has the government ever attempted to develop any set of objective standards by which banks may dispose of loan applications without fear of government intervention. Indeed, Justice does not even have a list of variables that it certifies as acceptable for use in determining creditworthiness. The result is that while the lender may apply traditional criteria—such as loan:value ratio, credit history, or applicant net worth—developed through years of banking experience, it is in fact playing Russian roulette with the whims and social predilections of its government overseers.

Yet another statute also comes into play. The Community Reinvestment Act (CRA) of 1977 requires government agencies to use their supervisory and licensing authority to encourage lending institutions to help meet the credit needs of communities in which they are chartered. The vagueness, if not the total opaqueness, of this mandate gives government lawyers and administrators an outlet for their creative energies since a lending institution can rarely be certain it is fully complying with the spirit of a law which barely articulates anything beyond a fuzzy statement of principle. Each year Federal Reserve Board regulators rate lending institutions from "poor" to "excellent" on the basis of their performance in meeting CRA standards, whatever they may be. The top ratings are highly prized because they are a key factor considered by regulators in passing on bank mergers, expansions, and acquisitions.

In addition, the Home Mortgage Disclosure Act of 1975 (HMDA) requires banks to provide the government with information on every mortgage application processed, including the applicant's race, sex, and income; the amount of the loan applied for; the census tract within which the property is located; and the disposition of the mortgage application. The information, made public each year, has provided the material for a long line of spectacular though ill-informed newspaper reports alleging widespread mortgage discrimination. These have in turn stimulated highly intrusive moves similar to the actions taken in Chevy Chase by government regulators. In something of a vicious cycle, data presented in a misleading fashion fuel excessive zeal by regulators who then use the misleading data to get their hooks into whichever lending institution they choose to target.

The journalistic use of HMDA data began in a big way when, in 1988, the *Atlanta Journal-Constitution* published a Pulitzer Prize–winning series of articles based on a statistical study of the data called, "The Color of Money." Comparing home sales in sixty-four middle-income black and white neighborhoods over a period of six years, the journal found that whites had received bank financing at five times the per capita rate of blacks.

What the paper did not do—but what it absolutely should have done to establish even a threshold case for discrimination—was to compare the *volume* of transactions in white and black areas with the *demand* for loans in the two areas. Turnover may naturally be more brisk in white areas, personal mobility greater, and property values more dynamic. Second, as later noted by David Andrew Price, the media critic for *Forbes* magazine, the articles included no analysis whatsoever of the basis on which individual loan applications had been accepted or rejected, another absolute essential to support a hypothesis of discrimination on the basis of race. But neither of these two glaring evidentiary deficiencies stopped the newspaper from accusing banks of waging "economic war" against black communities or from presenting an editorial cartoon depicting a black couple being directed to a mortgage bank loan officer, the latter clad in the hood and robes of the Ku Klux Klan. The report triggered a Justice Department investigation of Atlanta banking which eventually led to a consent decree against the Decatur Federal Savings and Loan Association, establishing the precedent that would later hang Chevy Chase and other mortgage lending institutions.

The issue of alleged mortgage discrimination was further inflamed by a 1992 study undertaken by members of the staff of the Federal Reserve Bank of Boston, which surveyed the results of 3,300 mortgage loan applications, of which 722 were minority, from banks serving both white and black urban neighborhoods. The study found no evidence of lender "redlining," but its data showed that blacks were, in the breathless words of the Boston Fed's press release, "60 percent more likely to be turned down than whites." Again, this kind of figure raises eyebrows but it is a long way from proving race discrimination because it tells us nothing about the decisions in individual cases. It may well be, for example, that the application of traditional factors legitimately considered by lending institutions in deciding whether to accept or reject an applicant may themselves correlate with race. And in fact, when we analyze material extracted directly from the Boston Fed data set, that is precisely the case. Table 9 presents some differences in average characteristics between nonminority and minority loan applicants, excluding only those who applied for mortgages on multifamily and rental units.

All of these factors related directly to risk. In each category, a neutral loan officer would conclude that the minority applicants represented a higher risk of default. And since the minority applicants on the average bring fewer assets to the table, the application of these neutral criteria have a *disparate impact* on them. Only by ignoring these factors—the true reasons for the difference between

Table 9. Minority Loan Applicants Present Higher Risk

Characteristic	Percent Nonminority	Percent Minority
Married	63	47
More than two years at current job	92	89
No bankruptcy, chargeoffs, or collection actions	95	85
Total expense to income ratio	32.7	34.7
Loan to value requested	76.5	87.4
Stated in terms of down payment	23.5	12.6
Monthly income	$6,487	$4,930

black and white mortgage approval rates—is it possible to pretend that the real reason is racism. But as banks cannot ignore such factors without courting high default rates, an objective loan officer would have concluded the minority applicant represented a higher risk of default.

Just as the *Atlanta Journal-Constitution* story led to the prosecution of the Decatur Bank, so did the Boston Fed study lead the Justice Department and the Federal Trade Commission to move against the Shawmut Mortgage Company, a bank which had, on its own, initiated a fair lending program which both agencies conceded to be an industry standard. Still, they insisted on a consent decree which would include compensation for minority mortgage loan applicants who had allegedly been injured by the bank's refusal to approve their loans in the 1990–92 period. All of the government's claims essentially came down to the single charge that Shawmut had not exercised the same degree of diligence in finding qualifying information on behalf of marginal minority applicants as it had for marginal white applicants and had, therefore, rejected some minorities who were as qualified as whites who received loans. While Shawmut denied the charge, it was in a difficult position since it was, at the time, seeking to merge with the New Dartmouth Bank, and the Federal Reserve Board was refusing to approve the merger until the allegations of discrimination were cleared up.

"We were, in effect, in regulatory jail," says Washington attorney Andy Sandler who, with his senior partner, Bob Bennett—President Clinton's defense lawyer—represented Shawmut, Chevy Chase, and other banks involved in disputes with the Justice Department. After months of reflection and negotiation, Shawmut agreed to the consent decree.

With the *Atlanta Journal Constitution* and the Boston Fed study serving as models, newspapers found the HMDA statistics a game that any number could play. Media investigations followed in Cincinnati, Pittsburgh, Detroit, and Dallas. And on 6 June 1993 the *Washington Post* proclaimed in its lead, "A racially biased system of home lending exists in the Washington area, with local banks and savings and loans providing mortgages to white neighborhoods at twice the rate they do to comparable black ones...."

Again, on its face, the statistic is meaningless since—even ignoring other factors—discussing supply without knowing demand could lead one to conclude, for example, that air conditioning manufacturers discriminate invidiously against residents of Anchorage, Fairbanks, and Nome. But, spurred by the *Washington Post* report, the Civil Rights Division began investigating Chevy Chase in mid-1994, and, at about the same time, lowered the boom on South Dakota's tiny Blackpipe State Bank and the First National Bank of Vicksburg.

Within a year, these three latest targets had followed Decatur and Shawmut down the consent decree route. Blackpipe's alleged offense consisted principally of a disinclination to finance homes located on the neighboring Wounded Knee Indian Reservation. With those lands under the jurisdiction and control of the tribal council, Blackpipe may well have feared that a forfeiture and repossession proceeding could produce the banking equivalent of Custer's Last Stand.

With respect to the First National Bank of Vicksburg, Justice charged that the Mississippi bank had "engaged in policies that discriminated on the basis of race in the extension of unsecured home improvement loans by subjecting its black customers to terms and conditions... that resulted in their paying more for their loans than similarly situated white customers." The evidence supporting this charge consisted solely of the fact that the bank offered two kinds of unsecured home improvement loans: a single payment loan to be paid in full at maturity, carrying a single interest rate; or, an amortized loan with a monthly payment, which often carried the more expensive "add-on" interest rate but where total interest charges were less due to the monthly reductions in principal. A review by the Comptroller of the Currency found that in 1992, 97 percent (59 of 61) of the bank's black customers received amortized loans while only 51 percent (64 of 126) of white customers received such loans.

In formulating its complaint, Justice did not suggest that the different interest rates for different loan packages were an unsound way of doing business. Nor did it suggest that black customers were in any way pressured or coerced into choosing the amortized loans or that the percentage of blacks and whites winding up with each type of loan reflected anything beyond so many voluntary individual choices. The position of Justice came down to the bizarre proposition that the provision of differentiated loan products at different prices amounted to illegal race discrimination because a relatively greater percentage of minorities chose the higher priced product, presumably because amortized mortgages were the more traditional way of doing things and may have provided the minorities with a larger "comfort zone." It would be hard to imagine the master of an antebellum Mississippi cotton plantation carrying the notion of racial paternalism any further than today's Department of Justice.

Despite the near unanimity of informed opinion on its misleading irrelevance, the HMDA data have been cited without caveat as evidence of mortgage lending bias in the press, on Capitol Hill, and, of course, throughout the Clinton administration. In his memorandum explaining and implementing his 17 January 1994, Executive Order, "Leadership and Coordination of Fair Housing in Federal Programs: Affirmatively Furthering Fair Housing," the president stated: "To address the findings of recent studies, I hereby direct the Secretary of Housing and Urban Development and the Attorney General... to exercise national leadership to end discrimination in mortgage lending, the secondary mortgage market, and property insurance practices." And in his State of the Union Address of 25 January 1994, Mr. Clinton included this call to action to his enforcement team: "As we expand opportunity and create jobs, no one can be left out. We must continue to enforce our fair lending and fair housing and all civil-rights laws, because America will never be complete in its renewal until everyone shares."

That effectively put leadership into the hands of Justice's Deval Patrick and Roberta Achtenberg (a senior HUD official battling alleged racism in the home insurance industry). In late September 1994, Patrick told a House subcommittee that while banks had long claimed that disparate treatment of blacks and Hispanics was a function of credit worthiness, "recent studies have laid this claim to rest. For instance, the Federal Reserve Bank of Boston concluded that African Americans and Hispanics have a 60 percent greater chance of being denied financing than white applicants with virtually identical qualifications." As we have seen, that statement is a patent misrepresentation of the Boston Fed data which showed that the cause of the different results was that black and white mortgage loan applicants did not have "virtually identical qualifications."

In his testimony, Patrick further indicated that Justice was committed to using "all legal theories that support a finding of illegal discrimination, including disparate impact as well as disparate treatment."

Months earlier, Attorney General Janet Reno had made clear her feeling that linking allegations of racism to intent was old-fashioned when she told the Fair Housing Summit organized by the White House, "Housing providers and lenders, as well as victims themselves, often believe that racial animus or deliberate premeditated acts of discrimination must be present to violate the law. This is not so. You can call it bad service, indifference, or even thoughtlessness, but when the consequences cause disproportionate harm to those protected by the law, it is discrimination."

So intent was the administration on expanding the application of its disparate impact theory from employment that the combined weight of HUD and Justice was brought to bear on Ed Brooke, a small Rocky Mountain businessman who owns a mobile home park on the outskirts of Golden, Colorado. When Brooke's engineers told him that his sewage disposal and recreational facilities could accommodate a total of 916 people, he decided to limit to three the occupancy in each of his 229 trailer spaces, thereby allowing for visitors as well as some future growth.

HUD became aware of the situation at Mountainside Mobil Estates and demanded that Brooke eliminate his residency limit. Why? Because it had a "disparate impact" upon married couples, allegedly in violation of the Civil Rights Act as amended in 1988. When Brooke refused, Justice jumped into the case; Patrick was delighted that he had found an ideal forum in which to establish this key legal building bloc in his pyramid of regulatory power. But unlike the banks who tend to cave at the first hint of adverse publicity, Ed Brooke chose to stand and fight on principle. Both the federal trial and appellate courts dismissed the government's case.

The government's yen to make disparate impact applicable to mortgage lending makes strategic sense since case and statutory law hold that without clear proof of business necessity the use of criteria having a disparate impact is tantamount to racial discrimination. And once discrimination has been established the government can go almost anywhere it likes to fashion a remedy. But is a disparate impact standard really relevant here? The doctrine, until now confined exclusively to employment situations, was first applied by the Supreme Court in *Griggs v. Duke Power,* which banned job requirements involving a high school diploma or satisfactory performance on reading and mechanical comprehension tests because, in North Carolina in the late 1960s and early 1970s, those requirements impacted more heavily against blacks than whites competing for the same jobs and had not been proven sufficiently job-related to overcome that negative.

However one may feel about the doctrine as applied to employment, the difference between that and a mortgage lending situation is obvious and fundamental. Applicants for jobs or managerial positions compete against each other for a finite number of openings. The employer weighs the merits of a qualified applicant versus those of other qualified applicants for particular jobs in what is, in effect, a zero sum game. By contrast, a bank considering the extension of ordinary or mortgage credit considers only whether the applicant is qualified, and it can extend credit to as many qualified applicants as apply for loans. Again, the mortgage applicant is not competing against anyone else, black or white, for the bank's dollar because even if its own assets are committed, the bank can find a secondary source to hold the mortgage, assuming the debtor is a reasonable risk. The only question involves the quality of the applicant's secured loan, not his or her relationship to other applicants.

Moreover, with today's huge secondary markets, the question on the lender's mind is often whether the contract will pass muster with "Fannie Mae" or "Freddie Mac." And if his bank rejects the application, there are dozens, perhaps scores, of other potential lenders ready to compete for the business. In this competitive market, discrimination along racial or ethnic lines carries the price of lost business.

If individual banks did practice racial discrimination on a large scale, two of the most visible signs would be a very low minority default rate, since only the best customers would obtain loans, and the operation of a highly profitable segment of the banking community—including a fair number of minority-owned and -operated lending institutions—taking advantage of the void left by their uninterested peers. In fact, nothing of the sort is happening. In the definitive study, "Mortgage Discrimination and FHA Loan Performance," by James A. Berkovec, Glenn B. Canner, Stuart A. Gabriel, and Timothy H. Hannan, undertaken for the Board of Governors of the Federal Reserve, differences in default rates were examined holding constant such borrower characteristics as credit history, loan:equity ratio, income, and many others. The result: For Hispanic, Asian, and Native American borrowers, default rates and default losses were statistically similar to those of white borrowers, while default rates and default losses were significantly higher for black borrowers. Moreover, minority-owned banks, on the average, were less profitable and have higher rates of failure than majority-owned lending institutions, suggesting there is no great untapped market of qualified minority mortgage loan applicants out there that has been denied access to loans by white-owned racist banks.

Again, a bank applying traditional race-neutral criteria to loan applicants may say "no" to a black relatively more often than to a white although both have equal incomes and seek to purchase homes of approximately the same value because there is a *correlation* between race and various factors that address the question of creditworthiness. But *correlation* is not *causation*. Most of the follow-up analysis to the Boston Fed study that created so big an initial splash has found little if any racial discrimination by lending institutions in the Boston area or elsewhere.

The American Bankers Association recently published a series of essays on the use of statistics in fair lending analysis which included contributions by the governor of the Federal Reserve System, Lawrence B. Lindsey. The compendium was edited by George Washington University economist Anthony Yezer, who said of the original Boston Study, "Simple models indicate discrimination. These apparently discriminatory results disappear as more data from loans files are added to the model. In the final analysis, the Boston Fed study shows the absence of discrimination in lending based on location." *In fact, in what may have been the most important if least publicized statistic in the entire study, 89 percent of whites and 83 percent of blacks applying for mortgage loans in the institutions reviewed had their applications approved.*

Further, as noted by senior General Accounting Office economist Mitchell B. Rachlis, the lending institution with the highest minority rejection rate in the Boston Fed study was itself owned and controlled by African Americans. *"Removal of this bank from the sample removed the effect of the applicant's minority status—the very coefficient that the Boston Fed analysts used to determine that discrimination was occurring"* (emphasis added). In other words, removing the minority-owned bank from the study would have removed even the erroneous suggestion of discrimination in the Boston Fed data.

Since 1992, studies of Houston; Washington, D.C.; and again

Boston have all found no evidence of substantial racial discrimination in mortgage lending. Yet the myth persists. On 19 July 1995, the day he reiterated his commitment to affirmative action, President Clinton said, "Just last week, the Chicago Federal Reserve Bank reported that black home loan applicants are more than twice as likely to be denied credit as whites with the same qualifications and that Hispanic applicants are more than one and a half times as likely to be denied loans as whites with the same qualifications."

In point of fact, the Chicago Federal Reserve Bank did no such thing. What Mr. Clinton appeared to be referring to was a paper by William C. Hunter, director of Research at the Chicago Fed, and Mary Beth Walker, an economist at Georgia State University, entitled, "The Cultural Affinity Hypothesis and Mortgage Lending Decisions." The paper does not deal with Chicago at all. It is simply a recomputation of the Boston data, except that it improves those data by removing entries that appear to have been gathered by poorly trained staff and that had been improperly monitored. Altogether 1,991 of the 3,300 Boston observations were discarded as unreliable. After cleaning the data, Hunter and Walker found "no evidence that loan officers in the Boston metropolitan area engaged in the practice of redlining..."—the same conclusion reached by every other serious analyst, even before the data were cleaned. Moreover, Hunter and Walker found that "for applicants with good credit profiles, race was not a significant factor in the accept/reject decision." They found, however, that all other things being equal, a minority applicant (black or Hispanic) with a bad credit history had "only" an 82 percent chance of gaining mortgage loan approval while a white with a similar history had a 90 percent chance of approval.

The difference was substantially greater when whites and minorities with poor credit histories and bad monthly payment:income ratios were compared. Here 70 percent of white applicants and 16 percent of minority applicants received their mortgages, and the authors theorized that "cultural affinity" between loan officer and applicant might play a substantial role in passing on unqualified or marginally qualified applicants. That situation, which affected a small fraction of all applications, may be the single credible evidence of disparate treatment found in any of the studies. What it means in practice is that banks must be alert for occasions when a marginally qualified white through his or her own advocacy tilts a loan officer toward taking a chance in circumstances where a minority applicant of similar qualifications either failed to try or was less successful. In an effort to address this problem, most of the larger mortgage lending institutions now have special committees which review minority loan rejections and can reverse the decisions that appear to have shown less flexibility than might have been expected in the case of a white applicant.

The Patrick/Achtenberg effort to extend affirmative action employment concepts to mortgage lending and insurance reached its high water mark in late 1993 and early 1994 when the administration proposed revising regulations under the Community Reinvestment Act to penalize banks for having a higher market share in white neighborhoods than in minority neighborhoods. Governor Lindsey at the Fed came out flatly against the rules, as drafted, and thirty-nine senators signed a letter questioning the direction of administration lending policy. The plan was quietly buried.

Patrick also ran into trouble with his galloping consent decree program. Using a bank's location of branch offices—increasingly irrelevant in any event to the conduct of mortgage business—its allocation of targeted advertising dollars, plus the volume of its business in one neighborhood or another to support allegations of race discrimination struck many as similar to nailing Tiffany's, Neiman-Marcus, or Gucci on similar charges for favoring posh boulevards and upscale suburban malls over Watts, Anacostia, and Bedford Stuyvesant.

As was the case with Shawmut, one reason the other targeted banks may have been so compliant is the government's power, pending completion of an investigation, to delay approval on everything from the opening of a branch office to a billion-dollar merger. "I call it regulatory jail because that's exactly what it is in terms of a bank's losing all freedom to operate," explains Bennett's law partner, Andy Sandler of the Scadden Arps firm representing Chevy Chase. Bennett negotiated the final deal while leading Chevy Chase's public relations offensive. These turned out to be delicate endeavors as each protestation of community involvement and racial sensitivity only intensified questions from lawyers, bankers, and journalists as to why Chevy Chase had caved in the first place. The firm reminded the curious that the bank was also about to initiate a major credit card campaign and hardly wanted to suffer months of racism allegations while attempting to peddle its plastic to the widest possible clientele.

Bennett and Sandler finally got their chance to stand up to Patrick in a case that created a highly visible split between the latter and Lawrence Lindsey of the Federal Reserve Board. The battle severely damaged Patrick's image of cocky invincibility. In September 1993, Patrick's office confirmed a story leaked to the press that Barnett Banks, Inc., of Florida was under investigation for racial discrimination in the handling of mortgage applications. At the time, Barnett was actively engaged in purchasing two other banks, Loan America Finance Corporation of Miami Lakes, Florida, and the Florida operations of the Glendale Federal Bank of California, the first transaction requiring approval by the Federal Reserve Board and the second by the Office of the

Comptroller of the Currency (OCC) which operates out of the Treasury Department.

During the summer of 1994, Patrick wrote to Governor Lindsey at the Fed formally notifying him that Barnett was under investigation and requesting that the Fed withhold approval of the purchase transactions under its jurisdiction. There followed a series of exchanges between Patrick and Lindsey in which Lindsey requested evidence of wrongdoing by Barnett and Patrick replied with summaries of the case but little documentation. Nonetheless, Patrick assured Lindsey that a complaint against Barnett would shortly be filed and that the evidence of wrongdoing was so strong that the chance was only "one in a million" that Barnett's racial discrimination was not deliberate. Lindsey meanwhile was conducting his own statistical analysis of Barnett's activity and could find no evidence of racial discrimination. He also examined CRA reviews with respect to thirty-one of Barnett's branches finding that fourteen were rated "outstanding" and seventeen others, "satisfactory."

On 21 September the Fed approved acquisition of Loan America, Lindsey saying the decision was "easy" because Justice had not disclosed its evidence. Patrick responded with his third and final letter to Lindsey, again saying the evidence against Barnett was strong and asserting that Attorney General Reno had entrusted him to bring a formal Fair Housing Act complaint against the bank, which he intended to do within twenty days.

This put Comptroller General Gene Ludwig on the spot. As part of Treasury, OCC lacks the independence of the Fed but, on a daily basis, works far more closely with it than with Justice. Ludwig and Patrick finally worked out a face-saving deal whereby OCC would approve the transaction on the basis of Barnett's record from July 1993 to July 1994, with Justice continuing its probe into the years 1991 and 1992. On 8 November the accord was announced at a press conference attended by Patrick at which he again claimed, "Qualified people were denied loans by Barnett for reasons totally because of race." He also indicated that "settlement talks" were under way with Barnett.

The following day Bennett released a statement emphatically denying that Barnett was in any sort of negotiations with Justice. In December 1995 Barnett announced it had been informed by the Justice Department that the case was being closed without prosecution. There was no settlement.

Lindsey's show of independence won plaudits plus a big sigh of relief from the banking community. In addition, the 1994 election of a Republican Congress brought with it some counterpressures against the administration to ease its regulatory zeal both as regards consent decrees and the heavy-handed use of the CRA.

Nonetheless, the policies of Patrick and his administration colleagues were having a profound impact on mortgage loan transactions, particularly by lending institutions whose immediate merger plans placed them at the mercy of federal regulators. A computer analysis of millions of mortgage loan applications for the year 1994 reported by the *Wall Street Journal* in early 1996 showed that home-loan approvals for blacks were up 38 percent from 1993 while loan approvals for Hispanics rose by 31 percent, for Asians by 17 percent, and for whites by 12 percent. Since black rejection rates changed relatively little in comparison to whites—31.2 percent versus 16.7 percent—the surge represented aggressive marketing both in lower income minority communities and among minorities living in predominantly white middle- and upper-income neighborhoods. Two of the largest initiatives came from banks actively involved in large mergers. Wells Fargo & Company, which is acquiring its former California rival, First Interstate Bancorp, pledged $45 billion for lower-income and small-business loans over ten years. NationsBank Corporation of

Charlotte, North Carolina, whose acquisitions include American Security Bank and several others, said it would make $500 million available in four Southeastern cities to as many as 10,000 borrowers with no down payment and no closing costs. In addition to these incentives, much of the new lending offered relaxed standards for such things as a borrower's credit rating, income, and level of debt.

The *Journal* found this not to be an unmixed blessing: "While such programs help people who otherwise might have no hope of owning a home, they may also distort the market, discouraging lending by others who are not ready to subsidize loans so heavily—and, ironically, squeezing traditional inner-city lenders."

The newspaper referred to the Boston Bank of Commerce, a minority-owned bank established to serve the city's desperately poor Roxbury and Mattapan neighborhoods. It had been substantially knocked out of the mortgage market by the flood of cheap credit. Ronald Homer, its CEO, noted, "There's a lot more credit on the street and in the short term, that's good for the community. But it hurts our bank, and over the long term, you have to ask how long these big banks are going to remain here when the regulators take the pressure off."

Another concern, articulated by Commissioner Lindsey, was that "tinkering with underwriting standards could create more social problems than it solves if the result is that more families default." The same concern was expressed by Ronald Homer in more practical terms: "You have to ask the fundamental question that if a person can't cover closing costs or doesn't have any savings for a down payment, what happens if the furnace blows?"

In fact, as early as the summer of 1995 both "Freddie Mac" and "Fannie May," as well as NationsBank, began noticing higher default rates among the inner-city beneficiaries. The result was the rapid acceleration of a practice known as "credit scoring," which has been around since the 1950s but which had been adopted by only a relative handful of banks in personal and commercial loan transactions and had been used hardly at all by mortgage lenders.

Credit scoring begins with the information, such as types of credit in use, length of time accounts have been open, and payment history provided by such major credit bureaus as Equifax, Trans Union, and TRW. The leading credit scoring consultant, Fair, Isaac, then takes all the information, weights it according to the relative importance of each factor in determining the probability of default on the applied for loan, and assigns the applicant a "score" between 200 and 400, the former representing the highest level of risk, and the latter, the lowest. The score can be used for the simple purpose of accepting or rejecting the loan application or to price loans based on the degree of risk. Together with accompanying "reason codes" provided by Fair, Isaac, the scores can be used to target areas that require additional explanation from the applicant or to suggest ways he can improve his credit behavior in order to qualify for a future loan. They can also be used as a device for routing each application toward streamlined consideration, ordinary underwriting, or the review committee that handles likely rejections.

Clearly, credit scoring can also formalize loan consideration procedures, employing a standardized, impersonal mechanism of documented validity for determining who gets a loan and who doesn't, and in the process, insulating the lending institution from charges of racial bias. A portent that things may be headed in that direction came in the fall of 1995 when "Freddie Mac," located in Northern Virginia, announced that it had decided to use credit scoring as an integral part of its mortgage acceptance process. A reluctant "Fannie Mae," located in the District of Columbia, followed suit. In private conversations, its officials expressed grave concern that the use of credit scoring would quickly become a hindrance to the acceptance of minority mortgage credit applications.

If that turns out to be the case, the effort by Deval Patrick and others in the Clinton administration to use the cherished concept of civil rights as a whip with which to beat lending institutions into changing practices which meet the tests of both tradition and sound business practice will have backfired. To inoculate themselves against federal harassment, the home loan industry will formalize its criteria, scoring potential applicants and, in the end, providing less credit to both whites and blacks who lack the paper credentials for a loan. Governor Lindsey's warning will have proven prescient: "Under current policy conditions, I would expect credit-scoring type procedures to be overwhelmingly dominant by the end of the decade. We will obtain the fairness of the machine, but lose the judgment, talents, and sense of justice that only humans can bring to decision-making.... The intended beneficiaries of our drive for fairness may in fact be those who suffer the most."

16

THE INSURANCE
DISCRIMINATION HOAX

The administration's foray into home insurance paralleled its efforts in mortgage lending—both were designed to impose affirmative action. But the standards used were developed in the employment sector, which is a vastly different milieu; mortgage borrowers and insurance purchasers are not competing against one another, because there is money or protection for all qualified applicants. Again like mortgage lending, large numbers of potential insurers can make money only by selling their product, as do the agents and brokers who represent them. In 1993, 1,136 companies in the United States wrote property insurance.

Insurance traditionally falls under state regulation. When Congress passed the Fair Housing Act (FHA) of 1968, it clearly stated that it had no intention of bringing home insurance under the purview of the act, and a 1988 federal court decision held that the Department of Housing and Urban Development (HUD) had no authority to regulate home insurance. But none of this prevented HUD in 1989 from writing regulations applying the FHA to home insurance carriers.

In 1993, the Justice Department, along with the National Association for the Advancement of Colored People (NAACP), brought the first major FHA home insurance discrimination case against the American Family Mutual Insurance Company, a Milwaukee insurer. Although American Family protested that insurance was not regulated by the FHA, the Seventh Circuit disagreed; it held that insurance was so integral a part of home ownership as to be covered by implication in the act ("no insurance, no loan; no loan, no house") and allowed the suit.

The allegations were that American Family used race as a factor in inspecting homes, overlooking deficiencies in white homes while those same deficiencies were used as excuses to deny coverage to blacks. One supervisor allegedly wrote an agent, "*Quit writing* all those *blacks!*" and later, "You write too many blacks. You gotta start writing good, solid premium-paying white people."

The alleged racism of one supervisor notwithstanding, American Family did underwrite 37 percent of the insurance business in Milwaukee's black neighborhoods and, during years of investigation and litigation, neither the government nor the NAACP produced a single individual who claimed he or she was denied a mortgage due to an inability to obtain home insurance, giving the lie to the court's nifty little slogan. Nevertheless, American Family took an Olympic swan dive and accepted a consent decree that sent shock waves throughout the industry.

The terms of the settlement provided a good window on how the Clinton administration really wants home insurers to behave. Under the decree, American Family committed itself to:

- Advertise in the black media.
- Hire at least four agents with offices in black areas.
- Permit the NAACP and the Urban League to develop

a "penetration strategy" for increasing black insurance clientele.

- Terminate the requirement that to obtain a "replacement" policy, the market value of the home must be at least 80 percent of the replacement cost.
- Eliminate the requirement that a home or property reach a stated "minimum value" in order to qualify for insurance.
- Employ credit checks that are made only to determine the likelihood of arson, rather than the ability to meet premiums or maintain the house in good repair.
- Sell policies at or below "market prices."
- Subsidize individual insureds, including closing costs.
- Provide a compensation package totaling $16 million, part of which would go toward compensating "discouraged applicants"—people who were discriminated against only in the sense of having heard or assumed that American Family was not interested in insuring blacks and hence declined to go through the "hollow gesture" of applying for coverage.

In paragraph after paragraph of the decree, the insurance company pledged to consider the *effect* of its actuarial practices on potential minority clients.

Jack Ramirez, vice president and chief operating officer for the National Association of Independent Insurers, reacted to the decree with public fury uncharacteristic of an organization that knows it must live with the administration in power. Terming the settlement the "ultimate affirmative action program," and the "most detailed micro-managing of a private business ever attempted," he predicted it would have pernicious effects upon the future conduct of the insurance business. "To avoid bludgeoning attacks by the government in the future," he predicted, "insurers will have to consider lowering the cost of urban insurance despite higher risks resulting from higher crime rates, older homes with deteriorating wiring or out-dated heating systems, and other similar factors. Consumers in other areas will pay the price of these subsidies through higher premiums. This distortion of the risk-based insurance market is not going to improve the quality of housing in any area."

Once again, the administration made no secret of its intentions to deploy its civil rights legal arsenal against sound and historic business practices. Roberta Achtenberg told a Senate committee in May 1994 that she was targeting seemingly race-neutral risk-based policies, such as minimum value or maximum age restrictions which have a disparate impact on minorities: "Black households are more than twice as likely as white households (47 percent of black households but just 23 percent of white households) to reside in homes that are valued at less than $50,000. Similarly 40 percent of black households but only 29 percent of white households live in homes that were built before 1950." On these grounds, the administration would seek to forbid companies from taking the age of a house or its value into account.

Since insurance has long been primarily an area for state regulation, there have been fifty different regimes regulating, overseeing, and studying the industry. Over time, no issue in insurance has been studied more often or from more different perspectives than the terms and conditions on which homeowners' insurance is available to inner-city residents. There have been and continue to be examples of individual racism, prejudice, and acts of discrimination. But in a highly competitive industry with hundreds of suppliers, agents, and brokers, the governing principle is actuarial risk. There are powerful if painfully obvious reasons for every standard the administration seeks to abolish:

- Old firetraps are bad risks and so require high premiums.
- People who cannot afford to modernize plumbing, wiring, and electrical fixtures are bad risks.
- Homes whose replacement value vastly exceeds their market worth are bad risks not only in terms of accident, but arson as well.

Moreover, "multi-line" underwriters—those who insure not only property but also automobile, personal liability, life, and health—must usually turn a profit in more than a single area in order to operate fruitfully. If, as is often the case in inner-city areas, automobile insurance cannot be profitably sold, fewer agents will be willing to set up shop to offer the remaining panoply of services.

Taking these factors into consideration, companies may deny coverage, restrict it, charge a lot for it, or avoid operating in certain markets, depending upon their assessment of actuarial risk and potential profit. The problem is mitigated somewhat by the Fair Access to Insurance Requirements plans in effect in most states with large minority populations, whereby insurers guaranty through pooling arrangements to provide at least basic coverage to high-risk clients. But getting insurance coverage through a *fair* plan tends to carry an onus and can sometimes impede the ability to obtain individual coverage the next time around.

All of these problems affect minorities more than others because they tend to be in the higher risk inner-city categories more than others. The problem was summed up adeptly by Robert W. Klein, director of Research for the National Association of Insurance Commissioners, in a 1994 paper: "The negative relationship between the extent of insurance coverage and minority concentration shown in previous studies is a matter of concern *but no analysis to date has adequately demonstrated that this relationship is even partially attributable to unfair discrimination by insurers"* (emphasis added). In other words, once again high risks tend to correlate, on average, with minority applicants, so on average they will find it harder to buy insurance. *But the reason has to do with risk, not racism.*

With the American Family consent decree in her pocket, the support of her secretary Henry Cisneros, and the enthusiastic backing of her Justice Department colleague Deval Patrick, Roberta Achtenberg set out to achieve her coup de grâce—development of a new set of regulations under the Community Reinvestment Act that would, in effect, revolutionize the insurance industry by getting rid of the core of actuarial practices that had the greatest disparate impact on minority groups. During 1994, four gala sets of hearings were held in Atlanta, San Francisco, Chicago, and New York to gather support for the changes. Witnesses included community activists, minority groups representatives, senior elected officials, insurance industry representatives, and state insurance commissioners.

To minority activists and their allies, it was simply a question of doing in insurance what had been done in other affirmative action areas years ago. William Lynch, chief counsel for the NAACP in the American Family case, offered the following: "The proof of specific clearly articulated company intention to discriminate should not be required. Even in the absence of such direct proof the regulations should prohibit practices which have racial discriminatory impact if the insurance company fails to demonstrate to HUD by clear and convincing evidence that the standard, policy or practice is a business necessity that cannot be achieved by business practices that are less discriminatory."

Among the scores of witnesses, however, not a single one testified that he or she had been unable to obtain homeowner's insurance on account of racial discrimination.

Several witnesses tried hard to edify Ms. Achtenberg. Richard W. Berstein of the Metropolitan Property and Casualty Insurance Company, spoke of the five-year effort his company had made to penetrate the inner-city market of Atlanta and to provide comprehensive homeowner insurance to the city's minority population. "Unfortunately, our underwriting losses in Georgia have grown faster than our earned premium," he said, proceeding to provide the data. "It is easy for critics to accuse the insurance industry and other businesses of charging higher prices or having fewer offices in inner-city neighborhoods because of a perceived systemic pattern of discrimination based on ethnicity of income level. The fact is, insurance prices reflect the risk characteristics of the property insured. The only systemic problem that exists is one of substantially higher losses in urban, inner city areas."

The insurance commissioner of Illinois noted that 93 percent of the homeowners in his state obtain coverage, one reason being that Illinois had removed restrictions on pricing, allowing the market to determine its own values.

And, pondering Ms. Achtenberg's desire to see insurance companies maintain meticulous records on the race of all applicants, Richard C. Hsia, New York State's deputy insurance superintendent, reminded her that many states forbid the accumulation of precisely that information in order to prevent bias. He stated, "We find sad irony in the current clamor for mandating reporting by insurers to track race, income, and ethnicity of individual customers. Applications for homeowners insurance do not, should not, and cannot ask for this information because these factors are not risk-related...."

How close were Deval Patrick and Roberta Achtenberg, encouraged by their superiors up to and including President Clinton, to bringing about new affirmative action standards to the fields of mortgage lending and home insurance?

Maybe as close as one court case with favorable results, affirmed by the Supreme Court.

Maybe as close as a rider tacked onto legislation—the real focus of the day's activity—like home district pork or a minority set-aside.

Maybe as close as a few hundred pages of proposed regulations that pop up in the *Federal Register* and take trained lawyers weeks to decipher, never make the news shows or even newspapers, but subtly and incrementally change the balance between statism and individual rights.

But then, in 1995, a Republican Congress came to town, and Patrick and Achtenberg soon found themselves on the defensive. Far from expanding affirmative action in insurance, Achtenberg would be greeted with a Republican proposal to restrict HUD's authority over insurance. Soon thereafter, Ms. Achtenberg announced her resignation, returned to San Francisco to run for mayor, and lost.

Her replacement, Betsy Julian, pledged to launch a dozen new investigations into racial discrimination in the areas of mortgage lending and home insurance.

17

THE CALIFORNIA CIVIL
RIGHTS INITIATIVE

In early November 1995, Tom Wood placed a call to Ward Connerly and begged him to take command of the effort to amend the California state constitution known as the California Civil Rights Initiative (CCRI). Wood, a professor who specializes in Far Eastern Philosophy, is co-author with Glynn Custred of the amendment, which would prohibit the state and its political subdivisions from discriminating against or granting preference to any citizen on the basis of race, sex, or ethnicity in employment, education, or the award of government contracts. Connerly, who is black, is a successful contractor, a leading Republican fundraiser, a close friend of Governor Pete Wilson, and a powerful member of the State Board of Regents. He had gained national prominence during the year while leading a successful battle to have the regents ban considerations of race in both student admissions and faculty hiring at state institutions of higher learning.

Wood told Connerly that the initiative was in deep trouble and that unless he was willing to take charge, it would not collect the nearly 700,000 signatures needed by 21 February to win a place on the November 1996 ballot. But Connerly was still absorbed with the regents battle which was about to enter a second round as supporters of race preferences in higher education sought recision of the ruling. Further, the issue had rubbed emotions raw and subjected Connerly to personal danger. His Sacramento office windows had been hit by bullets fired from passing cars; he had received a profusion of "hate calls," some of them threatening; and blacks openly accused him of being a traitor to his race. Neither he nor his family was ready for another round of political bloodletting.

But when Larry Arnn, a personal friend who briefly served as co-chairman of the CCRI and is president of the Claremont Institute, a conservative think tank, called, Connerly capitulated.

"I've always believed that people shouldn't be judged by their race," Connerly says simply, recalling the rather Gumpian admonition of his maternal grandmother, a full-blooded Choctaw Indian, "You can't tell a book by its cover." Moreover, Connerly is one of those ethnic rarities, a man who does not think in terms of racial identities, his own or anyone else's. "If I am betraying my people," he asks, "which people am I betraying?" recalling that in addition to his Indian grandmother, he boasts a French grandfather and a white great-grandfather. In personal terms, Connerly concluded that because of his regents stand, he was already heavily identified with the anti–affirmative action position, whatever its incarnation. And he felt there was little additional harm black political leaders could cause him. "I don't make my living in the black community. I don't wear black on my sleeve. I'm already a traitor to them. What the hell else, what more can they do to me?"

Connerly found the initiative as advertised, short on funds at the very moment when 85,000 signatures per week were needed to meet the deadline. Within a month, he had raised $400,000 and would raise an additional $200,000. By the end of February, more than enough signatures had been gathered to qualify CCRI for the November ballot.

The administrative snafus and political derring-do have blinded neither side to the importance of the issue and the potential stakes involved. A state with high Hispanic and Asian populations, as well as a black population measured in 1990 at 7.4 percent, California is also the state where racial preferences have been woven most deeply into the fabric of public life. The state university system had gone a long way toward a proportional admissions policy before a public backlash and the regents action forced some retrenchment. State contracts have for years had a 15 percent set-aside for minorities and another 5 percent for women. Some local governments have affirmative action hiring plans of such precision that specific jobs are designated in advance for members of one racial or ethnic group or another. A state constitutional provision requires all government agencies to continue with their affirmative action programs whatever holdings may come down from the U.S. Supreme Court or other judicial bodies unless the decisions apply to the specific plans involved—the same method of defiance used long ago in the South's "massive resistance" to desegregation.

CCRI threatens to change all that, and if affirmative action loses in California, it can lose anywhere. Opponents of the initiative will wage a bruising battle to defeat what Oakland Assemblywoman Barbara Lee has called "one of the most dangerous pieces of legislation I have ever witnessed." Assembly Speaker Willie Brown, now mayor of San Francisco and the unofficial leader of the opposition, has long since rendered judgment on it. "The thing's racist," Brown has charged. Eva Peterson, a well-known San Francisco civil rights lawyer, has described the initiative as "Willie Horton goes to college." And academics who should know better have argued that the measure could allow male gym teachers to pursue positions in female locker rooms and under-mine women's athletics in general. This despite language written into the proposed amendment that specifically preempts such anomalous results. Of course, that language too has been delib-erately distorted by opponents who claim it lessens the "com-pelling interest" standard by which excerpting to sexual equality must be judged in California.

Connerly agrees that CCRI raises issues of fundamental impor-tance and predicts the debate will show that it is the proponents of affirmative action who are really insulting blacks by arguing they need a perpetual helping hand. He says the debate will be "one of the defining moments in the state of California's history. It can be a good thing. It can make us realize that we are still making the correlation between pigmentation and ability. There's still the belief that a black person is not up to snuff."

In his office at Stanford University, Professor Paul Sniderman also sees CCRI as an event of singular importance in the nation's political history, which might set off a chain reaction that could ultimately discredit liberalism as a national political force. For the past decade, Sniderman has performed research on public opin-ion, race, and affirmative action, using the National Election Studies project—a massive survey of voter attitudes conducted in each election since 1986—as his data base. In an important 1993 book on the subject, *The Scar of Race,* Sniderman and co-author Thomas Piazza of the University of California at Berkeley ana-lyzed the responses to a massive attitudinal survey of Americans who voted in the elections of 1986. They offered several provoca-tive conclusions, and more will appear in an updated version:

First, 80 percent to 90 percent of white Americans believe deeply in giving blacks and other minorities an "even chance." Most favor measures to help the poor, and 61 percent approve making an "extra effort" to be fair through the sort of benign outreach efforts for minorities that used to be regarded as affirmative action before policymakers moved in the direction of race preferences. In this respect, Sniderman and Piazza are two of many public opinion analysts to document the fact that there has been a sea change in white attitudes toward race within the past generation, a profound move toward tolerance too often forgotten amid the emotions of contemporary policy debates.

Second, depending on the form of the question, 80 percent to 90 percent of white Americans reject both quotas and racial preferences.

Third, there is no significant statistical correlation between political philosophy and opposition to racial preferences, nor between one's level of racial tolerance and opposition to such preferences. Tolerant liberals are nearly as adverse to racial preferences as are bigots and conservatives.

Fourth, so deeply held is the opposition to racial preferences that the mere mention of it tends to influence the views of respondents toward minority racial and ethnic groups. In other words, a citizen whose responses ordinarily reflect little or no bias against blacks is more likely to vent antiblack bias in responses to questions that follow questions testing his attitude toward quotas and racial preferences.

Sniderman says his most recent research underlines his earlier findings. "If we define affirmative action as preferential treatment of one race over another, or double standards, it is opposed by conservatives and bigots nearly 100 percent of the time. But it is also opposed by liberals and those with highly tolerant racial attitudes 80 to 90 percent of the time." Even when Sniderman limited his sampling universe to the most liberal, tolerant 20 percent of the population, "affirmative action still gets hammered hands down."

Sniderman says that most citizens become incensed when they are informed that the government has imposed racial preferences in such areas as university admissions, jobs, and government contracts in order to help blacks and other minorities overcome the effects of past discrimination.

Most had no idea of the existence, or at least the extent of such programs. Sniderman says: "That issue, at the core of CCRI, has the potential for discrediting liberalism because government officials have been less than forthcoming in describing how affirmative action works in practice. They have found it easier to treat race preferences as an administrative matter than as a frankly debated issue of public policy." Sniderman warns of a divisive political period ahead: "I fear we have seen only the first act of what is likely to be a very long drama."

If Sniderman and Connerly are right, the appearance of CCRI on the November ballot will be a major political event with significant national consequences. Despite ferocious attack, the measure, according to all polls, continues to enjoy overwhelming support from rank-and-file voters, including more than 40 percent of black voters, more than half of all Hispanic voters, and nearly two-thirds of all Asian voters. Moreover, as the campaign intensifies, it could become a magnet issue drawing voters to the polls who might otherwise stay home, or influencing voters toward candidates who share their view on CCRI. If that happens in a significant number of cases, President Clinton could face more problems in a state critical to his reelection prospects than early polls suggest. And what happens in California could well prove contagious, inspiring backers of "copy cat" measures in as many as two dozen other states and building support for similar federal legislation introduced by Senator Bob Dole and Representative John Canady.

Surveying the political year ahead just prior to California's 26 March primary, John Herrington, the Republican state chairman, described affirmative action as "potentially as damaging to

Democrats as the abortion battle has been to Republicans." He said that the state party would "spend what has to be spent to make clear to voters what the issue is really about and who is on which side."

And CCRI is only one of several California fronts on which the battle against race preferences is being waged. Early in 1996, the Board of Regents reaffirmed its decision of the previous summer banning the use of race as an admissions or hiring factor by state universities. Governor Wilson has ordered race preferences in state hiring stopped, to the limited extent that can be accomplished through executive order. And he has also initiated a lawsuit seeking a declaration by the federal courts that all state racial preferences and set-asides are illegal, a decision which would relieve state and local officials of having to enforce the various preferences.

"Trying to put an end to racial and ethnic preferences is like turning a ship in the water," says Mike Antonovich, one of two Republicans on the Los Angeles County Board of Supervisors. "It is a slow process and you encounter a lot of resistance. But once you get going, you are as tough to stop as the preferences were."

It was, in fact, an effort by Willie Brown to expand California's quota policies that provoked the CCRI initiative. In 1991, Speaker Brown pushed his Education Equity Act through the state legislature, requiring state universities and colleges to admit and graduate classes of students that mirrored the racial and ethnic composition of the state's high school graduating classes. The timing was curious, coming as it did when the state university system was already under intense pressure to relax its rigid commitment to expand black and Hispanic representation at the expense of more academically qualified whites and Asians. Governor Wilson promptly vetoed the bill, and it never became law.

But it did command the attention of Tom Wood and his friend,

Glynn Custred, two conservative academics whose prior political involvement had involved little more than membership in the California Association of Scholars, the state chapter of a national organization that has spent much of its time battling the excesses of the political correctness movement on campus. The anger of the two professors at Speaker Brown's effort to impose legislated quotas on the public university system was rooted in both philosophy and experience. To both, it is axiomatic that preferences cannot be allocated on the basis of race without the excluded race suffering discrimination, and both regard it as a pervasion of American values to allow race or ethnicity rather than merit to dictate the outcome of an admissions process, an invitation to bid on a public contract, or the hiring of public servants. And, as professors, both have observed what they regard as the deleterious effects of bringing to a campus students who, as a definable racial or ethnic group, are markedly less qualified academically than their fellow students, and who, in many cases, require remedial courses even to begin coping with college-level work.

The essence of their proposed state constitutional amendment is contained in its first paragraph: "The state shall not discriminate against, or grant preferential treatment to, any individual or group on the basis of race, sex, color, ethnicity, or national origin in the operation of public employment, public education, or public contracting."

Subsequent sections declare that the law will not be retroactive, that it does not deal with "bona fide qualifications based on sex"—a provision taken from the Civil Rights Act of 1964 which, for more than two decades, has preempted the male gym teacher or male athlete seeking to win a place in female athletics—that it is not intended to invalidate any existing court order or consent decree, and that it shall not apply to action undertaken to establish or maintain eligibility for a federal program the loss of which would cause the loss of federal funds to the state. In its original form, the measure explicitly created a private right of enforcement in the courts; the current language does the same thing in more obscure fashion, a way of tiptoeing through the political minefield of antilawsuit sentiment in the state.

"To my way of thinking, this is a return to the principles if not the exact language of the Civil Rights Act of 1964 when we outlawed discrimination based on race and when sponsors of the law expressly disavowed the idea of preferences or quotas," says Custred. "In fact, they are two sides to the same coin. It is both theoretically and practically impossible to exercise a preference on behalf of one race or ethnic group without discriminating against another."

Connerly offers further evidence of the same point. "Each year we graduate 9,000 high school seniors with 4.0 GPAs [grade point averages]. Most of them are whites and Asians who played by the rules, and many want to go to one of our top two universities, Cal Berkeley or UCLA. If they lose their places because those schools accept blacks or Hispanics with GPAs of 2.9— maybe even from out of state—and they want to go to a comparable school, their parents have to borrow money to send them somewhere outside of California. And that defeats the whole purpose of state-supported higher education which is to provide a superior education to kids who can't afford to go to Harvard or Yale. If we can't do that, we shouldn't be in the business of higher education in the first place."

The intellectual integrity and vigor of the two academics is beyond dispute, even by those who disagree most fervently with their plan. But in terms of translating their idea into political reality, their names might just as well have been "Dead Wood" and "Frozen Custred." After submitting their proposed amendment to the attorney general the first time around, the two essentially waited for signatures to grow on the bottom of the paper. They didn't, of course, and the CCRI never came close to making the 1994 ballot. It was, to all intents and purposes, a dead letter.

Enter Joe Gelman, thirty-two, smart, tough, conservative, and idealistic. Gelman is also a Likudnik-style Zionist who had lived in Israel long enough to fight as a paratrooper in the 1982 Lebanon campaign. Back in California in the mid-1980s, he took a job with the well-connected Larry Weinberg, former head of the powerful American Israel Public Affairs Committee. In due course, he became chairman of the city's Civil Service Commission, an unpaid job.

Gelman at once saw the promise of the Wood–Custred idea. "First of all, it was the right thing to do," he recalls. "Second, I think it's something an overwhelming majority of Californians support. And third, quite frankly, it is a wedge issue, a way for Republicans to isolate Democratic candidates with those constituencies who want to use race as an entitlement for rights."

One of Gelman's first moves was to contact Ron K. Unz, president of Wall Street Analytics and a political unknown who financed his own challenge to Governor Wilson in the 1994 Republican primary, campaigning against both affirmative action and the punitive anti-immigration features of Proposition 187.

Unz needed no convincing over where public opinion stood on the question of race preferences, which he knew from his own polling was very strong and very deep, as are his sentiments on the subject. "I view this as an issue that can determine the future of America," he says. "Think about it. Over the last 1,000 years, the United States of America is the only example of a society which is large, successful, and multiethnic. And we succeed because we provide a system of values which everyone can adopt and which allows them to transcend their places of origin. Now instead you are starting to have groups growing up in America who are taught their rights depend on their ethnicity. I think that has the power to destroy America. And it would be a shame if America is destroyed by something which could have been cured by political courage."

Courage?

"The courage I talk about is the courage to defend a position you believe in even when the other side calls you a racist. Because if those of us who believe in equal rights under law are frightened off, the field will be left to the David Dukes, the Pat Buchanans, and the Jesse Helms, all of whom have used the anti-quota theme in their political campaigns with good results. That's not where this issue belongs."

In mid-December 1994, Gelman organized the meeting that gave CCRI its basic campaign structure in the months ahead, flying Wood and Custred down from San Francisco to join Arnn and Arnie Steinberg, a veteran GOP political strategist. Gelman quit his job with Weinberg and took over day-to-day management of the campaign. There were a few large donations, but $300,000 of the first $500,000 came from contributions of $100 or less. Steinberg estimated that about $1.2 million would be needed to obtain the requisite signatures to get on the ballot, while a fall campaign would cost anywhere from three to seven times that amount, depending on the opposition.

The early stages of the campaign proceeded with spectacular if deceptive success. A statewide poll showed overwhelming white and Asian support for CCRI with unexpected strength in the black and Hispanic communities. Even when the questions were tilted against the initiative, CCRI won majority support.

The press too descended on the issue, turning Wood and Custred into international celebrities in a matter of weeks. Steinberg and others attributed this to the fact that the media had been "blindsided" both by the support for Proposition 187 and the 1994 Republican sweep of Congress and were now overcompensating.

Adoption of the CCRI cause by Governor Wilson, soon to declare his presidential candidacy, also fueled media interest, particularly after his successful exploitation of Proposition 187's anti-immigrant sentiment during the past gubernatorial campaign. Finally, the potential impact on the presidential campaign itself was clear. Voters drawn to the polls by their opposition to affirmative action and racial preferences would surely vote against President Clinton in November, or place him in a position where, by endorsing the referendum or dodging the issue entirely, he would alienate a broad swath of his own constituency.

Wood prepared a "Speakers Manual" for pro-initiative debaters. The highly detailed analysis cited a number of injustices it would redress, but it also emphasized its limits, such as its non-interference with decisions by private employers and universities. A student assignment plan such as the bald racial quota allocations at San Francisco's Lowell High School would go by the boards, as would a Los Angeles City numerical "goals" policy which awarded a contract to a minority firm that had submitted a $4 million bid over a $3.3 million bid by a white company. On the other hand, race-neutral recruitment programs would continue, as would remedies, up to and including quotas, which redress proven official discrimination against individual claimants.

Wood also prepared debaters for two of the arguments opponents of CCRI were already making—that it would "turn the clock back" on the progress women and minorities had made and that reverse discrimination is rare to nonexistent since nothing in affirmative action policy mandates the acceptance of "unqualified" individuals for the school or job in question.

In addressing the first point, Wood noted that women and other minorities would continue to be protected against discrimination as they have been for a generation. "Opponents talk about turning the clock back, but they are talking about preferences,"

Wood wrote. "What they are saying, in other words, is that women and minorities can't compete unless the law gives them special privileges and treatment. This claim is baseless and demeaning to women and minorities."

As regards preferences to the qualified, Wood accused opponents of treating the term "preferences" the way Humpty Dumpty treated words in *Alice in Wonderland:* to mean whatever they wanted them to mean: "Preferential treatment is simply favoring or advantaging, period."

The running debate over CCRI has taken place on college campuses, in civic forums, on television, via radio talk and call-in shows, and in newspaper columns. Eugene Voloch, a young constitutional law professor at UCLA who immigrated from Kiev in the mid-1970s, participates frequently as an initiative supporter. He says he has become used to dealing with the demagogic debater tactics of opponents, ranging from veiled and not-so-veiled accusations of racism to exaggerated claims that federally funded projects would be put at risk or that women's athletic teams would suddenly be jeopardized by all those guys chomping on the bit to join women's teams.

But there are also serious issues. Voloch says, "The strongest potential arguments of the opposition are subtle and, therefore, rarely made in the debates; namely, that affirmative action is really a rough cut at dealing with existing societal discrimination, or that the bottom line is that an informal race-conscious private network continues to exist which must be neutralized by the race-conscious application of public policy."

And how would you respond?

"By describing the historic role of the law as a neutral arbiter of individual rights. You can't prefer one person on the basis of race or ethnicity without penalizing someone else on that basis. It is not a point that always wins converts because even when they know they have been discriminated against, white people often regard it as fair punishment for all that has been done to blacks over the centuries. And they dread being declared racist because they oppose what minorities say they need to level the playing field. But still, it is a point central to our society, and not to many others."

What about the question of self-esteem, that blacks, Hispanics, and perhaps others need to gain admission to the best schools, or win the good jobs, so they know it is possible for them to make it in this society?

"Self-esteem comes from learning and achieving, not from being told that you do not have to learn or achieve because this racist society owes you a favored place."

■ ■ ■

From behind her desk in an old but stately building on South Spring Street in what has become a center of Hispanic business activity in downtown Los Angeles, Teresa Fay-Bustillos disagrees. As the vice president and chief litigator for the Mexican American Legal Defense Fund (MALDEF), she has battled to establish ethnic entitlements in everything from jobs to voting districts. Brilliant, articulate, and thorough, she says she's an optimist regarding what legal and political battling can achieve, but a skeptic regarding individuals doing the right thing when not prodded by government. "I have a basic mistrust about relying on the goodwill of human nature to provide either legal or social justice for minority people," she acknowledges.

Formed in the mid-1960s, MALDEF has modeled itself after the NAACP Legal Defense Fund, but on behalf of the Hispanic population. Yet the situations of the two people are not all that similar nor is the strategy for blacks particularly appropriate for Hispanics. As Peter Skerry of the Woodrow Wilson Center has noted, Hispanic residential patterns are far more integrated than blacks'. And Hispanic communities tend to have far more stable family structures than those of blacks, which helps account for their greater level of entrepreneurship and upward mobility. They also intermarry at three to four times the rate of blacks—Ms. Bustillos's own father was of Irish–German descent—and face less discrimination in employment and at the polls. By any standard of measurement, their experience is roughly similar to that of other immigrant groups—Italians, Poles, the Irish, Jews, Greeks—who came to this country a century or so ago, not to mention the more recent Asian arrivals.

In one recent survey, the ten most common names of California home buyers included Lee, Martinez, Rodriguez, Garcia, Nguyen, and Wong. And increasingly the last name indicates little more than the race or nationality of one male ancestor. As of 1990, there were 1.2 million interracial couples in the United States, triple the number in 1970. During that period, the number of black–white marriages went from 65,000 to 231,000. In California, 15 percent to 20 percent of all marriages involve racially mixed couples, with 55 percent of Japanese Americans and 40 percent of Chinese Americans marrying outside their group.

What masks Hispanic success is that very many have arrived only recently and, in many cases, illegally. Skerry finds the greatest irony in MALDEF efforts to create voting districts based on overall population figures rather than eligible voters, given the heavy concentration of nonvoting Hispanic residents, many of them children, many others legal or illegal aliens. In 1990, for example, one heavily Hispanic state assembly district in Los Angeles cast a total of 25,000 votes, principally because most of its residents were ineligible to vote. In the same election, a predominantly white district with the same population cast 154,000 votes.

Ms. Bustillos supported Willie Brown's 1991 attempt to impose ethnic quotas on the state university system, and she endorses state efforts to provide government jobs and contracts to races and ethnic groups in rough proportion to their percentage of the population. "That is exactly the sort of thing government should be doing, opening the doors of opportunity for all of its people and making sure that fair numbers of all are brought inside," she maintains. She is against using Scholastic Aptitude Test scores to determine admission to the University of California, saying they cannot predict who will do well after the first year of college, let alone in the world of work beyond. She also dismisses standardized employment tests. "These tests are only one small partial measure of who will do well," she says.

Numbers, goals, and timetables are also important, she maintains, if for no other reason than to force employers to review their affirmative action performance and to make sure they are using the right methods to attract minorities. "If you had an advertising campaign, would it be wrong to judge its success by reviewing your sales figures?" she asks. Moreover, to maintain the pressure to be fair, you need a specific plan, and that means specific numbers and targets for employing minorities. And you need both private initiatives and unrelenting government oversight. Further, she insists Hispanics need affirmative action as much as blacks because "in the eyes of the majority, we are not white and we never will be."

And in the eyes of the majority, are Asians white?

"I don't know. When you look at universities, you might think so. On the other hand, I've been to meetings on affirmative action where the room is filled wall to wall with Asian contractors."

As all this suggests, affirmative action in California is far from the simple white-versus-black model appropriate to much of the rest of the country. In California today, blacks make up a shrinking

7 percent of the population. Hispanics were 25.4 percent as of the last census, but they are by now past 30 percent, and one out of every two babies born in the state has Hispanic parents. Chinese, Japanese, Koreans, Vietnamese, Cambodians, Filipinos, and other Asians form communities with overlapping interests in certain areas, but not others. In policy conflicts arising out of educational quotas or preferences, blacks and Hispanics will often join forces against whites and Asians. But where Asians have succeeded in having themselves listed among the "disadvantaged," set-aside disputes often leave white contractors alone to battle the race preferences. And in issues of government employment and voting rights, the interests of blacks and Hispanics often collide. Los Angeles County, which requires proportional ethnic representation in government jobs, has seen blacks and Hispanics battling over their "fair share" for a decade. Today, blacks constitute only 11 percent of the county population but have 28 percent of the jobs, while Hispanics, making up 38 percent of the population, have only 23 percent of the jobs. A case brought by Hispanics claiming discrimination is now in the courts.

John McDermott, a tall, grey-haired partner in the law firm Cadwalder, Wickersham, and Taft, has gone head to head with MALDEF in some of the state's leading voting rights cases during the past decade, winning most of the time. He sees the underlying issue in these cases—proportional ethnic representation versus a race-neutral government—as identical to that raised by CCRI. The issue is made more personal by his own background as a boy from a poor Ohio family who wound up graduating from Harvard Law School and working as a civil rights lawyer both in and out of government during the 1960s and 1970s. McDermott denies any inconsistency in values. "I grew up in a different civil rights era, where institutional race consciousness was the evil and color blindness was the remedy," he recalls.

But if individuals are not color-blind, doesn't official color blindness merely reinforce private racism?

"If people aren't color-blind, that's all the more reason why government must be. It is perfectly appropriate for government to enforce nondiscrimination. But when you move beyond color blindness to equal race outcomes, where ethnicity becomes the basis of everything from job offers to voting districts, you are not attacking racism, you are institutionalizing it. What's more, you've created institutions that stick around long after they are needed because people have built careers in government, at universities, and in business implementing race conscious affirmative action programs."

McDermott scoffs at suggestions that Hispanics need affirmative action because they have been victims of discrimination going back to the Mexican American War of 1848. He notes that at the time there were only 40,000 Latinos in the United States, that a majority of them were Spaniards, and that only 7,000 were residents of California at the time it gained statehood. Not only have the Hispanics come voluntarily—both legally and illegally— but most have arrived in California during the past quarter-century, two-thirds since 1970. "The socioeconomic status of Mexicans in the United States is a product of the socioeconomic conditions in Mexico which they brought with them when they came here," McDermott says. "It is not the product of racial or ethnic discrimination in the United States, and to maintain that it is, is fiction."

■　　■　　■

In the early stages of the CCRI campaign, timing was the critical issue. From the day the initiative was submitted to the attorney general, that office could take up to sixty days to give it a title, summarize its provisions, and project its financial impact on the state's treasury. Then the clock would start ticking, and CCRI forces would have 150 days to collect the signatures of the 694,000 registered voters in order to qualify for the November ballot.

Gelman focused on support mainly from the governor's office, the Republican National Committee, and the California Republican party, all of whom were happy to provide lip service, but little else. With his own presidential campaign taking shape, Wilson was not ready to turn on the spigot from his own list of potential contributors; others, with political sympathy for CCRI but not Wilson, regarded the effort as an integral part of his campaign and held back. At the same time, neither the state party nor the national committee was willing to commit much in the way of early resources to an operation they thought lacked political smarts.

National Republican leaders were only slightly more forthcoming. Senator Bob Dole and others vying for the GOP nomination could be helped by having CCRI on the November ballot, but their fundraising priorities were, of course, elsewhere. House Speaker Newt Gingrich assured CCRI that he could be counted on for support, but members of his staff and others urged him to focus instead on congressional issues of more immediate concern and to avoid a damaging attack on affirmative action without some alternative program in hand to ameliorate the condition of the nation's minority populations. Late in the year, Gingrich finally released his letter formally endorsing CCRI. In it, the Speaker wrote:

> The triumph of group rights over individual rights which has led to even greater government control over our lives, as well as crippling business and everyday life with the threat of *lawsuits, complaints, and grievances* must be reversed...

> *That means we must work to eliminate what I call*
> *"legalized discrimination,"* those programs put in place
> by government, which exalt group rights and give
> government far too much control over education and
> commerce (emphasis in original).

The letter urged recipients to sign a pledge of support for
CCRI. But by the time Gingrich acted, it was far too late to organize a national mailing of one million letters—the letter went out
only to 135,000 Californians.

In mid-December, Dole also formally endorsed CCRI in a *Los
Angeles Times* newspaper column.

Gelman had from the outset invited political trouble by assuming
a salaried role as CCRI coordinator while simultaneously serving as
Mayor Riordan's Civil Service Commission chairman. A man of
decency, integrity, and dedication, but with a touch of the kamikaze
in his political soul, Gelman sealed his own departure from the commission in November 1995 by churning out a press release herald-
ing the endorsement of CCRI—later denied—by Michelle
Park-Steele, the mayor's newly confirmed airport commissioner.
Park-Steele, who had all but sworn neutrality on the CCRI issue
during her confirmation hearings, resigned within days of the
embarrassing incident, as did Gelman.

The petition drive had suffered an earlier setback when Steinberg opted to strike a deal with the Democrats by virtue of which
the legislature would vote to place CCRI on the ballot in March
1996, when California held its presidential primary, rather than
await the outcome of the petition drive and thus a possible
November ballot placement. The move would have saved CCRI
backers the cost of a petition drive and would have virtually
guaranteed adoption of the amendment because a contested primary ensured a heavy Republican turnout compared with

Democrats who would stay away in droves with Clinton running unopposed.

For the White House and Democrats, the proposal offered to delink the November election from the CCRI campaign, perhaps saving the state for Clinton.

But when Steinberg and Custred showed up at Speaker Brown's ornate Sacramento office to cement the deal, they found they had been suckered. Brown had long since decided on unyielding opposition to CCRI and spent much of the hour session berating Custred, telling him at one point that he was "sitting in a black man's chair" in his office and that his seat at the university was also a "black man's chair." Steinberg's attempt at a managed settlement promptly collapsed, having done nothing to bolster GOP confidence in the team leading the campaign.

There was also difficulty getting prominent names and organizations to take a stand against their economic or political interests. Corporations anxious to preserve community goodwill and others who routinely fall back on "government pressure" to justify their own affirmative action programs would not endorse the measure. "This is not like an issue involving doctors, lawyers, insurance or tobacco, where the bucks just roll in from those with an economic stake in the outcome," Gelman noted. "Here, the only 'gain' for a business is to see pickets from [the American Civil Liberties Union] or Raza outside its fence. To help CCRI, you have to have ideological commitment. We need idealists."

Connerly confided he was "disappointed," not by the lack of support from businesses, but from individual CEOs. "CEOs of corporations have spines of Jell-O," he says. "They just don't want their names on anything that may be controversial. And they will say privately, 'Ward, hope you make it. We're with you all the way. It's the right thing to do. If we don't do this, California's going to be like Bosnia in another ten years.'"

But that's it. They fear boycotts and pickets.

"So I can understand it. I'm just disappointed. When democracy reaches the point where you're so chickenshit about standing up and being counted, freedom of speech doesn't mean a damn thing, because anybody can be intimidated by the NAACP, by the Urban League saying they're not going to hold their convention in California, by worry that we're going to have an 'R' stamped on our forehead if CCRI passes."

Not all of those who demurred or abstained were corporations or CEOs. The California branch of Associated General Contractors (AGC), a group which has been resolute in battling minority set-asides in the courts, declined to take a position on CCRI because of its reach into such areas as jobs and education in which AGC has no organizational interest. And an assortment of police organizations, many themselves veterans of anti-quota battles, elected to stay out of the CCRI fight so as not to provoke the Democratic establishment. Most intriguingly, the California Association of Scholars (CAS), which, like its national organization, has fought with tenacity against excessive political correctness and racial hiring on campus, declined to endorse the measure. In a speech to the Commonwealth Club of San Francisco, Jack Bunzel, a senior research fellow at the Hoover Institution, former president of San Jose State University, and a CAS member, said, "I feel that the yes or no direct democracy of the initiative process is too blunt an instrument to shape a more deliberative and nuanced response to such complex issues."

As is usually the case, supporters of race preferences felt no need for a "deliberative and nuanced response" to the issue. Cries of racism filled the air. Scare tactics regarding the measure's effects were rampant. Repeatedly, they charged that adoption of the measure would set race relations back thirty years, declining to explain how a measure that forbids official discrimination would reintroduce conditions that fostered official discrimination.

In terms of sheer intemperateness, Willie Brown outdid himself and his anti-CCRI colleagues in a September 1995 talk at California State Hayward, where Custred teaches, urging a form of student guerrilla warfare against the CCRI co-author.

"Believe me, if you treat him correctly, during the time you are in his class, by the end of the session he should really need therapy," exhorted the mayor (and former Assembly Speaker). "You ought to challenge him every day in every way. You should read ahead of him. You should do what you do best, to terrorize professors you don't like, and I guarantee he will be a basket case by the end of the year."

Sitting in his Sacramento office on a rainy Wednesday morning in mid-January 1996, Connerly contemplated Willie Brown's behavior in this and other racial preference battles with the bemused tolerance of a man who thinks there ought to be more black professionals and fewer professional blacks. He sees Brown as "a brilliant man" who could have been an extraordinary example for young blacks and other minorities had he chosen to emphasize the object lesson of his own career: that a man with pluck and ability can rise to any heights in this society. Instead Brown, in Connerly's view, stressed the roadblocks, and in so doing, gave new life to the notion of "separate but equal" at a time when it should have been disappearing from the American consciousness.

Connerly, like Brown, had come from the South, traveling with his family as a seven-year-old from Alabama's black belt to the more inviting California. He had grown up in the Sacramento area with black friends, white friends, Hispanic friends, and Asian friends; had been president of his college class; and for years has been a successful businessman. When asked his philosophy about race, he replies simply that it shouldn't matter: "A person does not choose his race, so he should not be judged by it."

Connerly sees CCRI as embodying this attitude. "You know, there are times when you can say, 'I had an impact,'" he mused. "You know, I'm not blowing smoke on myself, but if this thing makes it, I had an impact."

NOTES

A Note About the Notes

In a bibliographical note for each chapter, I sketch out the principal sources for that chapter, including interviews. In those cases where the work relied upon has, in my judgment, been adequately credited in the text, I make no further reference in the chapter notes. I try to include as well a number of sources, such as books and law review articles, that provided valuable background or perspective on the subject discussed, as opposed to specific facts.

Chapter 1: A Question of Discrimination

June O'Neill and Harold Orlans are quoted from their article in the collection, "Affirmative Action Revisited," *Annals of the American Academy of Political and Social Science* 523 (September 1992): 10–220. The views of Charles V. Hamilton, cited later in the chapter, are from his article, "Affirmative Action and the Class of Experiential Realities," in the same collection.

Glenn Loury's quote on the tax benefiting the black elite comes from the *San Diego Union,* 11 January 1995. His later quote on "the exhibitionism of nonachievement" comes from his prepared statement for hearings conducted by the Employer–Employee Relations Subcommittee of the House Committee on Economic and Educational Opportunities, 24 March 1995.

The quote from David O. Sears and Donald R. Kinder comes from their 1981 article, "Prejudice and Politics: Racism Versus Racial Threats to the Good Life," *Journal of Personality and Social Psychology* 40: 414–431.

Andrew Sullivan's quote comes from his *New York Times* Op-ed page piece, "Let Affirmative Action Die," 23 July 1995.

The account of the "Virginia (Law Review) Plan" is based on an interview with former editorial board member Rob Bell and other recent law school graduates who insisted on anonymity.

Robert L. Woodson's quote comes from his prepared statement to the U.S. Senate Committee on the Judiciary, 7 September 1995.

Professor Alex Johnson teaches a course on critical race theory at the University of Virginia Law School. Discussion of his views is based on materials distributed for that course, particularly his law review article, "Scholarly Paradigms: A New Tradition Based on Context and Color," *Vt. L. Rev.* 16 (1992): 913.

Randall Kennedy's quote comes from his law review article, "Racial Critiques of Legal Academia," *Harv. L. Rev.* 102 (1989): 1745.

Stephen L. Carter's quote comes from his book, *Reflections of an Affirmative Action Baby* (Basic Books, 1991).

Among the materials relied on for information regarding transracial adoption are R. Simon and H. Alstein, *Transracial Adoptees and Their Families* (1987) and Elizabeth Bartholet, "Where Do Black Children Belong? The Politics of Race Matching in Adoption," *University of Pennsylvania Law Review* 139 (1991): 1163.

My most helpful sources on the views of Martin Luther King Jr., and Malcolm X included James H. Cone, *Martin & Malcolm & America* (Orbis Books, 1991); David J. Garrow, *Bearing the Cross* (Morrow, 1986); and Bruce Perry (editor), *Malcolm X: The Last Speeches* (Pathfinder, 1989).

Justice William O. Douglas's quote comes from his dissent in *DeFunis v. Odegaard,* 416 U.S. 312 (1974).

The "Lift up your yarmulke" controversy involving Columbia University student Sharod Baker's anti-Semitic column in the *Spectator* student newspaper was the subject of a report in "Campus Newspaper's Excursion into a Bitter Free Speech Debate," *New York Times,* 1 November 1995, and two Nat Hentoff columns, "An Ivy League-Educated Antisemite," appearing in *The Washington Post,* 17 November 1995, and "College Degree in Anti-semitism," appearing in the *Village Voice,* 5 December 1995.

Arthur Schlesinger's quote comes from his book, *The Disuniting of America* (W.W. Norton & Co., 1992).

The source for Thomas Sowell's assessment of affirmative action abroad is "Affirmative Action: A Worldwide Disaster," *Commentary Magazine* (December 1989).

Shelby Steele's quote comes from his *New York Times* Op-ed page column, "Affirmative Action Must Go," 1 March 1995.

Chapter 2: A Failed Approach

Laurence Silberman's quote comes from his editorial page column, "The Road to Racial Quotas," *Wall Street Journal,* 11 August 1977.

Linda Gottfredson's quote comes from her paper, "Reconsidering Fairness: A Matter of Social and Ethical Priorities," *Journal of Vocational Behavior* 33 (1988).

June O'Neill's observations on the correlation between black test scores and black earning and employment were published in "The Role of Human Capital in Earnings Differences Between Black and White Men," *Journal of Economic Perspectives: A Journal of the American Economic Association* 4, no. 4 (Fall 1990).

On the impact of federal affirmative action regulation on black employment, the principal sources relied upon include:

Jonathan Leonard, "The Impact of Affirmative Action Regulation and Equal Employment Law on Black Employment," *Journal of Economic Perspectives A Journal of the American Economic Association* (1990).

———, "Affirmative Action: Symbolic Accommodation and Conflict," *New Approaches to Employee Management* 2 (1994).

John Donahue and James Heckman, "Continuous Versus Episodic Change: The Impact of Federal Civil Rights Policy on the Economic Status of Blacks," *Journal of Economic Literature* (1991).

Christopher Edley, Jr., and George Stephanopoulos "Affirmative Action Review," *Report to the President,* 19 July 1995.

Farrell Bloch, *Antidiscrimination Law and Minority Employment* (The University of Chicago Press, 1994).

Finnis Welch, "Affirmative Action and Its Enforcement," *AEA Papers and Proceedings* (1981).

On the workings of the EEOC and the OFCCP, interviews with the following:

R. Gaull Silberman

Jeffrey A. Norris

Larry Lorber

Leonard Biermann

Farrell Bloch

Charles R. Mann

Frank Erwin

On the workings of OFCCP, the testimony of Shirley J. Wilcher before the House Committee on Economic and Educational Opportunities, Subcommittee on Employer–Employee Relations, 21 June 1995.

On the workings of OFCCP, "Affirmative Action Workbook," prepared by the National Employment Law Institute.

On the early history and evolution of equal employment and affirmative action policy, Hugh Davis Graham, *The Civil Rights Era* (New York: Oxford University Press, 1990).

Important U.S. Supreme Court Decisions on affirmative action and employment reviewed include:

United Steelworkers of America AFL-CIO v. Weber, 433 U.S. 193 (1979).

Wygant v. Jackson Board of Education, 476 U.S. 267 (1986).

Local No. 28 Sheet Metal Workers International Association v. EEOC, 478 U.S. 421.

Local No. 93 Int'l Association of Firefighters v. City of Cleveland, 478 U.S. 501 (1986).

United States v. Paradise, 480 U.S. 149 (1987).

Johnson v. Transportation Agency, 480 U.S. 616 (1987).

Chapter 3: Strange Bedfellows

Many of the individuals and written sources relied upon in the preceding chapter were equally important to Chapter 3 and to the two following chapters on job testing.

In addition, the view of Fortune 300 corporations on the question of affirmative action was obtained from Jeffrey A. Norris, "Critical Issues in the Affirmative Action Debate: Executive Order 11246," *Special Memorandum* to members of the Equal Employment Advisory Council, 17 March 1995. Norris's 23 June 1995 testimony before the House Employer–Employee Relations Subcommittee raising concerns about OFCCP approaches to affirmative action during the Clinton administration was also significant.

The corporate endorsements of affirmative action were widely published in the press at the time, and most of those listed here were collected in the written statement of William T. Coleman, Jr., to the House Subcommittee on the Constitution, 25 October 1995.

Chapter 4: Merit Testing and Race

The chapter's principal source on the history of ability testing is Committee on Ability Testing, Assembly of Behavioral and Social Sciences, National Research Council, Alexander K. Wigdor and Wendell R. Garner (editors), *Ability Testing: Uses, Consequences and Controversies* (National Academy Press, 1982).

Other valuable sources include:

H. P. McCain, *The Personnel System of the United States Army, Volume 1, History of the Personnel System* (1919).

George D. Halsey, *Selecting and Inducting Employees* (Harper & Brothers, 1951).

Douglas H. Fryer and Edwin R. Henry, *Handbook of Applied Psychology* (Rinehart, 1950).

Anne Anastasi, *Psychological Testing,* fourth edition (Collier Macmillan, 1976).

American Psychological Association, *Standards for Educational and Psychological Testing* (1985).

Joyce Hogan and Robert Hogan (editors), *Business and Industry Testing* (Pro-Ed, 1984).

Lewis E. Albright, J. R. Glennon, and Wallace J. Smith, *The Use of Psychological Tests in Industry* (Howard Allen, Inc., 1963).

Marvin D. Dunnette and Leaetta M. Hough, eds., *Handbook of Industrial Organizational Psychology,* second edition (Consulting Psychologists Press, Inc., 1991).

Several of the authorities cited in the chapter were from papers collected in two special editions of the *Journal of Vocational Behavior:* volume 29, "The g Factor in Employment," edited by

Linda Gottfredson, December 1986, and volume 33, "Fairness in Employment Testing," edited by Linda Gottfredson and James C. Sharf, December 1988.

On the subject of the validity of employment testing, the following were among the most valuable of the dozens of articles authored or co-authored by Frank L. Schmidt:

Frank L. Schmidt, "The Problem of Group Differences in Ability Test Scores in Employment Selection," *Journal of Vocational Behavior* 33 (1988).

————, "Why All Banding Procedures in Personnel Selection Are Logically Flawed," *Human Performance* (Lawrence Erlbaum Associates, Inc., 1991).

————, John E. Hunter, Robert C. McKenzie, and Tressie W. Muldrow, "Impact of Valid Selection Procedures on Work-Force Productivity," *Journal of Applied Psychology* 64 (1979).

————, John E. Hunter, and Kenneth Pearlman, "Validity Generalization Results for Tests Used to Predict Job Proficiency and Training Success in Clerical Occupations," *Journal of Applied Psychology* 65, no. 4 (1980).

———— and John E. Hunter, "New Research Findings in Personnel Selection: Myths Meet Realities in the '80's," *Public Personnel Administration—Policies and Practices for Personnel Service* (Prentice-Hall, 1981).

Other important sources include:

R. Stephen Wunder, James W. Herring, and T. J. Carron, "Interpretive Guide for the API Test Validity Generalization Project," *Human Resources Series,* second edition, API Publication 755, (1982).

Leaetta M. Hough and Robert J. Schneider, "The Frontiers of I/O Personality Research," Personnel Decisions Research Institutes, Inc., 1995.

Frank W. Erwin, "A History of Federal Guidelines on Employee Selection Procedures," unpublished, 1995.

Mary L. Tenopyr, "The Complex Interaction Between Measurement and National Employment Policy," unpublished, 1995.

Jerard F. Kehoe and Mary L. Tenopyr, "Adjustment in Assessment Scores and Their Usage: A Taxonomy and Evaluation of Methods," *Psychological Assessment* 6, no. 4 (1994).

Wayne F. Cascio, James Outtz, Sheldon Zadek, and Irwin L. Goldstein, "Statistical Implications of Six Methods of Test Score Use in Personnel Selection," (Lawrence Erlbaum Associates, Inc., 1991).

In addition to interview sources cited above, interviews for this chapter include:

James C. Sharf

Frank L. Schmidt

Ted Carron

The leading Supreme Court cases in the area of job testing are:

Griggs v. Duke Power Co., 401 U.S. 424 (1971).

Albemarle Paper Co. v. Moody, 422 U.S. 405 (1975).

Wards Cove Packing Co., Inc. v. Antonio, 490 U.S. 642 (1989).

Chapter 5: The Red and the Blue

The account of the Birmingham Fire Department situation relies on, "Fighting Bias With Bias," *New York Times,* 21 August 1995, A1.

The account of the Nassau County police situation is based upon court documents in the case, *United States v. Nassau County,* 77 Civ. 1881, U.S. D.C. E.D.N.Y, plus interviews with James C. Sharf and William H. Pauley III, the attorney representing the county.

The case, *United States of America v. City of Chicago,* involving allegations of discrimination in the hiring and promotion of police has been the subject of a number of decisions over the years, including 385 F. Supp. 543 (1974), 385 F. Supp. 540 (1974), 385 F. Supp. 543 (1974), 411 F. Supp. 218 (1976), 420 F. Supp. 733 (1976), 540 F.2d 415 (Seventh Circuit, 1977), 631 F.2d 469 (1980), 663 F.2d 1354 (1981), 870 F.2d 1256 (1989).

The case has received extensive coverage in the Chicago and Springfield, Illinois, papers as well as the national press. Mayor Daley's quote is from the *Chicago Sun Times,* 19 March 1995, 11.

Chapter 6: Race and University Admissions

In addition to his interview, Richard Wagner provided a great many source documents on admissions decisions at the Cornell University School of Industrial and Labor Relations.

In addition to those cited in the chapter, information on affirmative action at Cornell was provided by Susan H. Murphy, vice president for Student and Academic Services, and by Joycelyn Hart, associate vice president for Human Relations.

Nan Keohane's quote comes from the Duke student newspaper *The Chronicle,* 29 November 1994.

Thomas Sowell's quote comes from his book, *Black Education, Myths and Tragedies* (McKay, 1972).

The cite on the landmark *Bakke* case is *Regents of California v. Bakke,* 438 U.S. 265 (1978).

The source for the figures on black faculty percentages is the *Journal of Blacks in Higher Education,* Spring 1995. The Summer 1995 *JBHE* is the source for the chart on declining black enrollment at several prestige universities; the Autumn 1995 issue for liberal arts colleges.

Chapter 7: "Three Hours to Live"

The chapter's five major sources on the Straight takeover are contemporary coverage by the *Cornell Daily Sun,* the June 1969 *Cornell Alumni News,* which was devoted entirely to the incident, "The Report of the Special Trustee Committee on Campus Unrest at Cornell," 5 September 1969, a special edition of the *Cornell Daily Sun,* commemorating the twentieth anniversary of the incident, 19 April 1989, and interviews with all of the principal players and dozens of mere participants conducted by university archivist Gould Coleman and preserved under the title, "Challenge to Governance," which were made available to the author in July 1994, twenty-five years after the event and which are now in the public realm.

I have over the years discussed the takeover with many of those present at the time, including my lifelong friend David B. Lipsky, the recently retired dean of the School of Industrial and Labor Relations, and my old government professor, George McT. Kahin, the latter an important opponent of the deal that ended the crisis; but I elected to rely principally on the contemporary accounts and analyses, particularly the rich archival material. Unless otherwise identified, the reflections of black participants in the takeover come from the archives.

Chapter 8: The Lonesome Dove

In addition to an interview with Professor Larry I. Palmer, the story of his battle to reform segregated housing and social patterns at Cornell is told in a paper trail of university reports and memoranda made available to the author.

On campus race relations generally, Chris Montgomery and Alicia Hughes, president of the student assembly, were among the many black students whose insight provided context to the chapter.

Chapter 9: A State of Excess

The words of Jesse Jackson were reported on ABC News *World News Tonight,* 20 July 1995. Panetta appeared on the CBS News program *Face the Nation,* 23 July 1995.

The principal source for the history of race-based admissions at Berkeley is the "Karabel Report," known more formally as *Freshman Admissions at Berkeley: A Policy for the 1990s and Beyond,* A Report of the Committee on Admissions and Enrollment Berkeley Division, Academic Senate University of California, Professor Jerome Karabel, Chair, 1989. A follow-up report, *The Implementation of the Karabel Report on Freshman Admissions at Berkeley: 1990–1993,* was authored the same committee, chaired by Professor David Leonard.

Figures on the percentage of minority students gaining admission to Berkeley through procedures complementary to GPA/SAT scores were reported in *The New York Times,* "Gains in Diversity Face Attack in California," 4 June 1995, and in the *Wall Street Journal,* "Campuses Mull Admissions Without Affirmative Action," 25 July 1995.

UCLA's minority admissions record for the year 1994 was the subject of the UCLA Senate Committee on Admissions, *Report to the Regents,* May 1995.

Gail Heriot's analysis of admissions practices at UCLA Law School and the impact on classroom work and campus attitudes was the subject of a memorandum to Peter Warren, Washington Director of the National Association of Scholars, made available to the author.

Chapter 10: Historically Black State Colleges and Universities

The cite on *U.S. v. Fordice* is 505 U.S. 717 (1992). Following remand, an exceptionally detailed opinion was issued by the U. S. District Court, N.D. Miss. 1995 WL 134597 (D. Miss.), 7 March 1995. The latter decision provides considerable detail on admissions policies and standard test results with respect to state institutions of higher learning in Mississippi.

The cite on *Bazemore v. Friday* is 478 U.S. 385 (1986).

The account of the Jackson March, along with the quotes attributed to Ben Chavis and the window of Jackie Ayers is based on the article, "Desegregation Called Peril to Black Colleges," *Los Angeles Times,* 1 May 1994.

The source for William H. Gray's quote is *Black Enterprise,* November 1994, 28.

Alex Johnson's quote comes from his law review article, "Why Integration Fails African Americans Again," *Cal. L. Rev.* 81: 1401.

William Blakely's quote comes from the *Baton Rouge Advocate,* 14 March 1994, 3B.

Source material on the performance of historically black colleges and universities was obtained from two scholarly papers:

> Ronald G. Ehrenberg and Donna S. Rothstein, "Do Historically Black Institutions of Higher Education Confer Unique Advantages on Black Students: An Initial Analysis," *Contemporary Policy Issues in Education* (ILR Press, 1994).

> Michael T. Nettles, "Student Achievement and Success After Enrolling in Undergraduate Public Colleges and Universities in Selected Southern States," Southern Education Foundation Initiative on Educational Opportunity and Post-Secondary Desegregation.

Chapter 11: Voting Rights: As Ye Sow... and Chapter 12: So Shall Ye Reap

Much of the background on Republican cooperation with minorities on voting rights issues was obtained from personal interviews with Benjamin Ginsberg and with internal GOP memoranda, speech notes, and other documentary material he provided to the author. Additional background on the same subject was obtained from:

Lee Atwater, "Altered States: Redistricting Law and Politics in the 1990s," *The Journal of Law and Politics* (Summer 1990).

Interviews with David Bositis of the Joint Center for Political and Economic Studies and Professor Merle Black of Emory University.

Mark F. Bernstein, "Racial Gerrymandering," *The Public Interest* (Winter 1996).

Chandler Davidson and Bernard Gronfman (editors), *Quiet Revolution in the South,* (Princeton University Press, 1994). The book was also an important source on the techniques practiced in certain Southern states to evade the intended consequences of the Voting Rights Act and the question of black electability in majority white districts.

Complete documentation of every Justice Department intervention in voting rights cases from the late 1960s through July 1995 was provided by the Civil Rights Division of Justice at the author's request.

Abigail Thernstrom, *Whose Votes Count? A Twentieth Century Fund Study* (Harvard University Press, 1987), provides a full account of experience under the act from its initial passage and of the 1982 amendment process.

The following were important sources on the electability of minority candidates in white districts:

Black Elected Officials: A National Roster (Joint Center for Political and Economic Studies Press, 1993). (The Center frequently updates its lists of such officials for all offices.)

Susan Welch, "The Impact of At-large Elections on the Representation of Blacks and Hispanics," *Journal of Politics* (November 1990).

Charles S. Bullock, III, and A. Brock Smith, "Black Success in Local Runoff Elections," *Journal of Politics* (November 1990).

Lani Guinier, "The Triumph of Tokenism," *Michigan Law Review* (March 1991).

"The Supreme Court, Racial Politics and the Right to Vote: Shaw v. Reno and the Future of the Voting Rights Act," a conference hosted by The American University Law Review and the law and government program of the Washington College of Law, *American University Law Review* 1 (1994): 44.

Peter Skerry, "The Ambivalent Minority: Mexican Americans and the Voting Rights Act," *Civil Rights in the United States* (The Pennsylvania State University Press, 1994).

On the relationship between the Congressional Black Caucus and the Voting Rights Act, the following provided important source material:

William L. Clay, *Just Permanent Interests: Black Americans in Congress 1870–1991* (Armistad, 1992).

Carol M. Swain, *Black Faces Black Interests: The Representation of African Americans in Congress* (Harvard University Press, 1993).

David A. Bositis, *The Congressional Black Caucus in the 103rd Congress* (Joint Center for Political and Economic Studies, 1994).

———, *Redistricting and Representation: The Creation of Majority–Minority Districts and the Evolving*

Party System in the South (Joint Center for Political and Economic Studies, 1995).

"The Effect of Section 2 of the Voting Rights Act on the 1994 Congressional Elections," *Report of the NAACP Legal Defense and Education Fund,* 30 November 1994.

David Ian Lublin, *Racial Redistricting and the New Republican Majority: A Critique of the NAACP Legal Defense Fund Report on the 1994 Congressional Elections,* unpublished, 1995.

L. Marvin Overby and Kenneth M. Cosgrove, *Unintended Consequences?: Racial Redistricting and Representation of Minority Interests,* unpublished draft, 1995.

David T. Canon, "Redistricting and the Congressional Black Caucus," *American Political Quarterly* (1995).

The following interviews provided source material on the variety of subjects dealt with in the two chapters:

Ralph Neas
Rep. Cynthia McKinney
Rep. William L. Clay
Rep. Melvin Watt
Rep. Nathan Deal
David Bositis
Trey Walker

The leading Supreme Court decisions in the period following adoption of the 1982 amendments to Section 2 are:

Thornburg v. Gingles, 478 U.S. 30 (1984)
Shaw v. Reno, 509 U.S. 630 (1993)
Johnson v. DeGrandy, 1994 U.S. Lexis 5082

Holder v. Hall, 1994 U.S. Lexis 5083

Miller v. Johnson, 1994 U.S. Lexis 4462

The account of reaction to *Miller v. Johnson* is based on *Washington Post* coverage of the decision and reaction appearing in separate articles appearing on pages A1 and A24, 30 June 1995.

Chapter 13: Education Versus Ideology

The principal sources on the subject of ability grouping included:

A collection of papers on the subject published under the title, "Ability Grouping," in *The College Board Review,* summer 1993.

Joseph S. Renzulli, *Schools for Talent Development: A Practical Plan for Total School Improvement* (Creative Learning Press, Inc., 1994).

————, "Common Sense About Grouping," unpublished, 1 June 1995.

James A. Kulik, "An Analysis of the Research on Ability Grouping: Historical and Contemporary Perspectives" (The National Research Center of the Gifted and Talented, February 1992).

Interviews were conducted with:

Joseph S. Renzulli

James A. Kulik

Albert Shanker

On school and student standards in Ohio, Dr. Robert Moore provided an interview plus documentation in support of standards.

The facts on Delaware student performance on standardized tests come from Defendants-Appellees Brief in *The Coalition to Save Our Children v. State Board of Education,* No. 95-7452.

On magnet schools an important source was Kimberly C. West, "A Desegregation Tool That Backfired," *Yale Law Journal* 103, 2567.

The cite on *Missouri v. Jenkins* is 1995 U.S. Lexis 4041.

Chapter 14: Whites Need Not Apply

Thomas C. Stewart testified before the Constitution Subcommittees of the House and Senate Judiciary Committees 22 September 1995.

The Supreme Court discussed the legislative history of set-aside programs in *Fullilove v. Klutznick,* 448 U.S. 448 (1980).

The 1995 Commerce Department Report *Characteristics of the Black Population* is the source for data regarding black self-employment rates.

The 1980 census figures on the employment of blacks in black-owned enterprises were reported in the book by Farrell Bloch cited in the notes to Chapter 2.

Ward Connerly's quote comes from his prepared statement to the Constitution Subcommittees, 22 September 1995.

The cite on *City of Richmond v. J. A. Croson Co.* is 488 U.S. 469 (1989).

Arthur Brimmer's Philadelphia disparity study was reviewed by the U.S. District Court for the Eastern District of Pennsylvania in

Contractors Association of Eastern Pennsylvania v. City of Philadelphia, Civil Action No. 89-2737, decided 11 January 1995.

Interviews with Deborah Barnes and Walter H. "Rusty" Ryland produced data and other information on Richmond's experience with minority contracting in the post-*Croson* period.

Nathan Glazer's quote comes from his editorial page column in the *Wall Street Journal,* 5 April 1995.

The Los Angeles affirmative action dispute between blacks and Hispanics, including Mamie Grant's quote, was reported in the *Los Angeles Times,* 13 July 1988.

Regarding abuses in the 8(a) program and other minority set aside programs, this chapter relies in substantial part on:

> Statement of James F. Hoobler, Inspector General of the U.S. Small Business Administration before the U.S. Senate Committee on Small Business, 27 July 1994.

> "Status of SBA's 8(a) Minority Business Development Program," Statement of Judy England-Joseph, Director, Housing and Community Development Issues, Resources, Community and Economic Development Division, General Accounting Office.

The cite on *Metro Broadcasting, Inc. v. FCC* is 497 U.S. 547 (1990).

Source material on the subject of white contractor problems with minority set-asides was obtained from interviews with:

> Arthur O'Donnell
> Mike Kennedy

Information on disparity studies and ongoing federal and state efforts to circumvent court decisions was obtained in several discussions with George LaNoue.

Information on the Regional Alliance for Small contractors was obtained from interviews with:
Mark Quin
Sioan Bethel

Information on the mentor program at the Port of Portland was obtained in an interview with Ron Stemple.

The cite on *Adarand Constructors, Inc. v. Pena* is 1995 U.S. Lexis 4037.

Chapter 15: The Mortgage Discrimination Hoax

The characteristics of the nonminority and minority loan applicants to Boston area banks were drawn from the raw data assembled by the Boston Fed by Professor Anthony Yezer of George Washington University specifically for the author. Yezer was also interviewed on the subject of interpreting HMDA data.

Published sources on the battle between Deval Patrick on the one hand and Lawrence Lindsey and Gene Ludwig include:
"Feds Back Barnett Deal Despite a Justice Probe," *American Banker,* 23 September 1994.
"Feds, Justice Sparring on Bias Issue in Barnett Deal," *American Banker,* 29 September 1994.
"Barnett's Thrift Purchase Is Approved, But Bank Faces Lending-Practice Probe," *Wall Street Journal,* 9 November 1994.
"OCC Approves Barnett Deal in Midst of Justice Dept. Probe," *American Banker,* 9 November 1994.

Chapter 16: The Insurance Discrimination Hoax

Roberta Achtenberg's testimony was delivered to the Senate Banking Committee, 11 May 1994.

Deval Patrick testified before the same committee on the same subject on the same day.

The Department of Housing and Urban Development's transcripts of the four-city Achtenberg hearings were an important source of information for this chapter.

Chapter 17: The California Civil Rights Initiative

The following provided useful information on CCRI during the course of interviews with the author:

    Ward Connerly
    Tom Wood
    Glynn Custred
    Governor Pete Wilson*
    Joe Gelman
    Arnie Steinberg
    Teresa Bustillos
    Ron Unz
    Paul Sniderman
    Ralph Carmona*
    John McDermott
    Eugene Voloch
    Mayor Willie Brown*
    Mike Antonovich
    John Bunzel
    John Herrington*

*Interview conducted pursuant to assignment for ABC News.

Paul M. Sniderman and Thomas Piazza, *The Scar of Race* (Belknap Press of Harvard University Press, Cambridge, Massachusetts, and London, England, 1993) provides important perspective on public attitudes toward race preference programs.

INDEX

Charlotte, NC, 247, 335-336
Chavis, Benjamin, 203, 383
Chevy Chase Federal Savings Bank, 317-318, 324, 333
Chicago Federal Reserve Bank, 331-332
Chicago (IL) police department, 112-117, 380
Chicanos, 194. *See also* Hispanics
Chinese. *See* Asians
Choosing by Color: Affirmative Action at the University of California, 197
Cisneros, Henry, 344
City of Richmond v. Croson, 290-291, 294, 296-297, 301, 304, 313, 389
Civil Rights Act of 1964: campus housing and, 174; enforcement and impact of, 10, 32, 354-355; merit testing and, 19, 72-73, 74-75; positive impact on black wages and employment in the South, 24; Title VI provisions, 137-141, 268; Title VII provisions, 27-28, 57-58
Civil Rights Act of 1991, 73, 99-100, 116-117
Civil Rights Division of the Department of Justice, 11, 27, 29, 57, 222, 226, 241, 317-318, 324, 385
The Civil Rights Era, 46
Civil rights organizations. *See specific organization by name*
Civil Service Act, 79
Civil Service Journal, 95
Claremont Institute, 348
Clark, Kenneth B., 17, 174, 179
Clark, Russell G., 275-279
Clark, Sen. Joe, 74
Clark College, 211
Clay, William L., 386
Cleveland, OH: busing, 271-272; police department hiring and promotion, 118; proficiency test for high school seniors, 268-269

Cleveland Plain Dealer, 272
Clinton, Bill: affirmative action address, 4-6, 8-9, 307; approach to set-aside programs, 307-310; Contract with America program, 251-252; Fair Housing Executive Order, 326; Goals 2000, 267-268
Clinton administration: Affirmative Action Review, 5, 31, 36, 37, 41-42; broadcast media quotas, 69-70; disparate impact and, 104-105; layoffs during budgetary cutbacks, 41; merit testing, 71-72; Piscataway (NJ) High School case, 53-54
"The Coalition to Save Our Children," 273, 388
Coleman, Gould, 170, 381
Coleman, William T., Jr., 40, 376
The College Board, 125
College Board Review, 265
College Entrance Examination, 87
Colleges. *See* Community colleges; Universities; University admissions; *specific institutions by name*
Columbia University, 16, 373
Commission for the Study of Retarded Children, 78
Committee for Psychology, 81
Committee on Classification of Personnel, 81
Committee on Special Education Projects, 160-161, 174
Community colleges: blacks continuing on to graduate from four-year college within six years, 207; California system, 185
Community Reinvestment Act, 320, 332, 344
Competency exams, 267-268
Cone, James H., 373
Congress. *See specific legislation and committees by title*
Congressional Black Caucus, 228-235, 237, 251-252, 386